# Surviving Zimbabwe

Catherine Buckle

Published by Catherine Buckle
P O Box 842 Marondera
Zimbabwe
Email: cbuckle.zim@gmail.com
www.cathybuckle.co.zw
©Catherine Buckle 2020


ISBN: 978-1-77925-230-2

Front cover ©Richard Buckle & Cathy Buckle
Design and Layout Kara Bishop
Fiery necked Nightjar illustration ©Margaret Shattock

Cover photograph: the three legged pot, a wood fire and a solar panel were the key to providing hot water and cooked food in life without electricity.

# ALSO BY CATHERINE BUCKLE

Farm invasions and political upheaval 2000 - 2002
- African Tears
- Beyond Tears


Letters from Zimbabwe and Diaspora Encounters 2000 - 2017
- Can You Hear the Drums
  Letters from Zimbabwe 2000-2004
- Millions, Billions, Trillions.
  Letters from Zimbabwe 2005-2009
- When Winners are Losers.
  Letters from Zimbabwe 2009-2013
- Finding our Voices.
  Letters from Zimbabwe 2013-2017
- Sleeping Like a Hare


Wildlife and Conservation Memoirs
- Innocent Victims
- Imire, the Life and Times of Norman Travers
- Rundi. Hand Rearing Baby Elephants


Children's books
- The Animals of the Shashani
- The Litany Bird
- Pookie, the Monkey That Came to Town
- Rusty Velvet

For many years Cathy Buckle wrote as "The Litany Bird".  The call of the Litany Bird seems to say "Good Lord deliver us"

# DEDICATION

This book is dedicated to my son Richard.

Survival depends not only on what you choose to remember
but also on what you are able to forget.

# CONTENTS

A mother's letter to her son

# INTRODUCTION

After writing a regular letter from Zimbabwe for twenty years describing our lives in a country in crisis, I've lost count of how many thousands of people have asked me why I stay. More appropriately for millions of Zimbabweans is the question: how do you stay? Surviving Zimbabwe through its worst years of collapse from 2004-2009 and then again from 2018 to 2020 (and still ongoing), forced us to learn a whole new set of survival skills, practical, physical and emotional, and to equip ourselves with survival tools. We didn't need to choose traditional survival tools such as a machete, fire starter or bow and arrow; instead our tools were jerry cans, water containers, solar panels, batteries and inverters. We had to re-learn recipes our grandmothers used; we had to barter and swop, shop in other countries, grow food in our gardens, pay school fees with fuel coupons or sacks of food, take our own bandages, injections and medicines if we went to hospital. We had to find our own sources of food, water and electricity and become less dependent and more self sufficient. Perhaps our greatest survival skill was being adaptable and prepared for anything. Surviving Zimbabwe was a journey into the unknown and it took courage and determination to keep walking along its route, always believing that in the end we, the ordinary Mums and Dads, sons and daughters, could and would prevail.

*"Surviving Zimbabwe"* is a collection of anecdotes, memories, hints and home-made rules on how we survived, and continue to survive, a country in crisis. Thank you to all the people who allowed me to use and tell their stories in this book. These are our stories of survival and perhaps they will help others who find themselves in similar situations; hopefully they will learn from our mistakes, something our leaders seem incapable of doing so far.

Cathy Buckle

Marondera,

Zimbabwe.

2020.

# A MOTHER'S LETTER TO HER SON

September 2003

Dearest Rich,

It's been three weeks now since the *Daily News* was closed down by the government. It's been a very scary time trying to work out how I'm going to support us both, pay the bills and put food on the table now that I've lost my job as a columnist on the paper and in between times waiting to see if I would be picked up.

The police said they were planning to arrest forty five *Daily News* journalists and reporters whose names were on their list and in the first ten days they arrested twenty four in Harare. Who knows these days who they're going to arrest and why. Every day I wonder if I'll be next and every night I wonder if I'll wake up in my own bed in the morning. Emergency plans are in place for you if anything happens to me. Always remember how much I love you.

As each day has passed since the closing of the *Daily News* the reality of it has slowly sunk in. Anger at democracy's voice silenced, disgust at people's acceptance, shock at what's happened and disbelief that the government can do this. 100,000 copies of the newspaper printed every day; ten people reading each paper; an estimated one million readers a day and yet there is this quiet, frightened acceptance of what's happened. I now realise the *Daily News* isn't coming back anytime soon so for me that means no job, no income, no way to pay bills, buy groceries, cope with our 460% inflation. I tried again to get a job last week, but no joy. I did get an interview for an office job but it lasted less than three minutes. She said if she had her way I'd start tomorrow but it was up to her boss. "That will have to go for a start," she said pointing to the little scrap of yellow ribbon I wore pinned to my shirt. The ribbon is my silent protest in support of all the farmers being arrested for farming. "It's the politics of your bravery that's the problem," she said, doubting I'd get the job. I didn't.

It's taken three years since being evicted from the farm but I've finally got to the point where I cannot support us. The money from *African Tears*, that was serialized in the UK Sunday Times, was going to keep us going for a long time but now that's gone too: the publisher in South Africa's taken everything: all the book sales and all the serialization money; he declared bankruptcy before paying me a single dollar and has got away with it. It has nearly broken me Rich; I fought it for two years with a lawyer, but I was throwing money away on lawyers, money we needed for food.

What have I done by consistently standing up for what is right, exposing the lies, contradicting the propaganda, speaking out for us all? Now this, three years later. Thousands of people have written to me these past three years, thanking me for speaking out, telling me how brave I am but when it comes down to the nitty-gritty, the bread and butter and the piles of bills, kind words don't help you to survive. What kind of a mother am I to have let this happen?

In the years to come, will you understand what I've done and why? Will you forgive me?

Always try and stand up for what is right Rich. One day you'll understand.

Your loving Mum

xxx

# CHAPTER 1

# SURVIVAL FOOD

It was impossible to believe that Zimbabwe could run out of food. Zimbabwe, known as the 'breadbasket of Africa,' a country that had for decades exported grain to countries in the region, fruit and vegetables to the UK, beef to the EU; how could we, once so productive and bountiful, run out of food? It was impossible to imagine a day when supermarkets would be empty, cafés and small family grocery shops would have no food to sell, restaurants wouldn't have the ingredients for a basic meal and giant grain silos would be empty cavernous shells. As hard as it was to believe, this is exactly what happened in Zimbabwe, starting in 2004 and getting steadily worse until 2007 and 2008 when there was nothing to buy. This was the end result of years of violent farm invasions and evictions, taking productive land away from experienced farmers, bad economic policies, massive government corruption, hyper inflation and a completely worthless currency. What do you do when supermarkets run out of food? How do you feed your family? How do you cook when the electricity is off for 18 hours a day and there's no gas to buy? Everyone found their own ways of surviving; these are some of our stories.

## HINTS AND TIPS

- Listen to the warnings and predictions of international food security agencies
- Be prepared for shortages, especially of basic commodities
- Stock up if you can
- Grow and produce as much as you can
- Protein is critical, get as much as you can, and if you can't find or afford beef (the Zimbabwean staple) look for eggs, nuts, chicken, smoked, dried or tinned fish, cheese, yoghurt, oats and lentils.


## BREAD IN THE BACK SEAT, TAKE-AWAYS IN THE BOOT: 2008

Sitting in a dentist's waiting room in Harare early one morning I watched a woman drive in, park and swing open the passenger door. The back seat of her car was filled from top to bottom with bread. On the floor, stacked on the seats and piled up against the windows and doors were dozens of loaves of bread.

"What going on?" I asked the dentist's receptionist.

"Oh that's Jane, she comes every day. She won't be here for long: watch!"

A steady stream of people started arriving, handed over their money and left carrying the maximum allowed purchase of two loaves of bread per person. In less than fifteen minutes the car was empty. Jane closed the car doors and came into the dentist's waiting room carrying two loaves of bread: one for the dentist and one for the receptionist.

"See you tomorrow," Jane said and then she was gone. It turned out that Jane had a relation who was a truck driver who travelled backwards and forwards to Mozambique every couple of days; he or one of his mates would buy the bread in Mozambique and bring it with them into Zimbabwe for Jane to sell. This was the perfect survival arrangement at a time when bread was as precious as gold.

At mid-day in another car park in another town a woman drives in and stops. She opens the boot and her take-away menu is already printed and stuck to the inside of the boot of her car: pies, hamburgers, sausage rolls, scones. All home-made and all sold out in a matter of minutes: no questions, no health regulations, no licence: survival at lunch time, for her and her customers.

## SURVIVAL PLANS: MUD UNDER YOUR FINGERNAILS

The obvious way to survive food shortages and empty supermarkets is to grow your own food, often easier said than done especially if you don't have a garden or plot. If you do have space to grow and water to irrigate plants in your garden, then getting mud under your fingernails is one of the most satisfying and rewarding things you can do. Quick growing hardy vegetables which don't take up a lot of space make survival so much easier: spinach, beans, tomatoes and carrots in the summer and peas, cauliflower and broccoli in winter. Spring onions and radishes all year round and potatoes and sweet potatoes if you have space. Piles of old car tyres stacked one on top of the other were a good plan for potatoes and garlic planted in between flowers do well and help keep the pests away too. I recruited friends all over the world who wanted to help, to send packets of seeds: easy and lightweight to post; hundreds of packets of seeds arrived in my post box for years, a few for me and the rest to give to people who I knew were struggling and had the ability to grow their own food. The old adage: give a man a fish and you feed him for a day, teach him to fish and you feed him for life, were particularly apt when it came to the seeds and veggie gardens.

Fruit trees became an obsession of mine when it came to survival and I started planting them almost as soon as I was evicted from our farm in late 2000 when it was obvious that Zimbabwe was going to head into a time of chronic food shortages as thousands of farmers were chased off their properties. At first you think that fruit trees will take too long to grow and you wonder how they will benefit your survival but once they start fruiting, usually after three or four years, they never stop if you look after them. The easiest, quickest ones are bananas, guavas, pawpaws/papayas and figs. With bananas the best way to start is to get two or three small suckers from a friend's banana plantation, settle them into as much compost as you can spare and then you'll never look back. Buy a pawpaw or papaya for breakfast and drop a few of the seeds into some rich soil and before you know it little trees pop up and you can easily transplant them to wherever you want them in the garden. Guavas grow easily from cuttings and figs grow beautifully from truncheons, even very large ones, giving you fruit within a year of planting them.

Slower to mature but well worth the effort are plums, peaches and apples. Mulberries are essential, giving you years of purple fingers, purple feet and purple bird splats on your washing hanging on the line but great for snacks, jams and puddings. Perhaps the most valuable tree you can plant in your garden is the avocado. Much slower to mature they are worth their weight in gold once they start producing: prolific fruits which are hugely nutritious and provide months of free food and all you have to remember is to not stand underneath them when they are fruiting. If you can swop avocado varieties with a friend and have a couple of trees that bear fruit at different times of the year, survival becomes even easier. The best way to start an avocado tree is to just plant a pip and up it goes. Another great way and always loved by the kids is to screw three matchsticks at equal spacing into the avo pip and then suspend it in a jam jar which you keep topped up with water just covering the bottom of the pip. Before long the white root emerges and coils in the water while the stem and leaves pop out at the top and when there are a few pairs of good strong leaves you can plant your avocado tree in its final location in the garden.

Vines and creepers take up almost no space and add a nice variety to the bounty from the fruit trees and veggie garden. Grapes are easy and produce well if you can summon your courage and prune them really hard in winter. Granadillas will happily climb and wind around a frame; they have gorgeous flowers which turn into deep purple crinkly fruits. Strawberries are incredibly prolific, putting out suckers in every direction and producing year after year but daily checks for slugs and snails are essential.

As easy as all this prolific produce may sound, there is also a veritable army of critters waiting to get stuck into the fruit as eagerly as you! Birds of all shapes, sizes and colours as well as fruit bats, beetles and wasps and if a monkey comes visiting you've had it. Every evening at sundown beetles took the first sitting in my restaurant, plums top of their list. Later at night a thump on the roof would alert me to a presence in the garden and I watched by torchlight as Pookies (Night Apes) stared back at me from the avocado tree, their eyes as red as brake lights on the highway and I knew that from there they would head to the plum trees for pudding, or the mulberries or figs or bananas, depending on the time of year and what was ripe. Genet cats and domestic cats came almost every night to snack, first on avocados that had fallen to the ground and then to look for rats and forage in the compost for worms and beetles. The only answer was to cover the trees with netting or get up very early to pick fruit before the birds or to be prepared to share. I tried to choose the latter whenever I could because of the massive environmental degradation and habitat destruction taking place everywhere in our lawless collapsing country. People seizing farms were burning decades' old orchards, chopping down trees, burning land and destroying habitat everywhere, leaving everything on the move from people and livestock to birds, mammals, reptiles and insects. My choice of sharing the produce wasn't always easy but the rewards of a spectacular bird in the fig tree or a

Night Ape eating plums was worth every mouthful of lost food, but when a pair of black collared Barbets and half a dozen Bulbuls and White Eyes gorged on every single green, seedless grape on the first crop of a new vine, I wasn't amused.

A friend on one of the few privately owned commercial farms still functioning in 2008 had far more important things to worry about than Night Apes and beautiful birds. Jane had to worry about the farm invaders on her property, the constant threat of violence and eviction and getting the crops out of the ground and sold before they were claimed by the intruders. Harvesting the crops and getting enough money to cover costs and keep going was a marathon undertaking. With inflation at over 1.8 million percent in mid 2008, Jane described the routine when she lifted the potato crop: "I used to load up the pickup with potatoes (such a good crop that year) deliver them in town, collect the millions, and go to tea at my friend's office. The trader across the road would see me, gallop across the road and change the millions into USD at a good rate."

### ROOTS, BEETLES AND A BLUE ENAMEL BOWL: JACK'S STORY: 2008

From as early as February 2008 international food security groups were warning that Zimbabwe was facing severe hunger. FEWSNET (Famine Early Warning Systems Network) said an estimated 4.1 million people, almost half of Zimbabwe's population, were in danger of starvation in the coming months and household food stocks had fallen to less than a month's supply. Community monitors reported people foraging for roots and berries and families reducing meals to one a day.

By October 2008 the dire warnings of FEWSNET eight months before had become a reality for millions of people. The word on everyone's lips was 'nzara,' hunger. Shops were completely empty, there was no food to buy and people in rural areas were hardest hit. The government had put a ban on international aid organizations distributing food aid, accusing them of trying to effect a regime change and in the villages people were digging for roots, collecting leaves and boiling beetles to stay alive.

The stores left from the previous season's maize crop had been depleted and everything that could be sold to buy food had been sold. People had nothing left to trade with: cattle, goats, chickens, furniture, clothes, radios: everything had already been sold in order to survive. There were traders who were going across the borders and buying food, selling it to whoever could afford to buy it but most people just didn't have any money and so they had to resort to nature and the old ways. Jack, a friend who had lost his job during farm invasions, had been forced to go back and live in a rural village and he described scenes unimaginable eight years into the 21st century.

"People are digging for roots from plants that our grandparents used to talk about, things we've never had to eat in our lives." Jack described how you first had to find the right tree or shrub that you had been told was edible and then toil, in the burning October sun, digging deep into the baked ground for dry, hard roots with thick skins. Then you had to go home, clean the roots and boil them for a long time, changing the water repeatedly. They tasted of nothing but at least the hunger pains went away for a little while.

"So many people are suffering with stomach cramps and diarrhoea," Jack said, hunger made them impatient and they ate roots that hadn't been cooked for long enough or that came from the wrong trees and shrubs. Other people were eating leaves and grass, boiling, mashing and mixing them into whatever berries or beans they had to make a meal go further. Jack nodded when I described sitting in a fuel queue in town at dawn watching someone collecting  the leaves of young weeds, black-jacks (*Bidens pilosa*), that sprouted along the railway lines in urban areas,  drops of dew from the steel rail tracks dripping  onto the ground enabling seeds to germinate in the harshest of conditions.

My story of a man collecting black jacks along the railway line faded into insignificance with Jack's story of the old woman who went from door to door in his village carrying a blue enamel bowl. At each house she held out a small, blue, chipped enamel bowl and asked if they could spare a little food. On the third attempt she got a couple of tablespoons of cooked sadza (thick maize porridge) and the old lady knelt on the ground and clapped in thanks with cupped hands. Jack said he felt so ashamed: for her suffering and for the state of the country.

Begging door to door for a few mouthfuls of food was the last resort and until that day came it was wild fruits that were the real life saver for people everywhere. In the area where Jack came from, it was the fruits from the Muhacha trees (*Parinari curatellifolia*) that had become the staple diet. The small, plum sized orange fruits were sweet and juicy early in the season but later when they were dry and floury, they were cooked, dried and pounded into a mash to make porridge. Too many muhacha fruits caused stomach cramps and diarrhoea but when you are hungry it's hard to stop eating.

"When the muhacha were finished, it was the mandere (chaffer beetles, *Eulepida sp*) we were searching for," Jack said, describing with vivid animation the frenzied swatting, jumping and running that was seen in the village every evening around sunset. The beetles feed on the leaves of Msasa trees, emerging at dusk and are easiest caught when in flight. The only source of protein for a lot of people, the beetles needed to be boiled for a long time before they were good enough to eat. The heads and wings had to be removed before cooking and some of the older villagers insisted that the water needed to be changed and the beetles boiled twice in order to get rid of a poison. Termites, stink bugs, locusts, green grasshoppers and flying ants were also on the protein menu as the seasons changed.

**THE PINK MARSHMALLOWS:**
**DAVID'S STORY: 2008**
3 packets of biscuits

16 slices of bread

1 large bowl of maize meal porridge

1 boiled egg

2 bowls of oxtail soup with added potato and pumpkin

2 large plates of macaroni and salad

1 litre of milk

6 cups of tea

2 scones

That was what David ate on the first day of an outing from the government supported residential institution where he was living. Thirty-three years old, 1.88 meters tall, David's arms and legs were painfully thin, ribs and shoulder blades clearly visible, his face gaunt and sculpted: eye sockets, cheekbones and forehead pronounced. David had weighed 77kgs before Zimbabwe's political and economic turmoil began in 2000 but by 2008 his weight was down to just 58kgs. The monthly government grant per person in the institution, which had previously been used to buy food, had simply stopped coming as the economy collapsed, leaving residents and staff in the institution in a desperate state.

Before the government's seizure of commercial farms, a steady stream of farmers in the area regularly delivered eggs, milk, meat, fruit and vegetables but that all stopped as the farmers were evicted from their properties. In 2008 David and 120 other residents were surviving entirely on maize meal porridge and cabbage. Eggs, milk, meat, rice, beans, vegetables, cheese and fruit were never available from empty shops, farmers were hardly ever coming with donations and vitamin deficiency was widespread. David had a shortage of vitamin B which caused him to have continuous ulcerous sores on his shins and ankles. At another government residential institution for mentally challenged adults, four residents died of malnutrition in 2008 and there were reports that a number of others had pellagra, a deficiency of nicotinic acid, a form of Vitamin B3, found in meat, fish and poultry.

At some stage during the years of hunger and malnutrition in Zimbabwe's crisis, David had collapsed and was taken by ambulance from Harare to a hospital in Marondera at some ridiculously exorbitant price but at least he was near his Dad and family GP. David's condition was serious and his Dad thought he was going to die. For four days the only movement from David was when the doctor did a lumber puncture. On the fifth morning when his Dad went to visit, the nurses couldn't wait to tell him the latest development. During the night David had got up, picked up his drip stand, gone to the toilet and had a pee. David then went back to his ward, got into the wrong bed, and went back to sleep! There was certainly nothing ordinary about encounters with David!

Added to his extraordinary intake on that first day, David also had one very large, family size packet of pink and white marshmallows. He ate the whole bag in one sitting! Vitamin content nil but his smile was worth every extravagant un-nutritious mouthful!

There was only one main survival lesson to learn from collapsing residential institutions and that was food: lots of it and with as much variety as possible. Pick it in your garden, buy it on the roadside, ask for donations from churches, friends and neighbours but never go visiting residential institutions empty handed and remember that the staff and employees are often as hungry as the residents.

## FAMILY HOLD BACK

FHB was always a big thing when visitors arrived unexpectedly and there wasn't enough food for everyone. Someone would whisper FHB (Family Hold Back) and the guests would be served first. In Zimbabwe's years of collapse FHB was changed to MHB, (Mum Hold Back) the natural sacrifice made by mothers everywhere that enabled millions of children not to go to bed hungry and we did exactly this for many years. Thankfully our children didn't know it at the time and hopefully they would never have to go through it themselves.

## HOPE DEFERRED:
## TSITSI'S STORY: 2008

"The years leading up to and including 2008 were incredible years of hardship with 2008 proving to be the hardest year of all. I remember on 31 December 2008 bidding the year good riddance. Never had a year been so hard in the history of my life in Harare, and every year since that year the level of hardship would be compared to 2008.

I was a single mother with two small children who were in primary school and I have vivid memories of times when I would have money to buy but the shelves in the shops would be empty of products, a few months later the opposite would be true: the shops could be full of products but I would have no money to buy as the rate of inflation kept galloping. One time I managed to buy a handful of potatoes to cook and feed the children; while the children ate the potatoes, I washed and fried the potato skins and ate those. In later years as I recalled those times a friend said to me that fried potato skins were actually a delicacy in some countries, but I'm positive the trend started in Zimbabwe in 2008.

When bread became scarce, I told the kids they would have to take the local staple food sadza as lunch in their school lunch boxes. My son did not mind but my nine year old daughter looked me point blank in the eye and said Highlands Primary School did not allow the kids to carry sadza to school. To this day I can't remember what we gave her instead. That year the school decided that they would bring back their tradition of school portraits, a tradition that had years before been shelved due to the economic hardships. Actually I think the school was fundraising because the cost was astronomical but as a parent of small children you never want to disappoint your children and make them feel like the odd one out and so I sacrificed and paid for those photographs.

Years later after I came across those photos, the one of my daughter especially was so sad, although she wore a huge smile, she looked so thin and gaunt with sunken eyes that I actually tore up the photo. I did not want a reminder of that year. But in your mind's eye you remember it all: it was a reminder of sadness, hardships, struggles that you cannot forget. Now that my children are young adults, I ask them about those days and if they remember them, it's funny because they have no recollection of those days, it's as if they never happened. They in their adulthood are now facing their own challenges, but I guess the fact that they do not remember is perhaps a testimony that nothing lasts forever and that at some point the tide always turns."

## IN PURSUIT OF PROTEIN: TURNING WEEDS INTO MEAT: CHRISTINE'S STORY

"When in the early 2000's meat started disappearing from the shop shelves, my husband and I started to breed our pet rabbits. The gardener was quite puzzled about why he wasn't required to pull out the weeds (like black jacks, khaki weed, amaranth and weed grasses) when they were barely a few centimeters high, as usual, but had to let them grow to 15-20 centimeters so they could feed our bunnies. Our suburban garden wasn't exactly manicured! We traded the slaughtered rabbits for fish with friends of ours who often went fishing, or for goods like flour and rice which other friends of ours brought in from Botswana, or for services, such as a hair cut!"

## HALF A LOAF IS BETTER THAN NONE: JOSEPH'S STORY: OCTOBER 2008

Joseph looked tired and dragged a hand over his gaunt face when I met him. "I'm not getting much sleep these days, always thinking about where to find food to save my family." Joseph has seven acres of land and is exhausted from the labour of trying to get some maize seed planted in time for the coming rains. "It's not proper maize seed, just good pips saved from last year's crop. My wife wanted to eat it because the kids are hungry but I said no, we have to plant something." Squinting in the bright October sunlight he looked out across his baked land: "I think I've got enough saved seed for about two acres but it's so hard to get the ground ready, digging it by hand like this. There are no government tractors to hire for preparing the land and I had to sell the two oxen I had for ploughing when all the mourners came for my father's funeral. If I can just do two acres it will give us something; it won't be enough but half a loaf is better than none."

## PEOPLE'S SHOP FOR RURAL VILLAGERS:
## SIMON'S STORY: 2008

In 2008 when there was no food to buy and the shops were empty, the Zimbabwe government introduced 'People's Shops' in rural areas to assist villagers to get food and presumably to calm an uneasy population following yet another disputed election and a new onslaught of violence.

Simon, a friend from a rural area explained to me how the 'People's Shops' operated. In Simon's village the names of the families in 120 households were listed by the Headman (in charge of the village). Each week ten households were chosen by the all-powerful Headman, with the families' names written on a piece of cardboard which was tied to a prominent tree in the village. These ten families were then allowed to visit the 'People's Shop' once during that week. The People's Shop was hardly convenient for the chosen villagers because it was forty kilometres away. For the rest of the villagers, they had to wait until their names were chosen; it could be next week or in twelve weeks' time, a very long time to wait when you were starving; something the government technocrats obviously hadn't taken into account when they came up with this absurd scheme.

If your name appeared on the list, if you had the money to buy the goods in the People's Shop, and if you had the bus fare to get to the People's Shop, you were entitled to buy the following items:

2 bars of bath soap

1 bar of laundry soap

1 jar of Vaseline

500 grams of salt

2kgs of sugar

2 kgs flour

500 grams washing powder

If you were unlucky enough to get to the People's Shop when stocks had run out then it was too bad and you were told you could try again in twelve weeks time when your name next appeared on the bit of cardboard tied to the tree in the village. Simon's name hadn't appeared on the tree yet, he'd been waiting for two months already.

## PROTEIN SURVIVAL PLANS: BROILERS

Rearing chickens in suburban gardens became a national past-time when we couldn't afford food and the supermarket shelves were empty. Of course there were by-laws against rearing fowl or livestock in suburban areas but the by-laws in my home town were impossible to get as local municipal authorities said they couldn't find them; an excuse we all knew was their way of preventing us from being able to identify and hold them to account for their own illegal activities. The unspoken word was if they (authorities) could get away with it, so could we.

There were three categories of chicken endeavors you could undertake: broilers, layers and roadrunners. Preparing to rear day old chicks in my suburban garden brought back very nostalgic memories as I had produced broilers for many years on our farm and had learned many practical tips along the way. It was essential to have a small, warm place where the day old chicks would start out. I knew from experience that the first few days to a week were critical to prevent mortalities amongst the chicks and so I laid thick cardboard on the floor in an outside storeroom and made a circle of cardboard around this; no corners for chicks to huddle in and get squashed. In the middle of the cardboard circle I made a thick bed of straw and hung a light bulb over it, the perfect incubator. Even though most of the time there was no electricity, the lights did usually come on for a few hours in the middle of the night which was when the chicks would benefit most from the heat generated by the light bulb. Water and feed containers were placed on the floor and these would be lifted as the chicks grew and could reach over the edges. The chicken food was found and purchased on the black market at vast cost and the day old chicks were ordered from one of the very few remaining farm stockist outlets left in our hugely diminished farming town.

On the day of their arrival I filled a small bowl with water and hard boiled one egg which I mashed very fine and spread out on a plastic tray: these were the two most invaluable tips I had learned from a friend which had helped to reduce mortality among the day old chicks to zero. Carrying the cardboard box of squeaking, cheeping day old chicks from the store to my car and carefully wedging them on the back seat, tears were stinging my eyes. This one simple thing had bought a flood of memories of the farm years back. How many hundreds of times had I done exactly this on the farm and how sad it was that it had all ended at the hands of a rabble who decided they wanted what we had worked so hard to establish; a rabble who were above the law, who had become the new law in Zimbabwe. Banishing those thoughts, I took my precious cardboard box home and went into the storeroom where I had left everything ready for their arrival.

Sitting on the floor I opened one corner of the box and lifted out the first soft, yellow, fluffy chick. Like any good mother I talked softly to the little ball of life in my hands before plunging its face and beak into the bowl of water, forcing it to take that first life-giving swallow of water. The chick looked shocked and surprised, I apologized with a sympathetic giggle and then lifted it over the cardboard wall and put it onto the plastic tray with the mashed boiled egg. Almost immediately the chick started to peck at the egg and I knew I had given it the best start in life, turned and lifted the next baby out of the box.

In 2003 the statistics for 25 day olds were:
- 25 day olds slaughtered at 48 days, average weight 1kg
- 25 day olds stock Z$5,550.
- 65kgs chicken food Z$30,346
- Total cost (excluding water, electricity, time) Z$35,896
- Selling price $2,000 per kg.
- Profit Z$12,000

As hyper inflation began to run, the income and profit from one batch of broilers wasn't enough to start another batch and so you had to dig deep if you wanted the protein. By 2006 you could add three zeros to these prices and by August 2008 you needed to add thirteen zeros because by then you were raising multi-trillion-dollar chickens.


## CRACKED EGGS AND THE PINK PLASTIC CUP: 2008

You have to be inventive, adaptable and prepared to lower your standards when there's no food to buy and in 2008 nothing was off limits. Health inspectors either turned a blind eye or no longer functioned at all and no one seemed to care or to take any notice of regulations. Being prepared to lower your standards became very visible with the sudden demand for cracked eggs in 2008 when the maximum amount of money you could draw from the bank a day was $500 and then only if you were prepared to queue for many hours to get it. $500 was enough to buy four and a half fresh eggs so when news got round that cracked eggs were selling for only $32 each there was a stampede to buy them. "Who cares about germs and salmonella when you're hungry," a friend said, "but make sure you cook the eggs well."

When it came to being inventive the man with the pink plastic cup took some beating. For months a man walked the streets of our town centre carrying a two litre bottle of milk and a pink plastic cup. In his jacket pocket he had a small bottle of water. He would call out 'mukaka' (milk) and people would stop, hand over a few bank notes and he would fill the pink plastic cup with milk which you could then either drink immediately or decant into your own container. Once finished the cup would be rinsed out with a little water from the bottle the seller had in his pocket and off he would go again. No one questioned where the milk came from, how clean or otherwise the cup was or how well it was rinsed after each customer.  This was survival: risky but essential.


## GOATS FOR MAIZE:
## PAUL'S STORY: 2008

Over the weekends the new entrepreneurs descend on rural villages from the nearest big towns and cities. It was the talk of the village when they arrived, and you could spot them a mile off. Wearing bright trendy clothes, dark mirrored sunglasses and with music systems blaring, it was obvious that they'd made a lot of money very fast and wanted everyone to know it. With egos and attitudes as big as their fancy new pick-up trucks, Paul said there was no bargaining with these guys, it's a simple case of take it or leave it. Their trucks are filled with maize meal which they swop for livestock. The price is one goat in exchange for a 10kg bag of maize meal, not enough grain to last a family of four for a week.

"Take the offer old man," they mocked scornfully as Paul tugged on the frayed, sisal rope around the goat's neck, hungry kids in the background. Humanity, compassion and empathy don't enter into the rationale of these new, get-rich-quick entrepreneurs in a country in collapse.

**PROTEIN SURVIVAL PLANS: LAYERS**

An easy source of protein to produce, maintain and sustain was layers, another venture I was familiar with and had considerable experience in, having reared layers and sold eggs from our farm for many years. Constructing a chicken run in a corner of the garden was easy: a few poles, some strong wire buried deep in the ground and a protected, roofed house where the nesting boxes were and which had a door to close them in at night and where they could shelter from rain. What I knew from experience was that layers loved to be able to scratch in the sand and have dust baths; they needed lots of sunshine and greenery to eat, clean water and they had to have properly formulated layers grain if you wanted a continual supply of eggs.

I knew that if I could get everything right each layer would give me an egg a day for a year to eighteen months and so I ordered six point-of-lay hens which came on the train from a producer a couple of hundred kilometers away. The train was due to arrive at midnight and there was no way I was going to leave my brand new layers sitting on a cold and windy platform all night so a friend and I went to the railway station at midnight to collect the wooden crate containing the six layers. I'm sure the guard at the station thought I was completely mad to be coming to collect a box of hens in the middle of the night but he just smiled and shook his head and I took my precious cargo home. Popped safely in my storeroom still in their box until sunrise, the layers emerged into their new run in the garden looking all clean and beautiful and nervous.

Clean water, fresh grain, lush green grass, warm sunshine and a pile of sand to dust bath in, what a life! I decided the layers need a bit of encouragement to start laying when they hadn't done anything for a month. Out came my little white pebble; the size and shape of an egg; I had used the pebble many times in the past to prompt and encourage the laying action. Depositing the white pebble in one of the nesting boxes, nestling it into the soft dry grass, the pebble looked exactly liked an egg and one by one the layers went to the nesting box, got in, scratched around a bit, got on and off the stone, pecked at it, huddled it in place underneath them and then got out again. Sure enough within a few days the hens began to lay and I took the pebble away again. Coincidence? Who knows but it always worked!

Soon there were six eggs a day, every day; enough for us and spare to sell, the income giving me enough money to buy more food. It wasn't all pain sailing with the layers because at least one hen always decided it was a rooster and would announce the sunrise, long before sunrise every day and start off both real and imposter roosters into a frenzy of cock-a-doodle-doo-ing all over the neighbourhood. There were the occasional escapes when a hen scratched a tunnel underneath the fence and got out into the garden and went on an orgy of feasting, scratching and uprooting anything and everything. Every day I would pull up weeds and throw them in for the hens, adding leaves from plants I knew they liked and grass cuttings. They loved kitchen scraps: tomatoes, anything green and almost all fruit including bananas, pawpaw, figs, guavas and watermelon. In the rainy season they loved snails and flying ants and these were collected in vast quantities, improving both my garden and the condition of the hens. The more sunshine and green grass they got, the nicer the eggs were, their yolks dark yellow and rich. I had never resorted to the antics of farmers who had added paprika to the layers grain which made the yolks of the eggs dark yellow, almost orange in colour; for my mind sunshine and green grass did the job far better!

Predators that came to help themselves included owls, snakes and genet cats all of which were looking for a free egg dinner and the sight or arrival of any of them would cause a huge ruckus of squawking, fluttering and crowing sending me running outside to see what had got into the cage and find a way of getting it out. I was very wary of snakes and could clearly remember the huge python that had coiled itself up very comfortably under a nesting box on the farm and the silly hen was actually sitting a few inches above it which I only discovered when I put my hand underneath her to see if she had an egg and I saw reptilian coils tightening slightly just inches away.

## BEEF IN THE PICK-UP; FLOUR IN THE ALLEY; ALCOHOL IN THE BLUE CAR WRECK: 2008

The smooth-talking wheeler-dealers who became the new barons of our collapsed country could source anything you asked for and kept everyday life ticking over, at a price of course. They trade on the black market in anything that's in short supply from fuel and foreign currency to bank notes and food, particularly the most in demand basic goods such as maize meal, flour, rice, sugar and cooking oil. They call themselves 'entrepreneurs' and if you aren't prepared to take the risk and buy from them, you go without. For a bit of black-market shopping all you needed was a box full of money and the inside information on where people with the commodities you wanted were trading that day. In one shopping trip you could meet the man in the red pick-up truck in a certain alleyway; he was selling beef and had an entire carcass in the back, covered by black plastic. You could go to a dark doorway down another alleyway and look for a guy with a wooly hat and dreadlocks; he was selling flour and sugar, or you could go to the broken blue car near the illegal kombi rank and get any type of alcohol you wanted.

## PROTEIN SURVIVAL PLANS: ROADRUNNERS

A very Zimbabwean way of rearing chickens was to produce what were known as Roadrunners. Basically these were chicks that had been allowed to hatch from fertile eggs and run around with the flock, scratching in the garden for seeds and insects and fed on scraps and maize grain. There was nothing refined or cosseted about Roadrunners; no hand feeding of vegetable scraps, flying ants and snails, these were sturdy, muscular and often fierce chickens that people sold live from their gates and that needed long, slow cooking but provided the much needed protein regardless.

# CHAPTER 2

# BARTERING AND SWOPPING

Old recipe books, secret ingredients and special techniques passed down from mothers and grandmothers were dug out of long forgotten boxes and trunks and brought back into service in the first decade of the 21$^{st}$ century in Zimbabwe. Faded, smudged handwriting on brittle, yellowed pages last turned by grandmothers became our most treasured possessions. Because of the collapse of our economy and empty shops we had to go back to the old ways and the old days and not be reliant on finding our necessities in supermarkets. We had to learn what the most precious ingredients were and to find the best, easiest and quickest recipes to use and then we had to go shopping and we learnt quickly what the priorities were.

Whenever you find a shop with food, whenever you cross borders or are bartering, swopping and exchanging, look first for the key items you need to maintain and replenish your survival pantry. These were the main items in my survival pantry:

| | |
|---|---|
| Flour | Rice |
| Oats | Sugar |
| Pasta | Lentils |
| Dry beans | Soya |
| Oil | Honey |

| Salt | Tea bags |
|------|----------|
| Dry yeast | Long life (UHT) milk |
| Milk powder | Baking Powder |
| Bicarb of soda | Soup powder |

## THE HUNT FOR BREAD AND ITS ALTERNATIVES

Bread shortages are a regular feature in a collapsing country. Sometimes they only lasted for a few days or weeks and other times they went on for months. The main problems were the supply of basic ingredients needed to make bread and the ability of bakers to keep up with escalating costs and remain viable. In Zimbabwe the government controlled the price of wheat resulting in a very small or negative profit margin for bakers. In Zimbabwe's 2000-2008 collapse, the shortage of bread was completely attributable to the lack of wheat production following the government's seizure of the country's main wheat growing farms between 2000 and 2008. In 1999, one year before the government began seizing commercial farms in Zimbabwe, the country produced 324,000 metric tonnes of wheat. By 2005 that figure had plummeted to 120,000 tonnes and by 2008 Zimbabwe only produced 38,000 tonnes of wheat. (United States Department of Agriculture)

Coping without bread is one of the harder things to manage, especially if it's one of the main staples in your diet and if you are trying to fill tummies in a hungry family. The first option was to buy flour and make your own bread which usually resulted in some very suspicious, heavy lumps that were a very far cry from the bread we used to be able to buy in the shops but the hungrier and more desperate we got, the fewer criticisms there were! The first obvious way to achieve the apparently perfect loaf was the bread making machine but this option soon lost favour with me because we only ever had electricity in the middle of the night so I had to get up at 1.00am to add the wet ingredients to the dry mixture I'd prepared in advance and press START on the machine. That wasn't too awful because I knew when I woke up in the morning there would be a lovely, still warm loaf waiting for me at the end of its three hour mixing, raising, kneading and baking programme. The problem was the electricity: if it flicked off, even for a second at any point during the three hour cycle, the bread machine didn't start itself up again and I'd get up to a  soggy, sticky pile of wasted ingredients.

In September 2007, in desperation, with nothing to eat in the house and a hungry teenage son due home from school that weekend, I went looking. Hunting for food in the empty supermarkets in my hometown never took long because they were always virtually empty, and you could scan down aisle after aisle of empty shelves and be gone in less than three minutes.  Sometimes there might be a line of washing up liquid or boxes of jelly powder or strips of condoms to buy, none of which were very useful when you were trying to survive! This September morning in 2007 however, happened to be my lucky day and I spotted a small rack with little half loaves of brown raisin bread on it. I bought two loaves (the maximum allowed per person), each one costing Z$300,000 dollars. If there had been a loaf of standard bread it would have cost about thirty thousand dollars, so I'd paid ten times the price for each of the little raisin bread loaves. That was when the hunt for home-made bread alternatives gained momentum and as the weeks turned into month's lots of experiments were tried. Flat bread, sour dough, corn bread, beer bread and others were tried but the favourites soon emerged. They all needed precious ingredients bought for vast sums of Bearer Cheque bank notes in alleyways or other suspicious places which had become Zimbabwe's black market supermarkets

## MELBA TOAST

I started out trying to navigate the bread shortages by finding inventive and palatable ways of using the bread I had hoarded and stored in the deep freeze. This was the same freezer which spent all of its time defrosting and partially re-freezing, depending on the intensity and frequency of the power cuts. The bread had very bad freezer burn and all the loaves on the bottom of the freezer had edges of blue mould (veins I called them, looking for a smile in the chaos) but throwing it away was definitely not an option and so melba toast hit the spotlight. Because the bread was stale and hard with freezer burn the veins got trimmed and the bread cut very thin, an easy achievement when it was partially frozen. Laid out on a baking tray in the oven and cooked in the middle of the night when the power came on, this made perfect Melba toast and soon we were all snacking on it, putting thin strips of avocado on it, dabs of home-made jam and dipping it into home-made soup. I began filling Tupperware containers with home-made Melba toast and taking them to my elderly neighbour who wasn't coping at all.

## WATER BISCUITS

Water biscuits (crackers) were attempted using a mixture of part flour and part corn flour, both bought on the black market and well past their expiry date, but they were not at all what I thought they would be. I guess I imagined lovely crisp crackers smeared with butter and topped with cheese and dabs of sweet chilli but instead the ones I made were hard and tough and not very palatable, and of course I didn't have the toppings, but they at least provided something solid to go with soup or stew.

## VETKOEK (PRONOUNCED FET COOK)

Now these were the business! All the Afrikaans ladies were cooking these yummy mouthfuls which I foolishly called doughnuts (but only once!) and was swiftly and firmly told that they were not doughnuts but traditional South African Vetkoek. They could be filled with sweet or savoury ingredients or eaten just as they were and lots of recipes were doing the rounds. The one that was the quickest, easiest, didn't need yeast and used the least ingredients was this one:

1 cup flour                              1 egg

1 teaspoon baking powder            1/2 cup water or milk

1/4 teaspoon salt                   oil to fry

Add the beaten egg to all the sifted, dry ingredients. Add water to make a soft sloppy dough. Heat shallow oil in a pot or pan and drop spoonfuls of the dough into the oil. Fry on both sides for a couple of minutes till golden. Cut them open while hot and fill with cheese, honey or jam or whatever you've got on hand or just pop them in your mouth just exactly as they are. The only problem with this recipe was that you tended to eat them as fast as they came out of the frying pan, so it was always worthwhile doubling the recipe.


## FLAPJACKS

For the less oily alternative, flapjacks were a great breakfast, snack or bread substitute, used minimal ingredients and were very quick and easy to make. There were lots of recipes but this one was my favourite because it was so easy and made a lot of flapjacks, useful for filling hungry tummies:

8 oz flour                          1/2 pint milk

1-2 teaspoons sugar                 1 egg

Make a well in the centre of the sifted dry ingredients and drop in the beaten egg and enough milk to make a smooth, thick batter. Beat well and then drop spoonfuls onto a hot, lightly oiled frying pan, flipping over onto the other side after a few seconds until golden.

## SCONES

Scones were another useful bread alternative and you could cut down on the amount of sugar to make them more adaptable. There were lots of recipes with all sorts of very surprising ingredients used to make them rise (including lemonade!) but my favourite were Benita's scones, the quickest and easiest never-fail scones I'd ever made:

2 cups plain flour                                4-6 teaspoons sugar
4 level teaspoons baking powder    4 dessert spoons milk
1 cup milk or 1/2 milk 1/2 water      1/2 teaspoon salt

Mix all the ingredients together with a spoon (quite a wet mixture). Turn it all out onto a well-floured board and cut out 8 large scones. Bake at 230 C for 12 minutes.


## SOYA

Love it or hate it, dried soya is an invaluable ingredient in your pantry when there's no food to buy. Soya is easy to store, quick and easy to cook and is lightweight, making it a perfect item for family and friends outside the country to send to you. Soya, also known as TVP (textured vegetable protein), usually comes as mince (granules) or chunks and it can be either natural or flavoured.

Not my favourite ingredient but really good for stretching meals, my first choice was to get plain soya which you can then flavour according to your own taste. For a long time I struggled with memories of a period in my young adult life when I had no choice but to eat soya and could well remember those slightly gelatinous, slimy bits in stews which were the soya chunks; the bits you move round and round the plate hoping you can hide under a cabbage leaf or 'accidentally on purpose' drop on the floor or give to the dog or cat when no one's looking. The only problem was that my Dad's pampered, fat ginger cat wasn't too keen on soya chunks either and so there'd be these strange little lumps left on the floor which you'd push under the table and hope no one would see.

By the time I was a Mum myself and trying to survive as everything collapsed around us in Zimbabwe, soya was a real life saver to me and had thankfully come a long way in its presentation and palatability, plus the fact that I had discovered chillies! Ahh thank goodness for chillies which got planted all round the garden, fruited prolifically and found their way into almost every savoury dish I concocted in the survival struggle. There would always be two separate dishes of food, one with chutney or tomato sauce for my young teenage son and the other with chilli for everyone else. For nearly two years we survived on soya, almost never having or being able to find or afford meat. I soon learned all sorts of ways to cook with soya and presented it as spaghetti bolognaise, cottage pie, hamburgers, meatballs, stew and casserole. I put it into pies, made endless mountains of soya chilli con carne and then there was Sos Mix, the life saver which came in parcels from my sister.

Sos Mix made of soya mixed with wheat and rice flour was definitely the favourite packet in the survival pantry. You simply poured the mixture into a bowl, added some cold water, let it stand for ten minutes to reconstitute and then rolled it into sausages, coating lightly with flour. Fried gently for a few minutes in a little oil they were delicious and there wasn't a hint that they were actually soya sausages. With a few fried onions and a splash of chilli or chutney, they were a great survival meal, bulked up with potatoes and veg. For a long time my son's favourite meal was bangers and mash which were presented as soya sausages and 'smash', instant dehydrated mashed potato. Smash became another essential ingredient in the survival pantry, small lightweight packets, easy to post and pack and quick to prepare by just adding boiling water and stirring into a mountain of mash. Smash wasn't my favourite thing at all but it was a life saver when it came to keeping food on the table.

Years later when I got an internet connection at home I met soya again and had a lot of reading to do, all of which helped to dispel even more of my bad memories. Apparently soya becomes even more palatable if you soak it in water for a few minutes to re-constitute it and then strain it through a clean cloth, throw away the water and squeeze any remaining water out of the soya before you cook it. Oh dear if only I'd known!

## THREE MEALS A DAY IN A SURVIVAL SITUATION

Being able to keep food on the table when shops were empty, and hyper inflation was in the multi millions was almost impossible and needed careful planning, creativity and inventiveness. Producing and growing as much food as you could was vital as were home-made recipes, black market shopping and securing a small but sustainable supply of critical basic ingredients. Three meals a day was difficult if you couldn't secure a supply of basic carbs such as bread, rice, pasta and maize meal which made for quick and filling ways to satisfy hungry families. Over time a handful of easy recipes made with minimal ingredients became favourites.

**HOME-MADE MUESLI**

1 kg oats

Half cup desiccated coconut (optional)

Half cup wheat bran

Half cup honey or sugar

Cup of oil

Mix all ingredients together in a big bowl. Microwave on high for two minutes. Stir. Repeat the process twice, stirring in between each two minutes. (Total cooking: six minutes)

Leave to cool and then, if you've got them, add chopped dried fruit and nuts, any variety and quantity. Store in a Tupperware container and have with yoghurt or milk and add sliced fresh fruit for the perfect, healthy breakfast every morning.

As extravagant as this recipe may seem if your country is in a state of collapse and you can't find or afford the ingredients, all the items except the oil and sugar are lightweight and perfect things to ask family and friends to pop in a parcel and post to you. All you need is less than ten minutes of electricity to make enough muesli for a month; well worth getting up in the middle of the night when the power comes on to undertake this simple process and secure one of your three meals a day.

## HOME-MADE YOGHURT

When my son was a little lad and had prolonged periods of ill health, yoghurt was one of the few things I could persuade him to eat, along with custard, mashed potatoes and gravy! Living out of town on our farm it wasn't always easy to get to shops and so I learned to make my own yoghurt using a recipe found in a very old recipe book. There were always containers of yoghurt in the fridge, easily replenished thanks to the twice daily fresh milk from our dairy cows. When Zimbabwe ran out of food in the mid 2000's I experimented with the recipe again and it became a staple for breakfast. To make one litre of yoghurt you need one litre of fresh milk 3 – 4 tablespoons of plain yoghurt and a flask. Bring the milk to the boil and remove from the heat as it starts to bubble. Allow it to cool down slowly until it is the temperature of a hot bath (when you can put your finger in it without getting burnt!) Remove the skin that has formed. Add three or four tablespoons of fresh plain yoghurt. Mix gently until it is incorporated into the milk. Pour into a flask. Wrap the flask in a thick towel and leave in a warm place for 24 hours by which time the milk will have turned to yoghurt. Decant into Tupperware containers and keep in the fridge or cold box and use within a week or so. Add fruit or honey or have it just as it is. You can reserve a few tablespoons of the home made yoghurt to start the next batch and can do this a few times until you can buy fresh yoghurt again.

## LENTIL AND CARROT SOUP

1 large onion finely chopped

1 cup orange lentils

1 cup grated carrot

1.5 litres water

Fry the onions lightly in a little oil. Add the lentils carrot and water and bring to the boil. Add salt, black pepper, chili, piri piri or paprika to taste. Reduce to a gentle simmer and cook for approx 45 mins.

This is the most delicious, healthy and filling soup; easy to make, affordable ingredients and it can be cooked outside on a wood fire, solar cooker or on a gas cooker if you are having extended power cuts. Lentils are very easy to post and good thing to ask family to send from outside the country. Turn the soup into stew by adding soya or fresh meat if you can get it, vegetables from the garden and add a few dumplings to make it go even further.

## DUMPLINGS

Dumplings are brilliant filler-uppers; they grow in enormous proportions when dropped into simmering soup, stew and casseroles and are best eaten straight away as they don't keep very well and tend to go tough, not that that's ever a problem as they are very more-ish.

2 tablespoons flour
1 level teaspoon baking powder
1/2 oz margarine
milk to mix
Pinch of salt
Mix flour, baking powder, salt and margarine and add enough milk to make a soft dough. Make into small balls and drop into simmering stew or soup for 10 minutes.

## HOME-MADE BUTTER

Cream from fresh whole milk
Salt to taste
Elbow grease
Making butter is easy but it needs lots of elbow grease and determination; an electric mixer is a huge help. You can make butter by hand either by whisking it in a bowl or even shaking it in a jar for a good ten minutes and a relay of helpers is very handy!

Pour fresh whole milk into large bowls in the fridge and allow the cream to rise for twenty four hours or more if you can keep it cool. Carefully scoop the thick cream off the top of the milk (a soup ladle works really well) and put it into a deep bowl. A good tip is to let the cream stand in the bowl until it gets to room temperature before you start mixing.

Using an electric mixer or whisking and shaking by hand, mix the cream until it goes thick and then mix it even further until it begins to turn or coagulate. When your cream starts to look like soft scrambled egg and clumps together with white buttermilk pooling in the bottom of the bowl, your butter is done. You know it's done when it starts to splash all over you, hence the suggestion to use a deep bowl. Pour the butter into a strainer over a bowl and drain off the buttermilk (save for making scones and rusks) and then rinse the butter under clean running water until there is no sign of any white buttermilk left. Using a wooden spoon press the butter against the side of the bowl and repeatedly squash out any remaining water in the butter. Add salt, mix and press again to get any hidden drops of water out and keep in the fridge or the coolest place you have. Butter making was another one of those middle of the night activities I indulged in so I could use an electric mixer!

Five litres of fresh whole milk will give you half a litre of cream which will give you 155 grams of yummy yellow butter.


**HOME-MADE COTTAGE CHEESE**

If your milk goes sour leave it until it completely separates: clear liquid at the bottom, curds at the top. Place a cloth (cheese cloth, mutton cloth, thin cotton or whatever you have) over a strainer or colander so that it hangs over the sides and is long enough to hold all the curds and be tied and squeezed, a tea towel works well. Pour the sour milk into the cloth over the strainer, twist and tie the cloth and squeeze gently to extract as much water as you can. Hang the cloth over a bowl to allow all the water to drip out or leave it in the strainer and put something heavy on top of it to push the remaining liquid out. Leave to drip for a couple of hours, unwrap the cloth and add desired flavourings such as salt and pepper, chives, garlic or other herbs and then put the cottage cheese into a Tupperware in the fridge. The perfect light supper on bread, crackers or toast this is easy, affordable and the perfect way to use up any milk that is going sour.


## HOME-MADE CONDENSED MILK

Survival wasn't only about bitter struggles, every now and again you also had to spoil yourself and treat the kids with something outrageously sweet. When we were kids a favourite treat was a thick slice of bread covered with thick butter and condensed milk. A nutrition disaster but well worth it as a rare treat. Making the bread was sorted, making the butter was done and because finding condensed milk was impossible, making condensed milk became a must.

1 cup milk powder

½ cup water

2/3 cup sugar

1tsp vanilla essence

Combine and cook for 2 minutes in microwave on high, beating every 30 seconds. Beat at the end. Keep in fridge and beat before using.

## SWOPPING AND BARTERING

Zimbabweans perfected the art of swopping and bartering as the years of collapse went on and we learned to be less dependent on formal shopping and service provision and become more independent.

## SCAVENGER HUNT SHOPPING:
## GERARD'S STORY: 2007

"In 2007 a simple grocery shopping trip turned into an adult version of a scavenger hunt. Had it not been true it would have had the makings of a great comedy. A call would come in saying that shop X had received cooking oil. However, shop Y had sugar and shop Z had mealie meal. (You could expand this list to include all the groceries you might imagine!) Then the fun begins. Before heading to the shop of choice you might need fuel which is only available in Avondale, today. Unfortunately you've unwisely run low on cash so first a trip to the ATM to draw the funds for the fuel. Borrowdale has a working ATM with cash (so the grape-vine tells you) so you rush there, draw the cash then off to get the fuel. Now armed for the excursion you begin the round trip to the four stores (in two suburbs) that you need to visit in order to obtain the ingredients needed for one cake you wish to bake. Of course the famous saying, 'teamwork makes the dream work,' was always at play so many of us used our network of family, friends and connections. Thus we could each hit one of the required stores in a short space of time to get what was required by ourselves and the others. Later that day, at school, tea or dinner, we would swop groceries and cash until each had all the items needed that day!"

## THE JUNGLE TELEGRAPH AND BREAD FOR BILLS: PENNY'S STORY

"I remember the phone lines being red hot with the latest news on where we could buy sugar, chocolate, flour and other things. More often than not it was in some garage tucked away in the suburbs full to the ceiling with all those difficult to find essentials and we helped each other through the 'jungle telegraph.' I ran industrial clinics a few hours a week, one of the clinics was for a well know bakery in Harare. At the end of each month I used to go cap in hand to coerce payment from them. More often than not they had no cash and so they paid us in bread. I would leave the bakery with the boot crammed with the precious commodity, happy that I was at least able to supply my family, friends and staff with bread."

## RICE AND PASTA FOR KETTLE REPAIRS: 2007

Visiting a friend, Linda, I was so relieved to see she'd finally been able to get her kettle fixed. I'd been worried that she was going to electrocute herself every time she boiled the kettle with its bent, twisted cord and flashes of naked wire shining at me: it looked like a tragedy waiting to happen. Linda couldn't afford to buy the new kettle she'd seen in a small appliances shop with a price tag of multiple billions of dollars so instead she popped into a little hardware shop nearby and their electrician offered to help. He dug around in a box of bits and pieces, sorted through plugs, fuses and bits of cable and eventually found a second hand cable that fitted the kettle exactly. Linda and the electrician settled on a trade: a packet of rice and 500grams of macaroni in exchange for a cable for her kettle. Linda was happy, the electrician had some food to take home and I extracted the little packet of tea bags and powdered milk I always carried round in my bag so we could have a cuppa together. This was survival Zimbabwe style at its best.

## BARTERING GOATS FOR SOAP: 2008

In 2008 when supermarkets were empty and basic every day goods were unavailable; everything had a value and a price when it came to barter deals. The Zimbabwean newspaper reported on a story of villagers in the Matobo district in Matabeleland South who were bartering goats for soap. Zimbabweans working in South Africa were bringing in boxes of soap and trading them for goats. The exchange rate in October 2008 was quoted in goats: one goat for a case (12 bars) of hard laundry soap. It wasn't clear how the goat would get through border and passport control but presumably it would just be pushed under the border fence where everyone, even goats, thought the grass was always greener, and the buyer was waiting on the South African side.

## THE BIRTHDAY CAKE BARTER: 2008

To say my son's 16th birthday was a very thin one was the understatement of the year and that was no mean feat in

2008. It was, after all, the year when inflation was completely out of control: over one million percent and increasing at the rate of 15% an hour according to local accountants. The milestone 16th birthday was in winter and it was a freezing cold day. The electricity went off at 5.00am and wouldn't come back on until 9.30 pm that night (load-shedding they called it) so it was going to be a long and boring birthday for a 16 year old boy. Schools had closed early for half term to allow for the re-run of the elections: 'disputed' and 'inconclusive' were the usual adjectives being used to describe yet another violent, contested election in Zimbabwe.

You can get a driving licence at the age of sixteen in Zimbabwe (and it's also the legal age of consent) so the choice of possible birthday presents should have been endless, but not this year. A home-made card with a fifty Rand note inside and a hug were about the best I could do and I sent up a silent message of thanks to friends and relations overseas who had posted parcels for Richie. At least someone was able to spoil him on this momentous day in his life

The lunchtime birthday treat, by request, came in the form of a mountain of instant mashed potato, which had arrived in a parcel from the UK: 'just add boiling water! 'This was accompanied by a fried egg, thanks to the six layers I kept in the garden to ensure a constant source of protein in the time of empty supermarkets, and a tin of baked beans. I had bought the baked beans months before on the black market and had been saving them for a special occasion. Baked beans for a special occasion, who would have believed we would ever get to this.

The real treat of the 16<sup>th</sup> birthday was unveiled at teatime: a chocolate cake made by a friend, Benita, and what a mission it had been. First I had to find and buy all the ingredients on the black market: flour, sugar and margarine were the easy ones, despite being outrageously expensive; eggs from my hens in the garden and, hardest of all, a small tin of cocoa powder. Most of my usual black market sources didn't have cocoa but: "Don't worry, we'll get it for you!" one guy in the car park behind the empty supermarket said. When the small 200 gram tin of cocoa came it cost more than I had paid for my car a decade ago and I hugged it to my chest as if it was gold!

The next problem was actually making, and baking, the cake. I took the ingredients to Benita, the friend who was going to stay up late at night to bake the cake because that was the only time she could be sure the electricity would be on and her oven would be working. Sixteen hour a day power cuts were an everyday occurrence and baking birthday cakes in the middle of the night was quite a normal activity for her. The day before the 16<sup>th</sup> birthday Benita phoned: the cake was ready to collect.

I set off to collect the cake with a twenty litre container in the back of the car. The lid of the container had a doubled over plastic bag underneath it to prevent the loss of even a single drop of the precious contents. The cake was as beautiful as I knew it would be, as light as a feather and exactly what I wanted, no icing or embellishments and all I had to do was add the birthday candles. Benita was delighted with her payment which was sloshing around in the plastic container: fifteen litres of petrol which I had bought on the black market. Benita's car had been parked for a month because of the chronic fuel shortages and so we were both equally happy with the barter trade for my son's 16th birthday: a chocolate cake for fifteen litres of petrol.

# CHAPTER 3

# SHOPPING ACROSS BORDERS

In 2007 and 2008 when supermarkets in Zimbabwe were empty, everyone who had a passport took to travelling to neighbouring countries to buy food to take back to Zimbabwe. Mostly this wasn't food to sell, but food to survive and this became the great food trek for millions of people.

## HEADING SOUTH: THE 2,400 KILOMETRE TRIP TO THE SUPERMARKET

My one tonne pick-up truck was so full that the headlights were shining up into the night sky on the way back from supermarket heaven. As ridiculous as it was, shopping in neighbouring South Africa had become essential when it came to surviving in Zimbabwe but everything about the trip to buy everyday groceries was an exercise in extremes and abnormality.

The planned shopping trip was going to take six days and entail a return journey of 2,400 kilometres. Two days for travelling, three days for shopping and one day for the inevitable recovery in a state of exhaustion. Armed with my passport and vehicle log book I had started at my local police station a fortnight earlier in order to get Police Clearance to take my vehicle out of Zimbabwe. The visit to the Police

Station left me wide eyed with incredulity. Despite being the only person there, I was ignored for quite some time while the people on duty chatted to each other and looked at their mobile phones. The door was broken and had a jagged hole at the bottom, perhaps where some poor soul had tried to claw his way out! Large square sections of the ceiling were missing and the walls were ringed with grime: at head height, rear end and hand level. There were two chairs for customers/visitors, one was just a frame with neither back nor seat and the other had no back and a cracked hardboard seat which looked in imminent danger of collapsing along one side. A bench covered with cracked and torn blue vinyl exposing filthy foam rubber stood just inside the door but it was distinctly uninviting. I chose to stand and waited, and waited. It took the official some time to locate a Vehicle Clearance Form which was found after sifting through piles of papers scattered across two desks.

"Have you got a pen?" he asked and I proffered mine, tight lipped in disbelief that anything functioned here at all. Once the form was filled in and the engine and chassis numbers had been checked on my vehicle outside, it was time for my thumb print to be made onto the police ledger book and the Vehicle Clearance form. The police station had no fingerprint ink and so a stamp pad was produced but it was bone dry. It took three attempts and the official holding my hand and pressing my thumb so hard into the stamp pad that I thought it would go through the bottom but eventually there was a faint purple colour on my thumb. With the official still holding my hand firmly, he pressed my thumb hard onto the ledger book and then the Vehicle Clearance form leaving a faint and mostly indistinguishable purple stain on both. He seemed satisfied and I left the moment everything was in order, relieved that I was legal, my vehicle was legal and I could get ready to go shopping.

My grocery list looked more like the requirements of a large residential institution rather than the needs of a small family but the provisions were intended to last for six months by which time, hopefully, some sort of a political solution would have begun to turn around the dire situation in Zimbabwe.

First on my shopping list were the bulky essentials: 100 litres of petrol (my mobility); 50 kilos of dog food (my security); 100 kilos of chicken food (my protein); and one car battery (my sanity) to run computer, radio and lights.

Then came the bulky basics:

50 kgs brown bread flour
50 kgs white flour
10 litres cooking oil
10 kgs rice
20 kgs sugar
10 kgs salt
100 packets of dried yeast
3 kgs baking powder
Then there were the extras - depending on how much money was left:

Tea Bags

Soup

Pasta and noodles

Tinned fish, meat, fruit and veg

Margarine

Mayonnaise, chutney, tomato sauce, chili

Light bulbs, fuses, plugs

Car, torch and penlight batteries

Washing powder, soap and toothpaste.

Finally, down at the very bottom were the luxuries - most of which I knew were just a pipe dream: coffee; marmalade; shampoo; biscuits; and luxury of all luxuries – chocolate, maybe!

Stepping into the first South African supermarket I was agog: eyes wide and mouth open, I felt weak at the knees: full shelves, aisles and rows overflowing and groaning with supplies. It was impossible to believe that it had been like this just a year ago in Zimbabwe until Mr Mugabe's government introduced price controls which emptied our shops and pushed us to the edge of starvation.

Where to start! There was so much choice, so many different brands, varieties, sizes and prices. All this food was just overwhelming and for a minute or two I just stood and stared at the opulence of it all, overcome with emotion and for the first time facing the reality of just exactly how low we had sunk in Zimbabwe and what we had learnt to live without; and that we had done it in a quiet, dignified manner, forever turning the other cheek. WOW! We Zimbabweans deserved medals, all of us.

Four days later, stone broke and with an estimated 800 kilos in the back of my truck, I headed home to Zimbabwe. As the Beitbridge border got closer I stopped feeling like a freak because now every car looked like mine: over loaded, overflowing, and groaning with food and supplies. It took three and half hours to get through the border - not because of searches and duties but because I refused to pay the bribes that every official from gate guard to customs officials and security men were looking for. A real bribe, mind you of US Dollars or South African Rand, not Zim dollars!

Ten minutes across the border and the change was dramatic: going from a first world to a fourth world country. Cars are replaced by donkey and ox carts; goats amble across the highway and naked children bathe in pools in the rivers. The view from the window, for hundreds of kilometres across Zimbabwe, was of empty fields, derelict farms and no food in our hungry, barren land.

There were eighteen road blocks on the eight hour journey from the border to my home town. Manned by pimply faced, painfully young policemen, always the questions were the same: Where have you come from; where are you going to, what's in the back of the truck. Sometimes the questions were subtle, almost pleading, more statements than demands: "we are hungry also": more often they were aggressive demands: "What have you got for us?"

## YOU DON'T WANT A PRESIDENT DO YOU? 2007

Driving back to Zimbabwe from South Africa after a week of food shopping and quick visits with relations, Steve's one tonne pick-up truck was loaded to the very top of the canopy. We had chosen to travel at night when there wouldn't be so much traffic and were getting near the small town of Ermelo at about midnight. Staying awake was an issue on such a long journey and so we tried to keep conversation going as much as possible. I didn't know anything at all about the town, but Steve said it probably can't have been far from Ermelo where his earliest childhood memories came from. A sucker for stories from "the old days" I asked Steve to tell me what he remembered. Steve's Dad, Daniel, was a soldier in World War Two, serving in the Royal Durban Light Infantry stationed in the desert for part of the war years. Steve's Dad only ever referred to it as The Desert but later Steve found out that it must have been the Western Desert, part of the Sahara, in Egypt and from there troops were later sent by sea to join other forces in Italy and Europe. Daniel had never talked much about the war but there was one story that Steve remembered hearing as a youngster, especially when he wasn't keen on what his Mum was dishing up for supper. All the men in Daniels' unit in the desert complained about how sand got into everything and one chap filled a salt cellar with sand and declared that he was going to take it home after the war. He said if his wife ever served him a meal he didn't like he would sprinkle sand over it from his salt cellar to remind himself what a bad meal really tasted like.

During the war years in Egypt, Daniel's best friend was a chap named Kenneth Wilson. Kenneth regularly got letters from his girlfriend back home in South Africa and felt sorry for Daniel who never got any mail. Kenneth asked his girlfriend if she would find a pen friend who would write to Daniel and keep his spirits up while they were at war and so far away from home. Daniel soon started getting letters from his new pen-friend, a girl called Agnes, who lived in Durban. The two exchanged letters and photographs but sometime before the end of the war they lost contact with each other. After the war Daniel was working as a customs officer in Durban and one day on his way home from work, he saw his pen friend Agnes walking along the pavement. Even though they'd never met face to face, they recognized each other straight away from the photographs they had exchanged. Daniel and Agnes resumed the friendship that had started in letters to and from Egypt and Durban. Agnes was the daughter of a lawyer; she smoked a pipe and could trace her ancestors back to King Louis IV of France. Daniel was a farmer's son and had grown up in the Freestate on Hoemoot Farm and gone to school every day on a donkey.

The thought of Steve's Mum smoking a pipe caused amusement and he explained: "I don't think Mom even smoked before getting married and leaving Natal. In the Free State they were dirt poor. I think Mom would have been classed as an 'uitlander' (foreigner/outsider) by the locals. They didn't go out and never went to see neighbours. Mom said she had smoked a pipe but I never saw this; I suspect she only smoked the pipe to annoy the locals!"

Daniel and Agnes seemed an unlikely couple, but they fell in love and soon got married; their first son, Steve, was born in Durban. In memory and recognition of Kenneth Wilson who had instigated the pen-friend relationship, Daniel and Agnes gave their son Steve the middle name of Kenneth. With his new young family, Daniel wanted to be in the open air and farming, so they moved to the Free State, to a town called Hoopstad. Daniel was earning five pounds a month looking after cattle, drilling boreholes and training horses; a hard life for low wages, especially when more babies came along.

Daniel heard of a job on Shashi Farm in Bindura, Rhodesia; he was promised thirty pounds a month and so the family decided to move. After visiting their families in Durban to say goodbye, the young couple and their four small children set off on the great adventure to start their new life. The journey to Rhodesia took five days. Daniel had a maroon Willies Jeep and would only travel at 30mph. Steve used to sit in the front between his Mum and Dad and when a car passed them, covering them in dust, his Dad would declare: "I'm not one of those cowboys! I drive at 30 miles an hour!" but even at that speed the Willies Jeep had frequent punctures and break-downsen. Steve remembered spending many hours in Ermelo one dark night when he was a little boy, waiting while the Jeep was being fixed. During the journey the family would stop at night and sleep on the side of the road: Daniel, Agnes and the baby sleeping in a tent, the other children sleeping in the car. They arrived at Shashi Farm in Bindura, Rhodesia on Christmas Day in 1953. Steve still remembered some of their early days on Shashi farm, and it made for good story telling in the middle of the night sixty years later on the road to Ermelo.

"We moved into a cottage on Shashi and the toilet was an outside long drop (a farm toilet) with a large tree over hanging it. One day Mom was going to empty a pot into the long drop when a big snake fell out the tree onto Mom's head, slid down her shoulder and arm and disappeared somewhere in the small building and Mom certainly wasn't hanging around to find out where. Mom went home and out came the Baby Browning. The gardener was called and by the time the two of them got back to the long drop the snake had gone. The hunt began for the big green snake in the green tree and then they spotted it; it was back up in the tree. Every time it was spotted Mom shot. Of the five shots Mom hit the snake three times killing it.

In the Bindura club there was a different toilet system which was called the thunder box and was just a hole with a seat on it and a bucket underneath it. Dad used to love to tell the story of the thunder box intruder. The bucket would be changed at regular intervals and one night at the club a man had gone to the loo. He came running back carrying his trousers gabbling incoherently that he'd been bitten by a snake. His buttocks were inspected and sure enough the bite marks were there for anyone who cared to look. The victim was taken to hospital for injections and the rest of the crowd then went to the back of the thunder box, where you change the bucket, ready to kill the snake, sticks and stones in hand. They gingerly opened the back of the thunder box, missiles poised and there, next to the bucket was a mother goose sitting on eggs, not a snake at all!"

Fifty five years later Steve and I were arriving in Eremlo in the middle of the night, giggling and chortling at the thought of the goose in the toilet snapping at some blokes exposed backside. His stories of the old days had made the journey seem shorter and kept us both wide awake. The roads through Ermelo were deserted and the story of the adventures of a young family half a century before lingered in my mind. Approaching a red traffic light, we slowed down and stopped. All our South African friends had told us never to stop at a red traffic light at night because that's when you'll get your car stolen. Car-jacking was apparently very common here although I can't imagine why anyone would want to car-jack Steve's hugely over-loaded old Mazda pick-up truck, except for the fact that it had about six months worth of food in the back.

Suddenly we heard a police siren, red and blue flashing lights lit up the intersection and we were being waved at to pull over. Two policemen, both with very heavy guttural Afrikaans accents asked us where we were coming from, where we were going to and what was in the back of the truck. I suppose we did look a bit suspicious in the middle of the night with this massive load on the back of the truck, so heavy in fact that the lights were illuminating half way up the trees rather than the road in front of us.

We had my open cage canopy on the back of Steve's pick-up, and everything was covered with a heavy, green, waterproof tarpaulin. Steve explained that we had come from Durban and were heading for the border.

"And what's in the back?"

"Just groceries," Steve replied, and we watched as their eyebrows went up and the two policemen exchange glances. I could just imagine them muttering to each other: "Groceries! Oh really!"

By all appearances it looked as if the police were going to inspect the contents of the back of the truck and despite it being the middle of the night I could feel beads of sweat along the top of my forehead and prickling under my arms; not because we were hiding or smuggling anything (which we weren't), but because it had taken us about two hours of very careful packing to fill the truck that afternoon. Again, and again we had to juggle boxes of pasta, bags of salt, cartons of soap, biscuits and toilet paper, sacks of sugar and flour and giant bottles of soft drink and cooking oil to get everything to fit in the truck. The thought of unloading six months worth of groceries onto the side of the road in a small South African town, and then repacking it all, in the middle of the night, was too awful to contemplate.

In the wing mirrors we watched the police walking round and round the back of the truck, not able to see anything at all because of the green tarpaulin.

"We're from Zimbabwe!" Steve said when the policemen reappeared at the window and that one word, Zimbabwe, seemed to be the magic wand that was going to get us out of trouble.

"Oh, from Zimbabwe hey! Is it as bad as we hear?" one of the policemen said.

"No, it's worse," Steve and I both replied at the same time.

"Agh shame man!" the policeman said. "It's OK! You can carry on."

Giggling under my breath we pulled back out onto the deserted Ermelo roads and the police car drove up again, alongside us in the next lane, and we both stopped at the next red traffic light. The questions from the police started again through our open car windows:

"Is there electricity? Are the shops really empty?"

We answered 'no' to the first question and 'yes' to the second, the traffic lights changed, and Steve pulled away again. The police were still in the lane next to us and we both stopped again at the next red traffic light.

"If it's such hell in Zimbabwe, why are you going back?" one of them asked through the window.

"It's home!" Steve replied. The policemen nodded, the lights changed and we pulled away again.

At the third red traffic light the conversation started again but this time from Steve: "You don't want a President do you?"

The two policemen roared with laughter, called out 'good luck,' turned off and went back on their midnight rounds of Ermelo and we headed off into the night, towards home, towards hell.

## SOUTHWARDS TO THE GREAT, GREY-GREEN, GREASY LIMPOPO RIVER: CHARLEY'S STORY

"One of our farm workers swam the great, grey-green, greasy Limpopo River, survived the crocs, got through the razor wire (probably because he was so thin from living on pumpkins and fresh air) and managed to get work on a farm near Tshipise hot springs in Musina. Sometime later he swam back over the Limpopo River with a television in a box strapped to his head. When he got to Harare he sold the television and was able to return to his family with some mielie meal [maize meal] and a few Rands to keep them going for a few months. His grandmother used to wake at 4.00am each day to walk to the lake to fish and collect mushrooms to feed the children: you can still see her standing knee deep near the lake Chivero spillway which is a treacherous but excellent way to get small bony fish. Turn a milk packet inside out and you've got the perfect container to put fish in and sell on the Bulawayo road."

## HEADING EAST: MOZAMBIQUE

The first stop every time we went through any border into any country was at the filling station, usually when the needle on the car was on E for Empty, not E for Enough, and sometimes even with the red light glaring ominously at you, warning that you were about to run out of fuel altogether. In Mozambique Manica was the first stop, the town where the buildings are old but solid and the highway is lined with trees whitewashed at the bottom and pollarded at about two or three metres to encourage the growth of a nice thick foliage on the top. The military looking trees always made me smile as they stood in straight lines, white stockinged legs and new shoots sprouting on top, standing awkwardly to attention in the searing heat displaying their fine Mohican haircuts. Then comes the nightmare of trying to understand a foreign currency, making sure you've got enough, checking you aren't being ripped off and usually giving up trying to convert the price from Mozambique Meticals into Zimbabwe's hyper inflation Bearer Cheques. Then with the car full of fuel, you head off for the marathon shopping trip to the huge South African Shoprite supermarket in Chimoio.

It's always very tense as you try and navigate around the very badly marked roundabout as you come into Chimoio, never sure if you're on the right side of road and not quite sure where to turn or how you'll ever be able to do it without having an accident as hundreds of people, motorbikes and roadside stalls crowd the roads in every direction. The earth is red, the dust smothers everything and the verges drop away steeply. Motorbikes zoom around in all directions, no one wears helmets and there doesn't seem to be a wrong side and right side of the road for bikers, or a limit to how many passengers they can carry; three was normal and five on a motorbike wasn't unusual at all. Someone's selling a red velvet lounge suite on the edge of the road, someone else is sawing planks and a compressor is roaring as tyre tubes are filled on the roadside. It's an understatement to say you have to have eyes in the front, back and sides of your head  but then at last you've made it and you sit in the supermarket car park  for a couple of minutes to calm down and reassure yourself you didn't hit anyone and the wheels are still on the car. Once inside the supermarket you can't help but feel completely overwhelmed by the huge selection of absolutely everything; it's like an Aladdin's cave of treasures after having come from Zimbabwe's literally empty shelves.

## THE PINK PAPAYA'S, MOZAMBIQUE:
## HELEN'S STORY

Helen Large who was working for a British Government Aid organization in Mozambique in the early 2000's, remembers the visits of Zimbabwe shoppers to the big Shoprite supermarket:

"I was living in Chimoio, just across the border from Mutare and started my own Backpackers lodge called The Pink Papaya. During those years of Zimbabwe's economic crisis I would often have guests from Zimbabwe come and stay with me, whilst they were on shopping trips to the Shoprite in Chimoio, which of course helped get me established. Despite the hardships they were going through, the Zimbabwe guests were a cheerful crowd and I would sometimes join them at The London Pub in Chimoio for sundowners in the evenings.

So it was a classic case really of one country's loss being another country's gain."

## HEADING SOUTH WEST TO BOTSWANA. THE LOVE GIFT: CHRISTINE'S STORY

"When the situation became really tough, especially for the old age pensioners (OAPs) in our church, we started putting monthly parcels together for them. We took the parcels to the OAP Retirement Homes and were shocked to find out how dire the situation was in those homes. For instance, at Jacaranda House they were given one toilet roll a month, one cooked and two cold meals, and just two cups of tea a day, to illustrate how tightly rationed the food and toiletry supplies were.

As so many items were totally unavailable in the local Bulawayo shops, we started going to Francistown once every two months to buy what we considered the bare necessities for the elderly, not just our church members but all the inhabitants of the three fairly small OAPs homes near our church, between 50 and 60 people. Our church contributed financially to this love gift project to enable us to import these essential goods for the pensioners, plus now and again a 50 kg bag of rice for the homes' kitchens. We did that for a number of years, until the situation had more or less normalised again."

## BLISS! NO SHOPPING FOR SIX MONTHS: GIGI'S STORY

"After losing our farms in 2005, my husband worked in Chimoio, but lived in Mutare. Shoprite shopping saved the day as did getting his vehicle filled up on the Mozambique side. In 2007 he worked in Afghanistan; I lived in Harare and still had one of the three children at home. His rotation was three months in Afghanistan and two weeks home. This certainly made me resourceful. I remembered that being kind and friendly whilst queuing in the bank for our "daily allowance" certainly went a long way. It opened the doors on where to find bread, meat or veggies and fuel, and many other things. I found such camaraderie in those days. Whilst queuing for fuel we made amazing friends. No use complaining as we were all in the same boat. With my husband working in Afghanistan it enabled me to be able to fly to Johannesburg and do a Makro shop which then got trucked down to Harare and delivered to my door. No shopping for six months, what bliss. Being able to help those that couldn't afford to do that was my greatest joy."

## HEADING NORTH TO ZAMBIA: ANNA'S STORY

"In the early years of Zimbabwe's collapse, Zambian people from across Livingstone city used to trek to Zimbabwe bringing bread, cooking oil and mealie meal and some other basic goods to Victoria Falls town and we used to buy from them. A loaf of bread was US$2 and two litres of cooking oil was US$10. I was a civil servant at the time and used to buy from the Zambian traders when I could get US dollars. The Zambian traders would arrive in Vic Falls in the morning and move about the townships, going door to door selling their wares. Then in the evenings they would gather around areas such as Jay's supermarket in the local township and in business shops in Chinotimba and Mkhosana townships. This made it easy for people coming home from work to buy what they needed direct from them. US$2 for a loaf of bread wasn't much for people working in the tourism industry but for everyone else it was difficult. I used to buy one loaf of bread for the whole week; it was for my daughter who was still at pre- school then and the rest of the time I would bake home-made bread for eating at home.

During this period my husband had left Zimbabwe for South Africa and he would send me basic foodstuffs. I would also travel to Kasane in Botswana to buy some other food stuffs for the child such as cereals, yoghurt, beef and other things that my husband couldn't send from South Africa. We soon realised that it was cheaper to buy in Zambia than to buy from the Zambian people selling in Vic Falls because they were charging a lot, sometimes even doubling the prices. The first time I went to Zambia I went with a friend who had gone there once before. We were allowed to use Border Passes instead of passports which made it easier and quicker for us.

We applied for border passes from the immigration offices. It wasn't a difficult process at all, you could do the passes in town or at the border office. You had to present your national

ID card, proof of residence in the form of Zesa or municipality bill or a letter from the local Ward Councillor. The Border Passes were valid for three months and the good thing about them was that you could cross the border as many times as you wanted.

I got myself a pass and off I went with my friend. Crossing both borders was simple and once across the border you could get to the shops by taxis which were expensive or kombis [minibuses] which were more affordable. Livingstone city had built a shopping mall close to the border, about 7km away and that's where we went shopping for the first time. We bought fresh hot bread and other basics there. I remember clearly that we bought an extra loaf of hot bread and my friend and I sat outside and devoured the bread; it was such a luxury and something we couldn't do back at home. It was an uneventful trip, but you had to carry a bag to hide your goods from baboons at the Zambian border. If you carried ordinary plastic shopping bags the baboons would grab your groceries.

Trips to Zambia for food became a regular occurrence. The Zim/ Zam border opened at 6.00am and closed at 10.00pm so there was always lots of time to go and come back in good time. We never planned our trips on the border times, but on the scorching heat; it was best to delay travelling until later in the day if possible. Most of the time it's very hot in Vic Falls so you would try to be in Zambia when they open for business at 9.00am so you could do your shopping and head home early before it got too hot. The border officials on both sides were very good; they understood our plight, which helped a lot.

Leaving home in Vic Falls to get to the border was a nightmare. We didn't have cars then and we would walk from Chinotimba to the border which is 3.5km away and then walk across the bridge because we needed to save money as much as possible. Sometimes, I would walk from home to the border and then all the way into Zambia as well if my money was short. If I was just going to buy mealie meal I would usually buy 12kgs which was enough for me but others would buy 25kg if they had a bigger household to support. The most painful thing was carrying the mealie meal back and we used to carry it on our heads. All around you could see men and woman carrying mealie meal on their heads because we couldn't afford the luxury of taxis. We would walk across the bridge carrying the mealie meal and a small bag with bread. Some people would be going as far as Mkhosana in Vic Falls which can amount to 10km from the Zambian side. Some would cross over to Monde village on the outskirts of Vic Falls making their journey about 22kms; it was a very long way to go for shopping.

On other trips, we would catch a kombi for 5 Kwacha to go the nearest mall which was off Mosi-Oa-Tunya road. We would window shop, check the prices of basic groceries and then walk to the city centre about 2.5 km away, checking prices from small tuck-shops on the way, looking for cheaper goods before we got to the centre and the big Shoprite and Spar supermarkets. When we finished shopping we would catch a kombi to the border and walk again from the Zambian border to home in Chinotimba or Mkhosana. Those who weren't so lucky with money would have to buy things in Zimbabwe that they could take to sell in Livingstone to raise the kwacha to do their shopping in Zambia. They would leave Vic Falls early in the morning and go and sell things like Mazoe orange crush in the Zambian townships until they made enough money to buy their mealie meal and come back home tired, dirty and hungry.

You would meet so many Zimbabweans over there in Livingstone that you would think that you were actually in Zimbabwe. The Zambian people were very good and understanding towards Zimbabweans; they treated us well as brothers and sisters. I don't recall any violence being perpetrated towards us like they had in South Africa; our only problem in Zambia was with the baboons trying to grab our hard earned groceries. For us in Vic Falls, Zambia and Zimbabwe have become like one country, we know each other. You can send them to bring you stuff from Zambia and they will reliably do so. We buy on credit from them and pay when we have money".

# CHAPTER 4

# ENCOUNTERS WITH OFFICIALS

Corruption, bribes and bureaucracy became our worst nightmare as Zimbabwe slipped ever closer to collapse. Civil servants had to implement an increasing mountain of new rules and regulations imposed by a government clinging to power and looking for control and revenue under every stone. The irony for civil servants was that as much as their bosses (who had access to US dollars) enriched themselves, built enormous imposing mansions and drove luxury vehicles, so the workers down the ladder got poorer by the day. Salaries and wages were paid in Zimbabwe dollars, hyper inflation reduced them to paupers and they had two options: leave the country or get onto the corruption gravy grain. Bribery and corruption seeped into every government department infected every official and every employee. Everyone wanted their cut of whatever you were trying to do whether it was to get an official document, travel on the roads, use a government service or cross a border. Officials at every level learnt that the longer they took to serve you, the more impatient you would get and the more likely you were to give them a bribe to work faster. It was a vicious circle: if you refused to pay a bribe you would leave empty handed or without satisfactory service; if you paid a bribe you made it worse for everyone else because it perpetuated a culture of expectation until everyone expected a bribe to do their jobs.


## DO'S AND DON'TS

- Always be polite
- Never argue or be aggressive
- Know your rights
- Don't pay a bribe
- Take a book to read
- Have certified photocopies of every possible document that officials may ask for: birth and marriage certificates, passport, driving licence, ID, vehicle registration book, vehicle insurance, police vehicle clearance, proof of residence and whatever else was relevant to the service you needed.


## DESTROYING THE EVIDENCE: 2006

Attending a Rotary lunch in 2006 the guest speaker was a court official and his topic was the destruction of evidence after convictions. The obvious items came up such as stolen property, equipment and money, when the owners couldn't be found, and then came the question of what happens with all the illegal substances that are seized, such as mbanje (marijuana). The court official said that mbanje was locked up until arrangements were made for it to be destroyed and this was usually done by incinerating it.

In the past when the problem wasn't so big, the court official said that drugs seized as evidence used to be burnt in the police yard or the courtyard under supervision. The serious and fascinating topic soon deteriorated into jokes and laughter when we heard how people who knew about the timing of the burning of seized mbanje would lean against the fence in the direction of the wind and get high on the smoke. Later, as the amount of mbanje being confiscated got too big to just burn in a heap or a drum in the police yard, they had to start taking it down to the local provincial government hospital and burn it in the incinerators. That apparently pleased the patients, so the joke went, because with the huge shortage of drugs in the country, the smell from the burning evidence helped anaesthetize them. The court official concluded his talk by saying that lately the problem has got much worse due to the shortage of coal and coke so the burning wasn't done and the evidence is mounting, literally!

## THE GOLD PANNING MAGISTRATE: 2007
When your country and its economy are in a state of collapse it usually takes the government of the day a very long time to admit to the situation and do something about it because the moment they do, they have to also accept responsibility for the collapse. In Zimbabwe's 2005-2008 collapse and again in the 2019 collapse, top level bureaucrats went on a frenzy of enriching themselves by engaging in fuel, currency, food, minerals and other black market activities; these were the tools with which to get rich in a collapsing country.  While workers couldn't even couldn't afford public transport to get to work, senior government officials would roar past in luxury

SUVs, the latest BMWs, Mercedes and even Lamborghini's. There were fuel barons, land barons, currency barons and mineral barons and you had to have connections to their networks to get anything that was in short supply. Meanwhile for the masses below them it wasn't about getting rich but about surviving and the tools to use were cross border trading, black market dealing and digging in the dirt for minerals, mostly gold and diamonds. One classic story reported in the Herald newspaper in 2007 told of a Magistrate who was about to appear in court in front of a Magistrate after being caught red handed while engaging in a bit of illegal gold panning: "The Magistrate, who was holding a panning rod, a pick and had folded his trousers knee high, dropped the equipment at the sight of the police officers and took to his heels."(sic) (The Herald, 2007)

## BORDER CROSSINGS AND TRAFFICKERS

Everything and everyone in need in a country in collapse creates an opportunity for someone else and the means of fulfilling those needs varies according to the depth of your pocket. A black market emerges for everything you can think of from bank notes, fuel, food and medicines to human traffickers who can escort you, for a price, through dense bush, raging rivers and razor wire across international borders. Or, if you want to go the legal route, there is always someone who, for a price, can get your passport stamped, jump you to the front of the queue, bribe immigration and customs officials and get you across the border with documents intact in a matter of minutes.

In 2007 and 2008 at the height of the country's collapse, there was no shortage of illicit dealings and night time 'people movers' travelling towards Zimbabwe's Beitbridge border post with South Africa. The situation was the same at border posts with all the country's neighbours: Botswana, Zambia and Mozambique but perhaps busiest was at the entry point into South Africa. The rule amongst road travellers going to these borders, especially at night, was: NEVER STOP AT A LAY-BY. The lay-bys on our potholed highways became drop off points, offices and waiting rooms for border jumpers and people movers. There were frequent reports of innocent travellers being attacked and robbed when they stopped at a lay-by to stretch their legs or have a break. The nearer you got to the border post the busier the lay-by's got with smugglers and traders buying and selling goods there.


## MRS GOLD TOOTH AND THE CEMENT:
## BEITBRIDGE BORDER: 2007

Arriving at Beitbridge border at 4.30am there were already three buses and well over 150 people standing in a queue to get into the immigration building. The line went out of the door, across the courtyard and circled three times around the yard. There was nothing to do but join the end of the line. Queue jumpers were everywhere, typical political types: arrogant, overweight, loud, overdressed, big sparkling gold watches; glaring at you, daring you to challenge them. It took over an hour and a half to get to the front of the line; little did we know that in the years to come that time would be considered as extremely fast and it would take eight to ten hours to get through the Beitbridge border post.

Finally out of Immigration, the problem started when we got to the exit boom to the South African border complex. It seems we only had two stamps on our little square exit slip and we should have had three. The gate guard was a woman in her thirties with a sparkling gold tooth in her front upper jaw. I don't know why but the gold tooth gave me the giggles: it seemed so out of place, so absurdly, outrageously ostentatious for a border guard who spent her days lifting a boom to let vehicles pass. The theme music from James Bond's Goldfinger got into my head making the suppressed giggles even worse and it was hard to concentrate on what Mrs Gold Tooth was saying but finally I paid attention:

"Give me some cement and I'll make a plan," she said miming that we should put money in the passport for her. My friend Steve who was driving didn't understand her and kept asking what the problem was, leaving Mrs Gold Tooth to repeatedly say she needed cement to be put into the passport; she expanded her mime to indicate getting something out of her pocket and putting it in the passport. I was a completely lost cause by that stage and didn't dare look at her or at Steve because of the giggles and so I looked out the window at the huge queue still waiting to be cleared at Immigration and the growing line of vehicles waiting impatiently behind us. Finally, Mrs Gold Tooth had either a moment of mercy or was simply bored with our stupidity and she snapped: "Oh go on!" and we did, fast.

As we navigated past traffic, money changers, hitch hikers and security personnel I explained to Steve the reason for my giggles and the glinting gold tooth that kept winking at me in the sunlight. As our laughter finally ebbed away Steve told me his story about shiny tooth fillings: "When I was a young farm assistant, I lived in a very nice cottage that belonged to the boss's son who was doing National Service. There was a young cook called Goliat. He was still learning but improving. I often shot food for the pot and also helped the crop guard with controlling pigs and baboons in the lands and would take Goliat with me. Goliat explained to me one day that his correct name was Goliath but pronunciation was a problem so everyone just dropped the 'h' and called him Goliat. When we were out shooting Goliat would watch and see where the empty cartridge cases fell and collect them. I asked him why he collected them. Goliat said that in the farm village there was a man who repaired teeth with brass and the cartridge cases were perfect for the dentistry procedures. Goliat even had several success stories of how tooth pain had been relieved with a bit of brass moulded over the painful tooth; it gave me the cold shivers."

As our mutual giggles died down and we set off on our marathon grocery shopping expedition I realised that perhaps I'd just learned another lesson in surviving border crossings when exiting a failed state: pretend not to understand and just play dumb, gold or brass teeth notwithstanding!

## LAY-BYS AND FUEL DEALERS: 2008

We left home at 3.00am, heading south to do our grocery shopping in another country in August 2008; it was an absurd reality of life for Zimbabweans trying to survive the country's collapse. At 6.00am we were in Chatsworth as the sun came up and we were greeted by huge Mukwa trees covered in pods that looked like prickly fried eggs but all eyes were needed on the road in order to zig-zag around the giant potholes. At 7.15am we got to Masvingo and had a short break to meet a friend briefly, drinking lukewarm coffee from a flask and eating sandwiches made with home-made bread the night before. Empty shops meant we couldn't even buy a cold drink or a snack on the road and soon we headed off again. Most of the trees were leafless and bare, preparing for their summer flush and a flock of ten guinea fowl rose up in noisy, laboured flight. In the middle of nowhere the 'Four Way Cocktail Bar' appeared: a run down, dilapidated building once someone's pride and joy. On the road between Masvingo and Ngundu Halt, the view was dry, barren and harsh: kopjes, aloes, Euphorbia trees and vast sandy riverbeds. Huge, life size, wooden carvings were on sale on the roadside: elephants, warthogs, eagles, giraffes and people. Further on, seemingly in the middle of nowhere, a man sat on a stone on the side of the road. As we approached, he held up a piece of cardboard. Written in smudged charcoal was just one word: 'PETROL.' Do we dare stop and buy some we wonder; a risky endeavour because you never know how clean or how pure it is. You wonder where and how a man on a rock could have found fuel to sell on the side of the road in a remote place like this; the answer lay ahead.

Ngundu Halt, at the turn off to Chiredzi, is a busy place: a market atmosphere with people milling around amidst cotton bales, goats, tomatoes and donkey carts. You pass through a densely forested valley and cross the Runde River, which is very wide with outcrops of huge, smooth black boulders, thick, deep sand and water in only a few pools. Then the Baobab trees start, giants marching through the barren bush, blazing a trail though the crackly, dusty lowveld. A maze of hundreds of potholes covers the road at Rutenga and continued until Bubye where the scene was of bleached dry grass and leafless trees. Between the Lion and Elephant Motel and the Beitbridge Border post there are more Baobabs, donkey carts and goats. Every few kilometres we pass fuel tankers stopped on the side of the road. Alongside the tankers are lithe, alert, men with plastic twenty litre containers. In cahoots with the tanker drivers they are siphoning off fuel to sell on the black market by the guys sitting on rocks in lay-bys.

The temptation to stop and buy twenty litres of fuel is very high, especially when your tank is almost empty and all of the filling stations have nothing to sell. There's a good chance that you'll be able to negotiate the price of the fuel with the man and his cardboard sign and you'll be able to buy it with local currency which you can't use once you get over the border, but even so, the risks are high. The best advice is don't do it! You've got no way of knowing if the fuel is clean, if the container is clean or has a sediment which you will then drain into your tank. You've also got no way of knowing if the fuel has been diluted or watered down and how far you'll get down the road before the problems of contaminated fuel bring you to a stuttering, jerking stop.

## LAY-BYS, GUMAGUMAS AND BORDER JUMPERS

On another food buying trip to South Africa we drove all night to avoid the endless corrupt police at road blocks, aiming to get to the border at daybreak. On the entire 650 kilometre journey from Marondera to Beitbridge (5.00pm to 6.00am) we saw a frog, a rat and one slender mongoose! Where, I wondered, were all the eyes in the night that we had seen on these long night-time road journeys when we were children? Eyes of civets and servals, night apes and genets, spring hares, owls and nightjars. Now the eyes in the night were of people: poachers, border jumpers and gumaguma's, the rough, tough young men who escort people across the border illegally: through the bush, along dusty tracks, across rivers and under the fences. These were the eyes of a country in collapse.

In one lay-by as we got nearer the border the picture of human trade was graphic. The big shady tree, concrete bench and picnic table where passing motorists could stop and have a drink and a sandwich, stretch their legs and take a break, had been taken over. Blankets were hanging from tree branches and draped over the remnants of the roadside fences. A small pile of firewood was stacked next to three flat rocks on the ground; the fireplace where the meal would be cooked before the border jumpers set out into the bush to bypass the border regulations. At other lay-bys the border jumpers and their gumaguma escorts were still there, waiting for more people perhaps or a better time of day, or night, before they moved. A big black pot filled with steaming maize porridge, a thick stirring stick in the bubbling sadza: breakfast almost ready.

Next, we passed a lay-by with plastic shacks held up with crooked branches for uprights. Black plastic and old, faded, yellow fertilizer bags formed the walls and roofs. Bare-chested young men are the 'hoteliers' of this roadside border jumper rendezvous. In this lay-by most of the people were women with babies and children, all well dressed, their suitcases, bags and luggage all piled up together, waiting for darkness and whatever terrors may lie ahead. It was the scene at this lay-by that left me feeling overcome with shame and empathy: shame that this is what our country had come to, the place that everyone is trying to get away from, and empathy for mothers so desperate that they would embark on such frightening journeys with young children in order to survive. Without money or passports there is no turning back for them, no other option than to embark on a journey into the unknown.


## BORDER MONEY CHANGERS

On either side of every border crossing there were always crowds of money changers as the country's collapse escalated. Always men, the money changers fiercely guard their patch and their pitch; they run alongside your vehicle calling out the rate, lock onto you and pursue you relentlessly, as close to the official buildings as they dare in the hope of doing a deal. They flick and wave handfuls of money in front of you urging you to do a deal, promising you theirs is the best rate you will find.

If you decide to use the money changers you have to have all your wits about you and preferably someone with you to check and double check because you can so easily be ripped off. Always check and double check the rate they are giving you and calculate how much you will get. Never hand your money over to them until you've received the full amount and don't change large amounts at a time. One common con of the money changers is to fold some of the notes in half so that both the top and bottom ends of the same notes are counted separately and only later do you discover that you only got half the number of notes you paid for. A helpful tip, learned after falling victim to this trick, was to insist that each single note is counted into your hand one at a time.

## BORDER OFFICIALS: 2003-2009

At the height of a country's collapse, everyone wants their cut when it comes to bribes and corruption and one of the most obvious places is where people are trying to get in and out of the country. Border officials at every level were involved in the corruption at the height of Zimbabwe's 2005-2008 collapse: customs, immigration, vehicle clearance inspectors, ZIMRA (tax) officials, EMA (Environmental Management inspectors) and even the person that lifts the boom to let you out of the border, such as Mrs Gold Tooth who we met in 2007 and would discover that there was one like her at every border crossing.

There is a price available for everything on the border corruption merry-go-round: to get to the front of the queue quickly; for an expired stamp in your passport; for an engine chassis number that can't be seen on your vehicle; for not declaring goods in your vehicle; for not searching your vehicle; for not delaying you at the boom gate; for not seizing perishable produce and so it goes on and on.

Sometimes the price could be as little as a bottle of Coke or a loaf of bread and if you left these items in plain sight on the back seat of the car it was almost an unspoken done deal. More often it was money that was wanted and if you took the moral high ground and refused to comply, you had to endure the inevitable anguish that followed. One painfully memorable occasion when a group of us were going to the coast for a week over Christmas and New Year I was on my high horse and not prepared to pay a bribe to the plump man at the boom who wanted something for himself. Eventually, when I wouldn't back down he simply said: 'everything out,' and he meant everything. For the next two hours the entire contents of my very full pick-up truck were unloaded onto the tarmac at the side of the boom. Every box, bag, trunk and container was opened; tents, sleeping bags and camp chairs littered the tarmac, everything was touched, turned over and inspected until eventually the New Year bottle of champagne was the prize he was looking for. Holding the bottle aloft he declared I was over the alcohol allowance and then I was done for. Two hours later: fined, Champers confiscated and with four sheets of A4 forms filled in, signed and stamped in excruciatingly slow motion, I headed back outside in the baking December heat with receipts in hand; the vehicle was repacked and the boom was lifted. Lesson learned!

**BORDER CONTROL: FOOT AND MOUTH DISEASE: 2007**

Arriving at the Beitbridge border post in what looked more like a farm truck than any of the other vehicles around, we approached the Foot and Mouth control area. It was late 2007 and as a farmer, even though I'm no longer allowed to farm in my country because of the colour of my skin, I felt pretty sure that the Foot and Mouth controls at the border were not going to be thorough, particularly because of Zimbabwe's state of collapse when the regulations had long since gone by the wayside because of no chemicals, no fuel, no transport, no inspectors or just no interest.

Foot and Mouth disease had always been one of the biggest fears with our breeding cattle on the farm. Whenever a cow was lying down with a fever, checking their gums and feet for blisters, wounds and ulcers was the first priority. Foamy saliva and stringy dribble were even more worrying and I'd make a note of the ear tag numbers and make sure that everyone knew to keep watching a feverish cow and be rigorous about quarantine, disinfectant and walking through the foot baths. Neighbours had foot baths on their farm driveways that people had to walk through and cars had to drive through.

With Foot and Mouth disease being so contagious and the necessary controls of culling infected animals and banning livestock movements and exports, surely this border disease control measure will be working I thought. Wrong!

At the border you were supposed to get out of your vehicle and walk through the foot bath which has sacking impregnated with disinfectant. We pulled up at the foot bath check point and got out of the car. The officials stared at us boredly. The foot bath was as dry as a bone. I raised my hands in question and lifted my eyebrows. "It's dry!" I exclaimed.

One of the officials yawned and said: "Oh, don't worry!" and signalled for us to get back in the vehicle and drive on.


## BORDER CROSSINGS, BRIBES AND CORRUPT OFFICIALS: 2009

The queue at the Beitbridge border post to get into South Africa from Zimbabwe was a massive four hour undertaking in early 2009. I'd done it twice in the last three weeks, once early in the evening and once at 3.00am in the morning and it seemed that the time of day or night was of no consequence. As fast as people reach the front of the queue so more join the back of the line, which I calculated held between 750 and 800 people all the time.

The South African officials, both Police and Immigration personnel, make no attempt to disguise their contempt for the flood tide of Zimbabweans. Surly, sullen and rude, they show no compassion whatever for Zimbabweans who, despite a decade of hell, are still polite, courteous and humble. No concession is made for women, children or pensioners and aggressive South African Policewomen patrol the queue shouting at people who are not standing one behind the other in a straight enough line or who have weakened and resorted to sitting on the ground.

"No sitting allowed here," they bark, waving their truncheons; "straight lines and standing only."

Touts locally called 'gumaguma,' the same name as the border jumper guides, weave in and out of the queue looking for easy touches. "You want to go fast," they ask? "200 Rand (20 US dollars) per person and I'll take you to the front of the line. Another 200 Rand and I'll take you all the way to the passport control counter." Police officers in uniform watch the touts and the bribery taking place right in front of them, but they do nothing at all and everyone grumbles that the officials are undoubtedly getting a cut of the deals which is why they don't intervene. Bribery and corruption seemed institutionalized in Zimbabwe and in 2009 and it seemed to be gathering pace in South Africa too.

## DRIVING LICENCE FOR A BOTTLE OF BRANDY: 2009

In the second half of 2008 when there was no food to buy and everyone everywhere was hungry, you could buy an identity document for 10 kgs of maize and 1 kg of beef. Without an ID in Zimbabwe you are stuck; you can't drive, get a passport, fill in any government form or even get a SIM card for a mobile phone. So a bag of maize and packet of beef was a small price to pay for an ID. Everything changed in mid 2009 when the shops were full of food again; the price of black market documents changed from food to money: real money, US dollars preferably. If you had the right connections and a stash of real cash you could buy a birth certificate or identity document for US$10; an Emergency Travel Document (ETD) for US$50 and a Zimbabwe passport for US$100. You could avoid being searched, harassed or detained at a road block for US$5 or US$10, depending on the state of repair of your vehicle and how many police are on duty at the road block (because they all want a cut of course) and you could buy a driving licence, after hours and at a discreet location, for US$100. "Gone are the good old days when you could buy a driving licence for a bottle of brandy!" a friend said.

## STORIES FROM THE ROAD BLOCKS: 2005-2009

Police checks, speed traps and road blocks became the scourge of the highways across Zimbabwe as the economic collapse escalated. By 2007 you could expect to encounter a ZRP (Zimbabwe Republic Police) road block every twenty or thirty kilometres and by 2008 you would be stopped once every ten kilometres. Corruption was the only explanation for the abundance of road blocks. Police were earning a pittance in a worthless currency and for them road blocks were a gold mine. The favourite procedure by police at a road block was to indicate for you to stop and when you did they asked for your driving licence which they immediately took and held onto, directing you to pull off the road, usually onto very eroded, steep verges. With the police detail holding your driving licence they would walk painfully slowly around your vehicle looking for something, anything, that they could fine you for. Very often they would stop looking at your vehicle and chat on their phone, talk to another officer or go away and pull another vehicle off the road, leaving you stranded and frustrated parked on the verge. You couldn't leave because they had your licence and so you were forced to wait, temper rising very quickly. There was absolutely no doubt that these interminable delaying tactics by the police were used to solicit bribes. The more impatient you got or the more of a hurry you were in, the more likely you were to offer them a bank note or two. As soon as that happened you were given back your driving licence and instructed to carry on with your journey. Legal experts told us that it was only legal for the police to see your driving licence, not to actually take it from you but in reality it was almost impossible to stop them from taking it. The obvious outcome of the whole rotten system was that the more people paid bribes the worse the problem got and the harder it was for those of us who wouldn't pay bribes to get away from the road blocks unscathed.

There were countless stories of how people who wouldn't pay the bribes dealt with their frustration. We heard of people getting their deck chairs out of the boot and setting them up on the roadside, chatting nonchalantly and telling jokes until the police got so annoyed at the spectacle they would tell them to go. "Carry On!" was actually the favoured phrase by police who couldn't find anything to fine you for and weren't making any headway in the bribery department. Another favourite story from the road blocks was the man and his wife who had a gas cylinder in the car and they set it up on the roadside and put on a small pot of water to boil and proceeded to make tea!

As the road block money making scheme continued, the issuance of tickets giving you fourteen days to go and pay a fine at your local police station was no longer an option. Very often police didn't have ticket books at all or they had strange looking, faded tickets sometimes without serial numbers which looked suspiciously like they had been photocopied. It was the same for receipt books: suspicious, without a police logo or ZRP identification. On one memorable occasion travelling with a friend, we were instructed to pull over; all the usual delaying tactics were employed by the policeman and eventually my friend demanded to see the policeman's official ID and force number. An argument ensued and the more my friend insisted that it was his right to see the ID and Force Number, the more annoyed the policeman got, eventually pulling out a crumpled photocopy of a photograph of a police car with a hand written ID number scrawled on the top! It was hard to keep hysterics in check and the policeman must have realised he'd gone too far and we were told abruptly to 'Carry On!'

Then came the era of what they called 'Spot Fines' which appeared to have replaced conventional tickets. The police would find some fault on your vehicle and fine you on the spot. The things they chose to fine you for changed from week to week and it was always helpful to ask around before you travelled so you knew what to expect and what particular item was the target of their fund generating project that day. The favourite ones were: fire extinguishers which they said needed recharging or weren't mounted on a bracket; green fluorescent vests, red breakdown triangles, wheel spanners and jacks, spare tyres. They always checked vehicle licence and insurance discs and another favourite of theirs, but the bane of our lives was the dreaded third number plate. This was a government sticker on your windscreen which had your licence plate, engine and chassis number and the Zimbabwe crest. At countless road blocks police would accuse you of 'tampering' with the third number plate sticker and make you pay a twenty US dollar spot fine. You could argue till you were blue in the face that you hadn't touched the sticker but they wouldn't have it. Their definition of tampering could include a part of the sticker touching another disc on the windscreen, a bit of dirt under the edge, it being on what they said was the wrong side of the windscreen, or in the wrong location on the glass or anything else they could think off.

As time went by we got to know where the road blocks would be and started to use them as maker points on regular journeys. On a regular route I travelled I could measure my progress by the location of the police road blocks: just past the honey sellers; under the big tree at the lay-by; in the long grass before the big kopje; near the graffiti painted on the flat rock; under the old fig tree; by the stall where they sell apples; just past the turn off to the rock paintings; half way down the hill where the mountain acacia trees are; near the thatched hut where they sell clay pots.

Regardless of where the road block was you never quite knew how it was going to turn out. I had a well practised procedure ready which I tried to always stick to: never have anything visible in the vehicle except water, switch the music off, take sunglasses off, open window a couple of inches, have driving licence at my side, have certified photocopies of every possible document they may want to see in the cubby hole, be polite, don't volunteer anything, don't argue and never, never, never pay a bribe.

Everyone had their own way of dealing with the police at the road blocks; one friend would always pick up police in uniform if they were hitch-hiking because she said this got her through every road block without ever being stopped. Another friend always had a copy of The Outpost in plain view on his dashboard or on the seat next to him. The Outpost is the monthly Police magazine and apparently the sight of the magazine always found favour and a friendly wave through the road blocks. Another friend carried a giant bag of boiled peppermint sweets in his car, Crystal Mints they were called, and he gave the police a sweet, much to their delight, but it didn't usually stop them from fining him if they were on a mission. A lot of people said the police had a 'target' of fines to meet every day and it certainly seemed that way in my home town when the police would even be in the suburbs fining people almost as they drove out of their gates first thing in the morning at 7.00am and by 11.00am the police had all gone, their target met.

My friend Verity had a classic plan that she used at road blocks at a time when the currency was absolutely worthless and cheques had become obsolete as they lost all their value before you even got to the bank to deposit them:

"When stopped and asked to pay some arbitrary fine, I smiled sweetly and reached for my handbag explaining that I didn't carry cash with me but would be happy to write them a cheque. As they hesitated and drew breath, I asked to whom did I make it out to, and that was that really. ZRP didn't want cheques! Every time I was sent on my way without paying a dime."

On another occasion Verity, always quick off the mark, had this lovely encounter: "Late afternoon, late October I am slumped over the steering wheel making my way home and was stopped at a road block where there hadn't been one before. The policeman asked for my driver's licence which he studied carefully, once or twice his gaze flickered back to my weary face. I leaned out the window and explained "that was when I was young and beautiful". His expression didn't change but he looked back at me, at the licence and said without any change of tone "Ah, Madam, you are still alright." Well, that made my day! I sat up straight, tossed my non-existent curls, smiled and made my way home with a lighter heart. I think he was really just being polite to an old lady."

Speed traps were a nightmare, not because you were caught speeding but because suddenly, out of nowhere there would suddenly be a speed sign for 60km/hr in a zone where the day before the limit had been 100km/hr. Hitting the brakes hard to try and get to 60km was pointless because the police would be waiting in the long grass just a few metres past the new 60km/hr sign. Often there would be loose sand or rubble around the base of the signs so there was no doubt they had been hastily erected and would just as suddenly disappear a few days later. The police showed absolutely no mercy with their speed guns, if you were 2km over the limit you had to pay their spot fine. As with every other traffic fine scheme the police came up with there were countless stories of the speed guns not being zeroed between one motorist and the next so even if you were doing 60km/hr, the speed gun would show that you were doing 100km/hr.

The worse the traffic/highway police became the more people became emboldened and it became common to see motorists having heated arguments at road blocks, refusing to hand over their driving licences, refusing to pay bribes or Spot Fines or simply just putting their foot on the accelerator and not stopping at the road block. The police response to this came with the dreaded spikes. At every road block you would see police with home-made spiked metal plates which they would slide out onto the road in front of vehicles to stop them, shredding their tyres instantly.

Nearly a decade later an article in the press by the Institute for Security Studies in South Africa, made the issue of spot fines, police having targets and the role of government in the whole corrupt affair very clear: "Central governmental collusion in this illicit process is readily apparent. Finance Minister Patrick Chinamasa has proposed raising the penalty for minor traffic violations by US$10 to US$30, and projected amounts accruing from road blocks (US$60 million) have been officially incorporated in the budget of the Home Affairs ministry. Police stations are given monthly road block revenue targets, and individual police officers are ordered to raise set amounts daily from fines." (Matyszak, 2017)

Being able to use humour was always a great way through a police road block if you could pull it off and Verity told this classic story involving her friends: "A couple I know ran a gift shop and had taken on a younger friend to assist in the shop. One weekend they all went out of town to stay with friends and made their way back into Bulawayo early Monday morning where they were duly stopped at a road block. The young policewoman asked where they had been and where they were going and my friend calmly explained "I took my wives out of town for the weekend."

The policewoman blinked, hesitated then asked him curiously "Do they get on?"

"Oh yes," he said enthusiastically, "they get on very well." Again, he was waved on his way without any kind of fine as the young policewoman was left wondering about white people and second wives!"

Out of town police road blocks were often treacherous affairs particularly if you were a woman travelling alone. In January 2009, approaching one of the numerous police road blocks a dozen kilometres outside of Harare, an assortment of armed security personnel were standing around. The sheer number of them was intimidating and you had no way of knowing if they would stop you or not. Sometimes they would stop you and other times they would completely ignore you; it was all a very hit and miss affair. There were police in khaki uniforms wearing fluorescent green vests; police in navy blue trousers and grey shirts; soldiers in army camouflage; other soldiers sporting red berets; youth brigade members in olive green uniforms and military police. I felt like I was in a war zone and there was no way of knowing if any of these police and soldiers were actually what their uniform indicated they were, why there were so many of them at the road block and what they were looking for. In the tall, uncut grass a tatty green tent offered protection for all these security personnel. A curl of smoke rose from under a soot blackened pot balanced on three stones above a small fire.

My knuckles white from gripping the steering wheel, I felt like a criminal and my heart sank when one of them indicated for me to pull over. The drop off from the tar looked to be a good eight inches or more and so I moved forward and stopped on the edge of the road. Immediately a very aggressive policeman came to my window and started shouting at me, demanding to know why I didn't stop exactly where he had indicated. He added a few more angry expletives and when I could get a word in I apologized and said the drop off was so steep there was a chance my car would roll on its side. "You are arrested," he said and walked away. I had no idea what to do next and so I sat there and waited, paralyzed, fearful for what was going to happen. Wrestling my mobile phone out of my pocket with shaking hands I decided to phone a friend so that someone would know what was going on and where I was, just in case things got nasty. Before I could make the call another policeman appeared at the window gesturing vigorously at me to "Carry On," which I did with much haste and anxious glances in the rear-view mirror. I had no idea what had gone on or why I wasn't arrested anymore but I certainly wasn't hanging around to find out.

Further out of town on the open road the road blocks were completely different. Every ten to twenty kilometres there would be a police road block and then, in between, under a tree or out of the long grass two policemen would suddenly appear and wave at you to stop. Nine times out of ten you could see it was a con: two bods wearing green reflective vests but with no police sign, drums or bollards. As time went on most people just drove past them but slow cars, minibuses and big trucks weren't so lucky. At all road blocks, regardless of the location, minibuses were always made to stop. In plain sight it was impossible not to see the minibus driver or the tout passing something in his hand to the police and then they would be free to go immediately, despite worn tyres, cracked windscreens, smoke belching exhausts and being overloaded with passengers: the bribe machine was in full swing.

## THE POLICE AND THE STOLEN MONEY THAT THEY STOLE!

What happened to all the money from spot fines and bribes was something we all wanted to know? You never saw lock boxes or storage facilities for all the cash police were taking at their road blocks so where were they putting it all out there on the highways? A friend who lived near a police road block described how he kept seeing the police going to a patch of thick scrubby bush around a big Msasa tree. Thinking they were relieving themselves in the bush, his interest was aroused when he saw a policeman bending down and putting something under a pile of leaves and then placing a rock on top of it; he was obviously hiding something. After days of watching the policemen going to exactly the same spot and bending down to conceal something he knew that this must be the hidden stash. The more we talked about incidents like this the more the stories of their hiding places came out: bags of bank notes stuffed into ant bear holes; pushed into hollows in tree trunks; in drainage culverts, under rocks.

The truth came out about police hiding their illicit bribes and spot fines a few years later, when a ten year old girl stumbled upon US$2,000 hidden in a plastic bag with some wild fruits hidden in pile of rubbish near a road block in Beatrice on Christmas Eve. The newspaper report exposing the story and the arrest of the two police officers on duty at the road block had this classic introduction in Newsday newspaper:

"National Police spokesperson Senior Assistant Commissioner Charity Charamba yesterday said police had launched an investigation into the case where traffic cops nearly lost about $2,000 stolen money, to a 10-year-old girl." (Newsday, 2014)

# CHAPTER 5

# MONEY MADNESS

**RULES TO LIVE BY WHEN YOUR CURRENCY STARTS TO COLLAPSE:**

- Get your money out of the bank
- Don't save your money
- Don't keep your money
- Convert your money into internationally stable currencies, minerals, non depreciating assets.
- Spend your money and stock up on food, fuel, assets

**PREPARE FOR:**

- Repeated devaluations causing deposits, savings and pensions to become worthless overnight.
- Being unable to withdraw salaries paid directly into banks due to very small maximum daily withdrawal limits.
- Banks run out of cash.
- No foreign currency available to anyone without government connections leading to massive black market demand and rising exchange rates.
- Requirements to apply to Reserve Bank for foreign currency to pay foreign bills, subscriptions, education fees, medical costs and imports.

- Businesses stop accepting cheques, credit and debit cards.
- Government prints money and releases increasingly higher denomination bank notes.
- Riots and unpredictable crowds outside banks

## SAVORY MONEY: 2004

In early 2004, there were no bank notes to be had anywhere. The banks didn't have any, shops and businesses didn't have any and no one had any change at all. If you purchased something for $92 and you gave $100, you had to leave something behind to change the total to suit the bank notes you had, give the shop the eight dollar balance or buy something else worth $8. Most shops littered their check-out counters with small items that you could take instead of change. Depending on what type of shop you were in your change might be a sweet, bubble gum or ballpoint pen (if you were in a supermarket); a roll of cotton, zip or packet of buttons (if you were in a fabric shop); a packet of envelopes, roll of Sellotape or A6 notebook (if you were in a stationers); a strip of biltong or half a beer stick (dry vorcs sausage) if you were in a butchery.

Some weeks before the 2004 cash crisis reached its peak, I had exchanged some forex (foreign currency) for Zimbabwe dollars. You didn't need a lot of British pounds or US dollars to get a huge amount of Zimbabwe dollars. With the deal done I got half a million Zimbabwe dollar Bearer Cheque notes and promptly broke all my own rules, hiding the cash to keep for an emergency. What a silly thing to do!

In the mid 2000's a lot of friends were leaving Zimbabwe as the country's collapse escalated and as they packed up to go they were always left with the strangest things which they asked you to get rid of. Things like knives without handles, strange  kitchen gadgets such as garlic pressing tools and ice cream scoops, house, car and garden tools, cleaning materials, half empty bottles, jars, boxes and Tupperware containers of food and always numerous jars of herbs and spices.

After a number of friends had left in quick succession, I suddenly realised that I had over a hundred little herb and spice bottles which filled two biscuit tins, two large Tupperware containers and a shoe box. Pushing them all to the back of the cupboard I left them until I felt emotionally strong enough to cope with getting rid of the last reminders of friends who had gone. Clean out time came a year or two later. The kitchen smelled like an exotic bazaar as jar by jar, box by box, I ruthlessly tipped out the contents of all the containers into a huge pile which I was going to burn. The glass and plastic jars and containers were going to be kept for the day, if ever that day came, when the dustbin truck came again. As the pile of herbs and spices got bigger the sneezing and streaming nose and watering eyes almost incapacitated me. Potions and powders, leaves and berries, seeds, bark, and liquids: soy, Worcester, brown sauce, chilli and numerous unknown home-made hot spice concoctions which smelled strong enough to launch a rocket into space.

When I got to the last container in the cupboard, a big round biscuit tin, I took all the bottles and jars out and saw that something had leaked because everything had sticky brown bottoms. Underneath the jars there was a sticky brown bag which I almost threw away with the stained paper which lined the tin. Then I noticed that there was something in the bag. In three thick piles held together with paper clips was the half a million dollars in Bearer Cheque notes that I had hidden away two years before. I put the whole lot in the sink, covered it with water and washing up liquid, washed all the money and laid it outside in the sun to dry. A few of the notes were too badly damaged and had to be thrown away so my half a million became four hundred thousand dollars and I knew I had to spend it straight away; it was by then enough to buy almost nothing. I decided I'd spoil myself and buy a box of cornflakes, a huge luxury that I hadn't been able to afford for years and the thought of having something other than mealie meal porridge for breakfast was intoxicating.

I should be so lucky! Arriving at the supermarket I discovered that a 300g box of cornflakes was Z$4,200,000 so I gave that a miss and reminded myself that I should be grateful I had mealie meal porridge to eat when people were starving. I filed my washed but still very aromatic Bearer Cheque notes into the bundle of money I carried in a plastic bag because it didn't fit in my wallet anymore and the smelly notes went back into circulation. It turned out that I could buy half a tin of baked beans for what had been my half million dollars! Knowing that half a tin of baked beans had cost me forty US dollars taught me a big lesson I'd never forget: don't save your money when your currency is collapsing.

**DELAYING PAYMENTS: 2006**

Wheelers and dealers, con artists and crooks pop up like weeds in a vegetable patch when a country's economy is in the process of collapse. Excuses of years past like the cheque's in the post, or the books are with the accountant, had been replaced by electronic scapegoats in the new millennium. Now the excuses had become: my computer crashed, a virus ate my hard drive, or the software isn't compatible. Whatever the excuses, the reality of delaying payments in a time of hyper inflation is huge. In March 2006 inflation was 780%, interest rates on deposits was over 400% and holding a payment back by a few days resulted in losses or gains of multi millions of dollars. On the 3rd March 2006 two deposits were said to have been made into my bank account, one for sixty four million and another for ninety four million dollars. It sounded like a massive amount of money but at the time a loaf of bread was sixty six thousand dollars, one single egg was twenty five thousand dollars and a bottle of shampoo was one million two hundred thousand dollars. By the 24th March there was still no sign of either deposit in my account and contacting the bank again, I was told that their 'software was incompatible.' When I asked exactly what that meant, they told me there were just too many zeros for the programme to recognize. On that day I calculated that if I had the one hundred and fifty eight million dollars invested at 180% interest, which was the investment interest rate at the time, in a month I would have earned twenty four and half million dollars in interest. I could have been making Z$819,000 every single day so the 'cheque in the post' and the 'incompatible software' excuses were as believable as pigs flying past my window! Delaying payments: a warning for some a get rich quick scheme for others, depending on your morals.

**ITEMS NEEDED DURING A CURRENCY COLLAPSE**

- Paper Clips – to hold the numerous bank notes together
- Elastic Bands – to contain piles of money
- Large bank bags, A4 envelopes and shopping bags – to carry bundles of money
- Cardboard boxes – to hold large 'bricks' of bank notes
- Money counting machines – to count the bank notes
- Backpacks– to carry the money when you go shopping
- Suitcases – to carry the money when you go bulk shopping
- Tin trunks – to carry your money to the bank or collect wages

**MANDATORY PRICE CUTS: JUNE 2007**

In June 2007 the government announced the enforced cutting of all prices by 50% to try and slow inflation which at the time was one thousand one hundred and eighty four percent. Accusing the private sector of profiteering, President Mugabe said his government was going to seize all the mines and nationalize them and take over all the companies. For consumers the nationwide 50% price slashing was a free for all bonanza, a huge bonus, but for businesses, importers and shops it was a death sentence. For a few days there was a stampede of people with rucksacks full of money buying up everything and anything they could get their hands on from food and clothing to TV's, computers, radios, furniture, appliances and equipment. Some were shopping for themselves and their families, others were buying to resell and then there were the unscrupulous black market dealers who were grabbing whatever they could. The enforced price cuts took no account of how much retailers had paid for their goods or what their profit margins were but it left them staring bankruptcy in the face after just a few days as they looked at their empty shelves, inflation of almost twelve hundred percent and no way to recoup their losses, resupply their stock or even keep their shops open.

The survival lessons here were not so clear cut. This was one of those very tough ethical questions: you could either go on a shopping frenzy and look out for number one or you could refuse to take part in what was simply State initiated looting and which you knew would destroy businesses. For me the answer was easy and it came when the government sent a 'Taskforce' to force shop owners and businesses to cut their prices by 50%. This Taskforce was made up of young men in army camouflage, (were they even soldiers we wondered?) police in uniform and large numbers of pimply faced Youth Brigade members. Shop to shop they went, followed by a Pied Piper rabble of friends, relations, black marketeers and hangers- on; they literally stormed shops and demanded loudly that managers cut the prices and waited while they did so, and then filled trolleys with all the goods themselves. It was utterly sickening to watch, heartbreaking to see people being forced to sell their goods for much less than they paid for them and there was absolutely nothing they could do to stop it. This was the equivalent of farm invasions in another guise: people destroying your livelihood with the permission of government while you stood and watched helplessly. Outside in car parks fancy vehicles with tinted windows were filled with mountains of goods and more rucksacks of cash were passed to their 'buyers' to go back and buy more. I felt physically ill  to be witnessing this; it was obscene and there was no way I was going to be a part of this orgy of organized looting because somewhere in the horror of surviving a failed state, you have to be able to hold your head up high and do the right thing.

## MILLION DOLLAR SHOPPING:  2007

Going shopping at Spar supermarket with two million dollars in my pocket in November 2007 I got to the till and had what used to be one of those embarrassing moments when I discovered I didn't have enough money to pay for my groceries. I say it used to be an embarrassing moment because in a time of hyper inflation running out of money when you got to the till was far more normal than having enough money. In my shopping basket I only had two items but there were no price stickers on the shelves or the items so it was always a bit of a wild guess as to whether you would be able to afford them when you got to the checkout counter. Two million dollars would surely be enough for my two items I thought.

I was wrong! One 400g tin of baked beans was Z$1.2 million and a two litre bottle of orange juice Z$870,000. In real terms those two items were far more expensive because three zeros had recently been removed from the currency so the tin of beans would actually have been Z$1.2 billion and the orange juice Z$870 million. I learnt two lessons on that occasion: You don't really need the orange juice was the first one and never believe you've got enough money in your pocket in a time of hyper inflation, was the second!

## INTO THE QUADRILLIONS: NOVEMBER 2007

In November 2007 Zimbabwe's Finance Minister Samuel Mumbengegwi presented a 7.8 quadrillion dollar budget and the only lesson we learnt was to expand our vocabulary! While he talked about a US$4.1 billion external debt; Z$209 trillion allocated for the 2008 elections and a budget deficit of Z$1,760 quadrillion, we got out our dictionaries and pen and paper to try and work out just exactly how many zeros there are in a quadrillion and how long those figures would be accurate for: a week perhaps before they needed to change them into quintillions.

**BANKS: BE PREPARED FOR:**

- Freezing of deposits
- Shrinking maximum daily/weekly withdrawal limits
- Cessation of communications with customers
- Unannounced new/increased bank charges for all services including: cheque deposits, cash deposits; bank transfers; telephone balance enquiries, personal balance enquiries, bank statements
- Continuous and unannounced raising of minimum balances
- Cessation of interest payments on savings and current accounts
- Charges to close bank accounts
- Reduced banking hours
- Closure of ATMs
- Closure of branches
- Collapse of banks

**BOMBARDED WITH BUREAUCRACY**

There were no better words than those of children's author Lewis Carroll to describe the continually changing government regulations when economic collapse accelerated: "Thick and fast they came at last, And more and more and more." The further your economy sinks the more you need to be prepared for an avalanche of bureaucracy. Rules, Regulations and Statutory Instruments come thick and fast as the government desperately tries to control an already uncontrollable situation. The rules change constantly: regulating prices, exchange rates, bank notes, money supply, interest rates, daily and weekly withdrawal limits, access to foreign currency and the ability to move money. In February 2008 the Zimbabwe government went into a frenzied scramble of new controls and rules and regulations but it was already far too late.

## CHEQUE LIMITS: FEBRUARY 2008

Notice from the RBZ (Reserve Bank of Zimbabwe) (February 2008)

"Individuals and companies can, with immediate effect, write cheques of a maximum limit of Z$10 billion dollars." The Governor of the Reserve Bank, Gideon Gono, said the new cheque limit was "aimed at promoting the use of cheques as a means of payment." Previously the maximum cheque limit was Z$500 million and we had all learned to use smaller and smaller handwriting in order to fit all the words and numbers onto our cheques. In reality, however, by the beginning of 2008 it was already almost impossible to pay by cheque as no one would take them because in the time it took for the cheque to be deposited, cleared and credited to your account, much of its value had been lost in run-away inflation. Government departments were still obliged to accept cheques but in shops everywhere there were signs: 'Sorry! No Cheques Accepted.'

## A DOG CHASING ITS OWN TAIL.

## CASH TRANSACTION LIMITS: 29 FEBRUARY 2008

At the end of February 2008, a new Statutory Instrument 21/2008 was released stating that it was illegal for companies and individuals to do cash transactions worth more than Z$250 million. Now the government were telling us how much of our own money we could spend, how daft was this! The reality of this absurd Statutory Instrument was that Z$250 million was only enough to purchase ten litres of fuel at the time; filling stations wouldn't take cheques or debit cards so what on earth were we supposed to do to get a tank of fuel for our cars; get in the queue six times to fill our tanks? It was a pointless regulation and joined the scrapheap with all the other desperate measures of a government which had lost the plot. The Bank Use and Suppression of Money Laundering Act went on to make it illegal for traders and parastatals to hold cash in excess of Z$500 million for more than 24 hours from the last trading hour. The Zimbabwe National Chamber of Commerce said the government's Statutory Instrument was "like a dog chasing its tail," which was an equally accurate description for everyone trying to keep up with the government's rules and regulations while out there on the streets there were no rules at all as everyone did their own thing.


## PRICE CONTROLS: FEBRUARY 2008

Not having learnt from the chaos caused by the 2007 enforced price cuts, or perhaps because of what they had personally gained in the process, in February 2008 the government's National Income and Pricing Commission (NIPC) again tried to control prices charged by retailers and private businesses. The NIPC announced the approval of price increases of a number of commodities which were to be valid for the following three months. Instead of allowing prices to be charged in line with restocking and import costs, government again chose the clenched fist line of control. It was a pointless exercise because in the six months since the 2007 enforced price cuts, companies had closed down and jobs had been lost; in those outlets that had survived, the prices of goods had crept up every week in order to try and keep pace with inflation and restocking costs. The NIPC set prices that were absurdly low and totally unrealistic; another frenzy of forced price cuts and shopping orgies ensued. When this happened inflation was officially quoted at over one hundred thousand percent, 100,580.2% to be exact, and all we knew for sure was that this move would make it impossible for shops to restock their shelves and there would be less and less goods to buy.

Some of the items in the NIPC increased price controls list:

| COMMODITY | QUANTITY | NIPC PRICE (Z$) | MARKET PRICE (Z$) |
|---|---|---|---|
| Bread | One loaf | 200,000 | 3,500,000 |
| Brown sugar | 2ks | 7,360,276 | 12,000,000 |
| White sugar | 2kgs | 7,944,249 | 15,000,000 |
| Cooking oil | 2 litres | 24,600,000 | 55,000,000 |
| Chicken | 1kg | 15,913,043 | 25,400,000 |

| COMMODITY | QUANTITY | NIPC PRICE (Z$) | MARKET PRICE (Z$) |
|---|---|---|---|
| Milk | 500mls | 1,464,000 | 4,500,000 |
| Rice | 2 kgs | 2,880,000 | 35,000,000 |
| Cement | 50kgs | 84,765,364 | 107,300,000 |
| Mealie meal | 10kgs | 152,400 | 40,000,000 |

## DIARY NOTES: TWO BEERS, 28 MARCH 2008
## (PRE ELECTION DAY)

At the end of March 2008 by all accounts Zimbabwe appeared to be at its lowest ebb. We were about to go into a general election and it seemed unimaginable that the electorate would vote for more of the same. Shops were empty, inflation was 355,000 percent, one US dollar bought 70 million Zimbabwe dollars and an estimated quarter of our population were living and working in the Diaspora, sending money home to support their families. Knowing that the importance of documenting events in our country was to ensure that we and others would be able to learn from our history, I described what I saw the day before the elections:

"It is the day before the elections, I feel compelled to describe this day – may it be the last of this hell? The world is calling this the most important election since Independence in April 1980. It's Friday today, Richie is at home because schools broke up two weeks early because of the elections.

I collected Peter, an elderly neighbour, for our usual Friday shopping routine and dropped him at the post office where he had business to do. When I picked him up an hour later Peter had bought virtually nothing as the shops are empty. But he did have his cigarettes which he'd bought on the black market! I took him to TM and OK supermarkets, but they were both empty, aisle after aisle of empty shelves. Peter said he'd been living almost entirely on charity again this week along with my home-made bread, milk I bought him from the farm and a couple of tins of sardines that had arrived in a parcel. He says there have been countless occasions in the past six months when he would literally have starved if it hadn't been for me. As we got out at Spar supermarket, he told me that for the first time in a year he has bought himself two beers. He says one is for tomorrow: D Day he calls it, to toast getting to the elections and the other beer is for the day the elections results are announced – to toast real change, or perhaps to commiserate, he says, he is pessimistic.

Inside Spar only two tills are staffed and at one counter is a well-dressed skinny woman and she is buying every single bottle of orange juice in the store, there are dozens of them. They are five litre bottles, all imported and each one costing 300 million dollars! Part way through the adding and packing the woman asks for an interim total. She and the teller both put their fingers on the computer screen to count the number of digits as there are so many. The interim total is 37 billion dollars. "No problem," the skinny woman says, "keep going" and more bottles of orange juice go through the till.

Aside from the orange juice there's almost nothing else to buy in Spar. There are a few bags of small, soggy, sprouting potatoes and in the cold freezers which would normally have butter, margarine, cheese, yoghurt, bottled and canned drinks and processed meats, there is nothing except for a few bags of small over-ripe lemons. The only reason we've come into Spar is because they have an in-house bakery where we can buy bread. While the great orange juice purchase continues at one check- out counter, the rest of us wait in a long, long line at the other counter, each of us buying one or two loaves of bread or a small bag of buns from their in house bakery: it's all we can afford and all we're allowed to buy anyway. It takes ages to check out, the long delay due to the time it takes the cashiers to count all the bank notes. I buy three Chelsea buns (without icing) and each one costs 5 million dollars (actually 5 billion before they took zeros off)".

## MONTH ON MONTH PERCENTAGE INFLATION 2000-2008

|     | 2000 | 2001 | 2002 | 2003 | 2004 | 2005 | 2006 | 2007 | 2008 |
|-----|------|------|------|------|------|------|------|------|------|
| Jan | 55 | 57 | 116 | 208 | 628 | 133 | 613 | 1,593 | 100,580 |
| Feb | 48 | 57 | 116 | 220 | 602 | 127 | 782 | 1,729 | 165,000 |
| Mar | 50 | 55 | 113 | 228 | 583 | 123 | 913 | 2,200 | 355,000 |
| Apr | 53 | 56 | 114 | 269 | 505 | 129 | 1,092 | 3,714 | 736,604 |
| May | 58 | 55 | 122 | 300 | 448 | 144 | 1,193 | 4,530 | 1,800,000 |
| Jun | 59 | 64 | 114 | 364 | 394 | 164 | 1,184 | 7,251 |  |
| Jul | 53 | 70 | 123 | 399 | 362 | 254 | 993 | 7,634 | 220,000,000 |
| Aug | 53 | 76 | 135 | 426 | 314 | 265 | 1,204 | 6,592 | 231,000,000 |
| Sep | 62 | 86 | 139 | 455 | 251 | 359 | 1,023 | 7,892 |  |
| Oct | 60 | 97 | 144 | 525 | 209 | 411 | 1,070 | 14,840 |  |
| Nov | 56 | 103 | 175 | 619 | 149 | 502 | 1,098 | 26,470 |  |
| Dec | 55 | 112 | 198 | 598 | 132 | 585 | 1,281 | 66,000 |  |

(Central Statistical Office)

## SUPER-HYPER INFLATION: 2008

In 2008 Zimbabwe hit the record books as having the second highest inflation rate ever recorded in the world, beaten only by Hungary in 1946. Zimbabwe's inflation rate was 100,580% in January 2008, 355,000% by March and 231,000,000% in August 2008. The Zimbabwe government stopped announcing inflation figures after August 2008 and by mid November monthly inflation was estimated to be 79.6 billion percent with year on year inflation estimated to be 89.7 sextillion percent in November 2008 when prices doubled every 24.7 hours. (Hanke & Kwok, 2009)

Hearing economists saying that prices were doubling every 24 hours was one thing, living it was another. Nicky told this funny story of the reality in our daily lives: "My husband and I went and met some friends in Bulawayo at the Tin Cup one Saturday afternoon for a few drinks. As the good Zimbabweans we are, each guy took his turn to buy a round, but before the afternoon was over and by the time the guys towards the end of the queue bought their round the prices had gone up! We all had a jolly good laugh."

The numbers and percentages were bad enough but coping with it was a nightmare. There was no way to prepare for this stage of the country's collapse and the only thing to do, if you could afford to, was to buy US dollars, as often as you could, as much as you could. We watched each new absurdity with a mixture of disbelief and contempt as our government lost control completely and economists called it a state of super-hyper inflation. We didn't even know if there was such a term and there was certainly nothing at all 'super' about it.

In May 2008 inflation went into seven digits for the first time and was 1.8 million percent. The government reacted by introducing higher denomination bank notes in the form of a one hundred million dollar note and a two hundred and fifty million dollar note. It didn't help at all. Another devaluation loomed, the last one had been the removal of three zeros in August 2006. In the following three months the exchange rate between the US dollar and the Zimbabwe dollar went into what economists called a 'frenzied freefall.'

| 23 May 2008 | 1 US$ | = | Z$500 million |
| 6 June 2008 | 1 US$ | = | Z$2,4 billion |
| 20 June 2008 | 1 US$ | = | Z$20 billion |
| 25 July 2008 | 1 US$ | = | Z$700 billion |

On the first of August 2008 ten zeros were removed from the currency. With that announcement ten billion dollars became one dollar. On paper it looked like this: Z$10,000,000,000 yesterday becomes Z$1 today. On the first of August 2008 the maximum withdrawal limit from my bank was two hundred dollars, the day before it had been two trillion dollars. A set of new bank notes and coins, which had apparently been sitting in the vaults of the Reserve Bank since 2007, were released on the first of August when the ten zeros were removed. The old and new values looked like this and left all of us carrying pen and paper to try and make sense of it all (calculators didn't have enough spaces for all the zeros):

## NEW NOTES AND COINS, 10 ZEROS REMOVED:

## 1 AUGUST 2008

| | | | |
|---|---|---|---|
| 10 trillion | = | $1,000 | (new note) |
| 5 trillion | = | $500 | (new note) |
| 1 trillion | = | $100 | (new note) |
| 250 billion | = | $25 | (new coin) |
| 200 billion | = | $20 | (new coin) |
| 100 billion | = | $10 | (new note and new coin) |
| 50 billion | = | $5 | (new note and old coin) |
| 20 billion | = | $2 | old coin |
| 10 billion | = | $1 | (new note) - old coin |
| 5 billion | = | .50 | cents - old coin |
| 2 billion | = | .20 | cents - old coin |
| 1 billion | = | .10 | cents - old coin |

## DIARY NOTES: FIFTY BILLION DOLLAR STAMPS: 2008

Trying to get our heads round the fact that yesterday's 50 billion dollar notes were only worth five dollars today was mind boggling; everyone everywhere was doing sums: on scraps of paper, on the back of till slips and even with sticks in the sand. Suddenly we realized we had to mentally add ten zeros to the quoted prices to work out how much things cost, or take ten zeros off to work out how much money we were handing over. To make matters worse both the old and new currency notes were operating side by side so we had fifty billion dollar notes and five dollar notes in our pockets and they were both worth the same amount!

I had a little wad of 50 billion dollar notes in my purse and like a helpless child I handed them all over the counter to the lady in the Post Office, smiled stupidly, and asked her to give me as many stamps as the handful of notes could buy. I laughed and shook my head as she smiled back at me in sympathy; we were all in the same boat in this absurd situation. She handed me eight stamps, each one had cost fifty billion dollars and was only enough to post a local letter.

"How can this go on?" she said, "how much longer?"

I shrugged and smiled but didn't answer because I don't know, I don't think anyone does. When I got home I looked at my eight single fifty billion dollar stamps. Long gone were the days when the stamps had their values printed on them, such as one dollar or ten dollars, now they just had two words printed on the bottom right hand corner: 'Standard Postage.'

## DIARY OF ABSURDITY: BANK WITHDRAWAL LIMITS
## SEPTEMBER 2008

In September 2008 the maximum daily withdrawal allowed from banks by individuals had increased from one thousand to twenty thousand Zimbabwe dollars. At the time twenty thousand dollars on the black market was equivalent to twenty British pence or about sixteen US cents. After weeks of only being allowed to draw out one thousand dollars of our own money a day, this twenty fold increase sounded huge but in reality was another pointless exercise in control by a government whose coffers were dry.

At 8.00am at bank opening time, there were already hundreds of people queuing outside all the banks and building societies. People said they'd been waiting in line for over three hours, since before sunrise. None of the ATM cash dispensers were working and the hot topic in the queues was where the banks were suddenly going to find enough bank notes to fill this massive demand.

By 8.30am there was chaos everywhere in my home town. Driving had become impossible as the crowds of people trying to get into banks had swelled into multiple thousands. Queues had disintegrated into huge crushes of people who filled the pavements and spilled out into car parks and onto the main roads. As the clock ticked well past opening time nothing was happening and more and more people arrived to try and get their money out of the banks.

Repeated attempts to get into any of the banks was a waste of time. It was standing room only with many hundreds of people already crammed into banking halls. Queues, if you could call them that, wound round and round and back on themselves until a sea of people were squashed up against each other and the physical temperature of so many people in the banking halls was palpable. Still no one was moving, none of the lines were shortening and it soon became obvious that no one was being served. There was no money to withdraw!

Police in uniform, soldiers in camouflage and large numbers of youth militia, (who everyone called Green Bombers), tried to jump the bank queues but this time it was to no avail because there simply was no money to be had. None of the banks or building societies in the town had received any money from the Reserve Bank in Harare and by 10.00am it was all over. Gradually the word got out, and people believed it: go home, there is no money.

**MONEY, MONEY, MONEY: EXPLOSION OF THE NOUVEAU RICHE: SEPTEMBER 2008**

On the 1st September 2008, a month after ten zeros were removed from the currency there were five sets of Zimbabwean currency in our wallets and in circulation in the country. While we navigated between the new Zim dollars, Bearer Bond Notes, 'Special Agro-Cheque' notes and two different sets of coinage, the well-connected government elite and nouveau riche (fuel, food, currency and black market barons) were as busy as ever making more money than they could ever spend. Anyone with connections to government was able to buy US dollars at ridiculously low exchange rates from the Reserve Bank which they sold on the black market at massively inflated rates. This gave them huge profits enabling them to buy back even more US dollars than they started with and double their money after just a few transactions. I was as confused as most people about how this could actually be allowed to be happening but the luxury cars, lavish lifestyles and multi story mansions being built in a time of complete collapse were explanation enough. These were the fruits of corruption; looting at its best. Watching the exchange rate was essential as it changed weekly and then daily as the economic collapse gathered pace. It was this exchange rate that enabled Zimbabwe's explosion of nouveau riche people in a time of extreme deprivation: people with extreme wealth and arrogance but very little class.

**DIARY OF THE VERY STRANGE 20,000 DOLLAR NOTE: OCTOBER 2008**

With your daily bank withdrawal limit of twenty thousand dollars cash, if you are lucky enough to get it, you can't even buy a single orange on the street. A 65 gram packet of two minute noodles is this week priced at 117 thousand dollars, meaning you'll have to get in the huge bank queues every day for six days and by then it's inevitable that the price of the noodles will have gone up; how can we survive this?

Most people have no choice but to queue at the banks where lines form as early as 2.00am. All day, every day the bank queues are being controlled by police with dogs and scuffles are breaking out more and more frequently as tempers flare and desperation rises. If you can get one, the new 20,000 note (released in August 2008) is cause for both concern and amusement. The note has no metal security thread and displays a peculiar Zimbabwe Bird which looks distinctly thin and misshapen and sits on the note at a skewed angle; much like we look actually and fitting testament to the state we're in. This was definitely one of the bank notes worth keeping; tuck it away in the back of the cupboard and sell it to collectors when this insanity is over.

## DIARY OF RAGE: WE WANT OUR MONEY: OCTOBER 2008

"Don't go anywhere near CABS," was the word on the streets of my home town early on Monday morning. CABS (Central Africa Building Society) is one of the main building societies in operation in Zimbabwe, has low bank charges and minimum balance requirements and is a popular choice for easy banking. Ever since last month's increase in the daily cash withdrawal allowance, there has been an incessant queue of hundreds of people trying to withdraw their own money. The latest unrest at CABS was audible rather than visible. When news got out that bank notes hadn't arrived from the Reserve Bank in Harare, customers were being told to go away and come back after lunch. This has become an almost daily message and people have just about reached breaking point. An angry buzz that sounded like a swarm of bees at first, rapidly grew into shouts, chants and raised tempers: 'We want our money!' 'Give us our money!' crowds demanded. As the noise level rose more and more people swarmed forward. All semblance of a queue collapsed as people ran from all directions bringing traffic to a complete standstill. Two people running from the other side of the road slipped and fell in the purple Jacaranda flowers that are lying in thick carpets on our pavements and streets everywhere. It's so painful to see our country collapsing like this and obvious that the situation is at breaking point but it's just a question of when.

## STORIES IN THE BANK QUEUES:
## UNIVERSITY LECTURERS: NOVEMBER 2008

In November 2008 life in Zimbabwe revolved around the bank queues: this is where we meet our friends, make phone calls and send text messages (if we can get through on the very congested and over-subscribed government controlled phone lines). In the bank queues the discussions are always about the collapse of our country, pick any topic you can think of and there's always a horror story waiting to be told. There is no shortage of time for the story telling either as we have to queue at the banks for a good two hours every day in order to withdraw the daily limit which is presently enough to buy just two loaves of bread – if we can find bread that is. By the end of the week the daily limit will only be enough to buy one loaf of bread because the prices are rising so fast.

Standing in the bank queue which must have been about five hundred strong a few days ago, I met a young woman I'd been talking to a few weeks before, a university student who'd been telling me about the water crisis on campus. This time she told me she should have been at the University attending lectures right now but nothing was happening at UZ, not because of the water shortage but because now there were no lecturers. Lecturers aren't allowed to say they are on strike or they'll lose their jobs, so they simply say they aren't working! Because their salaries are controlled by government regulations, UZ lecturers are earning amounts that make even basic survival completely impossible as they are being paid less than the equivalent of fifty US cents a month, yes a month! There was an audible gasp from people in the queue who couldn't help but listen to our conversation because the queue was so tightly packed. This salary madness is the same for government school teachers and most civil servants who take home 90 thousand Zimbabwe dollars a month at a time when a single loaf of bread is 200 thousand dollars. As the stories are told and the numbers revealed, people in the queue murmur in sympathy, mutter in disgust and hang their heads in shame at the diabolical state we're in.

## EXCHANGE RATE ZIMBABWE DOLLAR TO US DOLLAR

### FIRST DOLLAR

| Month | Year | Zimbabwe $ | US$ |
|---|---|---|---|
| | 1980 | 0.63 | 1 |
| | 1983 | 1 | 1 |
| | 1997 | 10 | 1 |
| | 2000 | 100 | 1 |
| Jun | 2002 | 1 000 | 1 |
| Mar | 2005 | 10 000 | 1 |
| Jan | 2006 | 100 000 | 1 |
| Jul | 2006 | 500 000 | 1 |
| 1st August | 2006 | 3 zeros removed | |

### SECOND DOLLAR

| Month | Year | Zimbabwe $ | US$ |
|---|---|---|---|
| Aug | 2006 | 650 | 1 |
| Sept | 2006 | 1 000 | 1 |
| Dec | 2006 | 3 000 | 1 |
| Jan | 2007 | 4 800 | 1 |
| Feb | 2007 | 7 500 | 1 |
| Mar | 2007 | 26 000 | 1 |
| Apr | 2007 | 35 000 | 1 |
| May | 2007 | 50 000 | 1 |
| Jun | 2007 | 400 000 | 1 |
| Jul | 2007 | 300 000 | 1 |
| Aug | 2007 | 200,000 | 1 |

**SECOND DOLLAR**

| Month | Year | Zimbabwe $ | US$ |
|---|---|---|---|
| Sep | 2007 | 600 000 | 1 |
| Oct | 2007 | 1 000 000 | 1 |
| Nov | 2007 | 1 500 000 | 1 |
| Dec | 2007 | 4 000 000 | 1 |
| Jan | 2008 | 6 000 000 | 1 |
| Feb | 2008 | 16 000 000 | 1 |
| Mar | 2008 | 70 000 000 | 1 |
| Apr | 2008 | 100 000 000 | 1 |
| May | 2008 | 777 500 000 | 1 |
| Jun | 2008 | 40 928 000 000 | 1 |
| Jul | 2008 | 758 530 000 000 | 1 |
| 1st August | 2008 | 10 zeros removed | |

**THIRD DOLLAR**

| Month | Year | Zimbabwe $ | US$ |
|---|---|---|---|
| Aug | 2008 | 1 780 | 1 |
| Sep | 2008 | 590 000 | 1 |
| Oct 7th | 2008 | 2 300 000 | 1 |
| Oct 14th | 2008 | 10 700 000 | 1 |
| Oct 21st | 2008 | 1 220 000 000 | 1 |
| Nov 8th | 2008 | 669 000 000 000 | 1 |
| 1st February | 2009 | 12 zeros removed | |

## THE LESSON FOR THE ZEROS 2005 - 2009

Always have a paper and pencil at hand because calculators aren't big enough to display the numerous zeros that appear when you get into the realms of hyper inflation. Work in threes: three zeros a thousand; six zeros a million; nine zeros a billion; twelve zeros a trillion; fifteen zeros a quadrillion; eighteen zeros a quintillion. By early 2009 Zimbabwe's bank notes were already in trillions, prices and salaries were in septillions but most of us didn't even know how many zeros that was. It didn't matter how many times the government took zeros off the currency, the reality was that by 2009 we had all lost everything and were starting our lives, savings and pensions from scratch, regardless of how old we were.

## THE 'NEW FAMILY' OF BANK NOTES: FEBRUARY 2009

On the 1st of February 2009 Reserve Bank Governor, Gideon Gono, removed twelve zeros from the currency. One trillion dollars had become one dollar and Gono smirked as he said: "Yesterday's trillionaires, I am sorry, will not be able to buy their favourite drink today." (Was he talking about orange juice I wondered or was it the imported Scotch whisky he meant, the drink of choice for a lot of senior government members.)

Sweating profusely throughout the presentation of Zimbabwe's latest monetary policy, Gideon Gono was at pains to explain that Zimbabwe had not 'dollarized,' (converted into US dollars) but instead had legalized the use of multiple currencies in Zimbabwe. "If we had dollarized," Gono said, "then we would need permission from the owners and printers of that currency."

Gono announced the introduction of a 'new family' of bank notes ranging from 1 dollar (previously 1 trillion) to 500 dollars (previously 500 trillion) but didn't acknowledge the fact that you can't buy anything in Zimbabwe dollars anymore. Everything from fuel to food, clothes, spare parts and equipment is charged in any of the multiple currencies now in circulation – any currency that is except for Zimbabwe dollars. Despite having the highest inflation and fastest shrinking economy in the world, Zimbabweans had already mastered the art of switching between US dollars, British Pounds and South African Rand and can do calculations and conversions almost instantly. Within a week Gideon Gono's 'new family' of bank notes was as good as dead, everyone preferring to trade in US dollars, British pounds and South African Rand.

## THE 'BASKET' OF CURRENCIES: 12 APRIL 2009

On the 12$^{th}$ April 2009 Economic Planning Minister Elton Mangoma announced the suspension of the Zimbabwe dollar. Trade commenced in what was called a "basket of foreign currencies" including the South African Rand, Botswana Pula, UK Pound, Indian Rupee, Euro, Japanese Yen, Australian Dollar, Chinese Yuan and United States Dollar.

## THE AFTERMATH, TRILLIONAIRE TO PAUPER. ZIM DOLLARS TO US DOLLARS: APRIL 2009

The last bank statement I received from Barclays Bank was almost two years ago in August 2007. Despite paying me no interest on my money for over three years, Barclays said they'd stopped sending statements to their clients because they couldn't afford to do so. This is despite the fact that for years they've been charging us for everything you can think of including withdrawing and depositing cash; using the ATM; depositing out of town cheques; ledger fees, administration fees and even for scribbling your account balance on a scrap of paper at the enquiries desk. I found our recently that they also charge me every time I phone them and ask for my bank balance.

When I enquired from Barclays how much money I had in my bank account I was told that I wasn't in their system anymore. My current account has been closed, without warning or notice, 'due to insufficient funds.' Despite the fact that I had nine trillion Zimbabwe dollars in my account a few months ago, and hadn't spent a cent of it, all my money evaporated when twelve zeros were removed from the currency. Overnight nine trillion dollars was reduced to nine dollars and this, the bank teller told me, was lower than the bank's allowed minimum balance to keep an account open.

It's a bank account I've held since I left school 35 years ago and for the first time in my life I have no ATM card, no credit or debit cards and no cheque book. It's a chillingly impotent feeling for all Zimbabweans who've been robbed of their life savings, which they entrusted to the banks, and have instead been left entirely dependent on cash under the bed.

The US dollarization of the Zimbabwean economy has left all the banks virtually deserted, car parks empty, Managers and Accountants on leave. Banks are being manned by bored security guards, and one or sometimes two yawning tellers. "What's going to happen to us and our jobs," the bank's Accountant said to me when I was querying the closure of my account. I didn't respond. There's not a lot of public sympathy for bank executives who did nothing to reassure customers, or stand up for our rights during all these years when there haven't been enough bank notes to go around and we've been waiting outside their big glass doors begging to be allowed in. While Managers and Accountants sat closeted in their offices, we queued in our thousands for hours at a time outside banks we had supported for decades but if we were lucky enough to get in we were only allowed to draw out miniscule amounts of our own money: maximum daily withdrawal amounts that weren't even enough to buy a single loaf of bread.

Banks are now trying to persuade individuals and companies to open 'foreign currency' bank accounts where we can deposit our US dollars but not write cheques or withdraw cash from ATM machines. I don't think so!

It's an understatement to say that there's a serious lack of trust on the part of depositors who have no guarantees that once they put their US dollars into the bank that they'll ever be able to get it out again, or if it will even still be there tomorrow. No one's forgotten the shocking, outrageous admission by Reserve Bank Governor, Gideon Gono, recently that he had removed funds from private bank accounts in order to pay for electricity and grain imports for the country.

In case anyone was having second thoughts about depositing US dollars into banks, trust plummeted even further when scores of depositors gathered in an angry crowd at one bank to try and withdraw their own US dollars. Bank workers told the customers they didn't have any money to meet the withdrawal requests; some people said they'd been trying for a week to withdraw their US dollars. When the mob proceeded to another branch of the same bank, the senior executive took refuge in another building and refused to meet the customers saying they should go to the bank's head office.

## LOST SAVINGS:
### PENNY'S STORY: 2009

As hard as it was to force ourselves not to save our money during the years of economic collapse, some people never did manage to get their heads around it and break the savings habit of a lifetime. Penny related this heartbreaking story of a domestic worker who lost everything and didn't find out until it was far too late: " She saved most of her money and it was put in her Post Office savings account every month. When Zimbabwe switched back from Bearer Cheques to US dollars in 2009, she went along to the Post Office to find out the balance in her account only to be told she would have to pay in $10 to keep her book open, all her saving had gone."

## LOST SHARES: 2009

Investing in shares is pointless when your economy is in collapse and there's galloping hyper inflation. One friend told of the five quintillion dollars he had invested in Old Mutual. When the Zimbabwe economy stabilized in March 2009 shares were converted into US dollars which were then the official currency of the country. My friend's five quintillion dollar shares were only worth US$91.

# KEEPING TRACK OF THE BANK NOTES

| Year | Month | Currency |
|---|---|---|
| 1980 - 1993 | | $2, $5, $10, $20 notes |
| 1994 -2000 | | New $5, $10, $20, $50, $100 notes |
| 2001 | | $500 note |
| 2003 | August | Travelers' cheque $1,000, $5,000, $10,000, $20,000, $50,000, $100,000 |
| | September | Bearer cheque $5,000, $10,000, $20,000 notes |
| | October | Z$1,000 note (bank note with silver security thread) |
| 2005 | October | Bearers cheque $50,000, $100,000 notes |
| | February | Bearer cheque $50,000 (new) note |
| | June | Bearer cheque $100,000 (new) note |
| | June | Bearer cheque $100,000 (new) note |
| 2006 | 1st August | Three zeros removed |
| | August | Bearer cheque notes 1c,5c,10c, 50c, $1, $5, $10, $20, $50, $100, $500, $1,000, $10.000, $100,000 denominations. (This is not a misprint! Actual bank notes for one cent, five cents, ten cents, fifty cents and all the dollar denominations were released as paper money) |
| 2007 | March | Bearer cheque $5,000, $50,000 notes |
| | August | Bearer cheque $200,000 note |
| | December | Bearer cheque $250,000, $500,000, $750,000 notes |
| 2008 | January | Bearer cheque $1 million, $10 million notes |
| | March | Bearer cheque $500 million note |
| | May | Bearer cheque $100 million, $250 million notes |
| | May | Special Agro Cheque $5 billion, $25 billion, $50 billion, $100 billion notes |
| | 1st August | Ten zeros removed. Bearer Cheques replaced with notes |
| | August | $1, $5, $10, $20, $100, $500, $1,000, $10,000, $20,000 notes |
| | October | $50,000 note |
| | Novemeber | $100,000, $500,000, $1 million notes |
| | December | $10 million, $50 million, $100 million notes |
| | December | $200 million, $500 million notes |
| | December | $1 billion, $5 billion, $10 billion notes |
| 2009 | January | $20 billion, $50 billion notes |
| | January | $10 trillion, $20 trillion, $50 trillion, $100 trillion notes |
| | 1st February | Twelve zeros removed |
| | February | $1, $5, $10, $20, $50, $100, $500 notes |

**GETTING RICH ON EBAY**

Founded in 1995 and based in San Jose, California, eBay became one of the best places to make money from Zimbabwe's bizarre seven year currency printing absurdity. From the time Zimbabwe went into the fantasy world of Bearer Cheques a market sprang up on eBay, increasing with every new ridiculous denomination that Zimbabwe's Reserve Bank released. By 2020, ten years after Zimbabwe's first currency collapse and one year into our second economic crisis, this is what you could get on eBay for some of Zimbabwe's 2001 – 2009 bank notes:

| | | |
|---|---|---|
| 10,000 dollar note | on eBay | 27 US dollars |
| 20,000 dollar note | on eBay | 6 US dollars |
| 50,000 dollar note | on eBay | 5 US dollars |
| 100,000 dollar note | on eBay | 3 US dollars |
| 500 million dollar note | on eBay | 4 US dollars |
| 1 billion dollar note | on eBay | 6 US dollars |
| 10 billion dollar note | on eBay | 6 US dollars |
| 20 billion dollar note | on eBay | 6 US dollars |
| 50 billion dollar note | on eBay | 3 US dollars |
| 10 trillion dollar note | on eBay | 5 US dollars |
| 50 trillion dollar note | on eBay | 13 US dollars |
| 100 trillion dollar note | on eBay | 41 US dollars |

## MAKING MONEY FROM MONEY

With seventy one Zimbabwe dollar bank notes released between August 2003 and February 2009 it was obvious that there would be significant interest from collectors but it went much further than this and making money from money resulted. While most of us just had boxes of worthless bank notes stacked up in the corner and others threw them away or used them to fuel cooking fires in the endlessly long electricity cuts, there were also the clever ones.

A friend who emigrated in 2015 told this fascinating story of how Zimbabwe's trillion dollar nightmare helped them start their new life. It all started in Mutare in March 2009 when prominent Zimbabwean Roy Bennett, incarcerated for punching MP Patrick Chinamasa in Parliament, was to appear in court for a bail hearing:

"We gathered peacefully after dark at the Magistrates Court where Roy was expected to arrive for his courtesy accommodations. There was a large MDC presence outside the courtroom. We were singing and chanting for his release. Needless to say it turned ugly and the riot police tear gassed everyone and we escaped by running into buildings.

Well the exuberance was quashed temporarily but revived for Roy's court appearance the next day. Coincidentally, while I was part of the large crowd waiting outside the court for the trial, the crowd started to buzz with a different energy. My husband owned a shop at the time and I got word that he had been arrested for trading in US dollars. He was in handcuffs and being escorted into the charge office at the court house. Of course high drama in itself but they seized the US$300 currency he had. When he was being charged and the US dollars they had confiscated were being receipted, they gave him a very large stash of crisp mint $100 trillion notes in sequence. These they said were being paid to him as compensation for the seized US dollars because they insisted that transparency was key! Nothing ever happened after that, I think they just wanted the US dollars! The box of $100 trillion notes were worthless at the time and were put in storage with all our other junk and forgotten.

We were emigrating in 2015 pretty much as economic exiles with meager savings. I was browsing Facebook and noticed an advert for $100 trillion notes paying US$10 each. We thought 'yeah!' a possible windfall if we could find them as they could have gone out with a lot of accumulated junk. Well luckily they were safe! The Z$100 trillion notes ended up being worth between US$50 and US$100 each. Well needless to say trading them became a very lucrative activity for several months. We made tens of thousands out of the beautiful crisp bank notes signed by Gono. That waste paper yielded a far more comfortable set up than our real money savings could. What a windfall. We were lucky."

## BANK CRASHES IN ZIMBABWE: 1998 - 2015

The collapse, closure and liquidation of banks was inevitable during the years of Zimbabwe's economic collapse; some were done according to the rules and others just involved closed doors and a runner in the night. It all began in 1998 and was reported in the press as a "serious crisis."

"The unprecedented closure of a local merchant bank has caused panic in Zimbabwe's financial sector once touted as the second most stable in Sub-Saharan Africa after South Africa. The United Merchant Bank (UMB), owned by controversial Black tycoon, Roger Boka, had its licence revoked last week after it was discovered that the bank could no longer meet depositors' claims, and that its liquidity ratio was too low to meet debt obligations and other liabilities. Although government officials have fallen over themselves to create an image that all is well, banking experts are sounding an alarm".

"This is really a serious crisis. We have not had a crisis of this nature in the history of this country. It's a crisis of an unparalleled magnitude in the sense that it will affect the entire economy," says Theresa Moyo, economics lecturer at the University of Zimbabwe, and a specialist in banking. Soon after the news of the bank's fall, the stock exchange lost five percent of its value. The UMB crisis has wiped off some 127 million US dollars in the values of all firms listed on the ZSE in the last seven days. ... Boka, one of the most vocal proponents for the government opening up the space for more blacks to gain entry into Zimbabwe's white-controlled economy, has several other business interests which, according to sources, are not doing very well. It is alleged that he used UMB depositors' money to help his Tobacco Auction Floors, which are said to be the largest in the world. This season's low tobacco prices on the floors affected his repayment of the borrowed money to the bank.

...The UMB, insiders say, was "just giving loans without respecting the principals of prudent bank management, which are profitability, prudence, solvency and liquidity." Some of the clients who received loans were really "high risk clients". Boka never insisted on security, because the understanding was that he was trying to promote indigenous (Black) business, and therefore was not too rigid on demanding collateral, one source indicated." [sic] (Machipisa, L. IPS, 1998)

Things were to get much worse in the decade that followed. In July 2003, the Depositors Protection Corporation was established in Zimbabwe. The DPC listed the following bank closures since 2003:

2004    Century Discount House

2004    Rapid Discount House

2006    Sagit Finance House

2012    Genesis Investment Bank

2012    Royal Bank of Zimbabwe

2013    Trust Bank Corporation Limited

2014    Capital Bank

2015    Interfin Bank Limited

2015    Allied Bank Limited (formerly ZABG)

2015    AfrAsia Bank Zimbabwe Limited (formerly Kingdom Bank)

2015    Tetrad Investment Bank

No payments were made to depositors of the following banks which failed prior to the establishment of DPC in July 2003: United Merchant Bank; Universal Merchant Bank; Zimbabwe Building Society, and First National Building Society.

No compensations were made to depositors of failed banking institutions whose resolution methods did not entail liquidation: NDH 2005; HighVeld; Intermarket Bank; Original Trust Bank; Royal Bank and Barbican Bank whose assets were sold to ZABG in 2005. (Deposit Protection Corporation, Harare, 2003)


## DEMONETIZATION OF THE ZIMBABWE DOLLAR: JUNE 2015

Six years after the collapse of Zimbabwe's economy and the introduction of trading in US dollars, the government of Zimbabwe made an announcement about the lost savings of a nation. In a Letter From Zimbabwe in early July 2015 I wrote: "It's taken six years for the government of Zimbabwe to put a value on the money that turned to ZERO in 2009 and frankly for most people, who had become paupers through hyper inflation, it's a pointless exercise. The Central Bank announced that bank accounts with balances up to 175 quadrillion Zimbabwe dollars will be paid a flat amount of five US dollars; yes, just five US dollars. Bank balances of over 175 quadrillion will be paid at what we are told is the UN exchange rate of US$1 for every 35 quadrillion Zimbabwe dollars. In numbers it looked like this:

US$1  =  Z$35,000,000,000,000,000

Cash customers can apparently walk into banks with their old Zimbabwe dollar notes and will, with 'no questions asked,' get US$1 for Zim$250 trillion. For most of us the cost of taking the old notes to the bank will be more than the US cents we will get back in our pockets. There is a 'demonetization window' from the 15th June to the 30th September to exchange every 35 quadrillion Zimbabwe dollars we have into one US dollar and after that the Zimbabwe dollar will be officially dead, no longer legal tender. The Central Bank announcement said: "Demonitization is not compensation for the loss of value of the Zimbabwe dollar due to hyper inflation, it is an exchange process." (Buckle, C. 2015)

In 2020 Zimbabweans were still waiting for compensation from the Zimbabwe government for the loss of value of the Zimbabwe dollar, our lost savings, pensions and investments.


**WE DID NOT LEARN FROM OUR OWN HISTORY: 2019**

The South African Rand and US Dollar became the most commonly traded currencies in Zimbabwe from 2009 until 24 June 2019 when the Zimbabwe government banned trade in all currencies except their new Zimbabwe RTGS/Bond dollar (ZWL) and the whole cycle of economic collapse and hyper inflation started all over again. Zimbabwe's government had, it seemed, learnt absolutely nothing from its own mistakes.

# CHAPTER 6

# THE BULLET IN THE SCHOOL TOILET

For parents, keeping our children in school was the top priority during the collapse of Zimbabwe. At home our lives were in turmoil due to farm invasions and evictions, losing our homes and livelihoods, horrific political violence, harassment and persecution. Particularly in farming and rural areas, having our children in school was critical: an oasis for them in lives which were in a continual state of upheaval. The familiar routines of school, knowing they were safe and able to be normal, helped them to cope with what was happening. In the classrooms and playgrounds our children discovered that what was happening to them was also happening to many of their classmates; there was comfort in knowing they were not alone.

For teachers and administrators schools became places where children needed so much more than books, lessons and homework in those awful years. During the 2004-2009 collapse of Zimbabwe children needed extra emotional support, counselling, empathy and gentle handling. How well I remember the call from a teacher who knew our farm had been seized and needed me to know that in my son's class was the child of a farm invader and that some unpleasant encounters were taking place. Or the call to say my son needed special coaching as he was writing words upside down and back to front. Or the occasion we arrived at the junior school gates one morning to find the place surrounded and barricaded by chanting, aggressive land invaders. Or the time the Headmistress and other Head teachers from private schools around Marondera were arrested for charging "unapproved" fees and were put in police cells; or the bullet in the toilet, a story best told on its own.

Schools in rural areas regularly found themselves having to answer to political players: staff forced to make donations to political events; schools forced to close for political rallies; teachers harassed, intimidated, arrested, threatened and chased away if they spoke out, dared to protest or were suspected of being opposition supporters. The list of abuses under the gaze and often the instruction of our own government went on and on.

In rural and urban areas school administrators had the immense and relentless task of trying to remain functional and viable in the years of hyper inflation. School fees constantly had to be reviewed, budgets changed, and parents called on to give more, bring more and do more to keep the schools open. In government schools particularly, conditions for teachers became untenable. Salaries did not match inflation; teachers could not afford to support their own families and many had no option but to leave for other countries in order to survive.

Our government had much to answer for, their desperate need to retain political power crushing the education of a generation of children and driving away our country's finest educators. The tragic irony was that so many of our leaders' own children were not at schools and universities in Zimbabwe during the years of Zimbabwe's collapse; their children were studying in South Africa, UK, Europe, USA, Singapore, Australia, New Zealand and other safe and stable countries. It was the classic Orwellian mantra: "All animals are equal, but some animals are more equal than others."

## THE BULLET IN THE SCHOOL TOILET: MAY 2004

The Headmistress of my son's junior school, Gill Martin, was arrested and spent the night in a cold, dirty police cell at the beginning of the second school term in winter 2004. Gill was one of a number of Head teachers at private schools arrested for charging 'unapproved' school fees at a time when inflation was around 500%. Later we heard that Gill was the angel of the cells that freezing night, singing with her cell mate, their voices bringing cheer and hope to everyone incarcerated in dark, cold cells. It was the start of the most bizarre incident and one which affected countless teachers, parents and children. I wrote in my diary:

"Went to drop Darren (Richie's friend) off at the school boarding hostel at 5.00pm only to find the gate locked and all the kids' school trunks, which had been left there earlier in the day, abandoned in the dust outside the fence. The guard said the police had ordered the hostel closed and the school shut and that we should all go home.

Darren and Richie loaded the trunk into the back of the truck and climbed in next to it. It was nearly dark and getting cold already. On the way home they opened the trunk and extracted a giant packet of apricots, big yellow gob-stopper sweets that were hard on the outside and soft in the middle. Darren and Richie had gouged a hole in the bag and were tucking in mightily. I had also loved apricot sweets a lifetime ago when I was a little school girl so it was hard not to take the one they held out to me, which immediately made me an accomplice enabling them to get off lightly."

The next morning Kevin Martin, our GP and the Chairman of the Board of the school, went to the police station to find out what could be done for his wife Gill and the other arrested Head teachers and the police arrested him too. A fortnight later I picked my pen up again and summarized the insanity that followed:

"Gill had been in prison. Kevin had been in the outside lock up at the police station – detained in a cage like an animal and we could see him pacing up and down from outside on the main road. We heard later that they let him out to go and treat his patients at his surgery; what an absurd situation. The police had closed the school down and put their men inside the school premises to stop anyone from getting in. All week the school was closed until finally we heard that school would be open on Monday and I dropped Richie off at 7.00am; there was no problem and he was happy to be seeing his friends again.

On Tuesday Richie said he had sore eyes, but everything looked fine, so I stood my ground and took him to school anyway. By 10.00am the school phoned and asked me to come and fetch him, he wasn't feeling well. I got Richie home and after thirty minutes on the couch watching a video, he seemed absolutely fine.

Richie was out of school the rest of the week: four visits to the doctor but aside from a little patch of eczema on his face which the Doc said was probably stress related, there was nothing to worry about: no ear problems, no temperature, no pain.

Monday the following week Richie still begged me not to take him to school; the patch of eczema had got bigger and redder on his face. Something was definitely up so I went to the school to see Gill. It seemed the kids had found a live bullet in the toilets, left behind by the police and it had caused a scare in the playground with lots of whispering amongst the kids. Richie couldn't talk about it but Gill thought because the children all knew that she had been arrested and Kevin had been locked up in the outside cage at the police camp, lots of their fears had resurfaced. Then when the children had seen police at the school gates and in the school grounds and then found a bullet in the toilet, it was all just too much. Flashbacks and bad memories came back for many children who had been traumatized during farm invasions, witnessed frightening encounters between their parents and police, and even seen their parents being arrested and taken away from their homes on farms."

Later Richie and I talked about it all, joked about the apricots, bought a replacement packet (which we proceeded to eat), watched a video together that afternoon and the next day he went back to school happily. Behaving normally and maintaining the routines of everyday, including going to school, were the best healing when it came to surviving this absurdity of Zimbabwe's ugly politics. After this one small incident in an urban junior school in Zimbabwe I found myself thinking more and more about children in war zones, about child soldiers and the horrors and terrors in their young lives and hoping that one day governments, all our governments, would be held to account.

## THE 'DONATION': OCTOBER 2004

By the third term of 2004 when inflation was officially quoted at 250% but was in reality closer to 650%, according to independent economists, the little local junior school had almost completely run out of money. They couldn't afford anything from wages to toilet cleaner and everything in between. A message went out to parents to attend a meeting to take place after the school gala when a lot of parents would be present. The only item on the agenda was what to do about parents who hadn't paid the 'donation.'

Some months before, as the school had struggled to stay afloat, a meeting had been held and it was proposed that parents would make a donation to supplement the school fees which had already been paid as the government had not responded to the school's request to raise fees to keep up with inflation. The proposal had been approved by parents and now the problem was what to do about parents who hadn't paid the donation and parents were bitter as those who had paid felt they were subsiding the children whose parents hadn't paid.

The PTA was chairing the meeting with the Headmistress and Chairman of the Board observing. Once the PTA outlined the prevailing dire financial situation facing the school and the need for all parents to pay the donation, tempers flared instantly.

"We want to know who hasn't paid," someone from the audience called out. There was a murmur of agreement and the Headmistress asked us again and again:

"Are you sure you want the list read out?"

Three times the Headmistress asked and by then most of the audience were calling out: "Yes! Who are they that haven't paid?"

The Headmistress said that it wouldn't be right for her to read the list out and that it was up to the PTA to decide, with our agreement, and then to read the list out themselves. A show of hands was called for, the proposal endorsed, and it was agreed that the names be read out.

The PTA Treasurer stood up and read out the list of parents who had not paid the donation. There were a lot of names, over fifty of them, and with so many names very few stuck in your mind but there was one parent who stood up at the end. He was shaking with anger, his rage palpable. "I have been shamed," he said. "Never have I been so insulted. This is a lynch mob."

You could have heard a pin drop in the audience, but the man hadn't finished.

"No one better come near me, phone me or tell me to pay after this. If they do, I will shoot them."

There was a collective gasp of shock from all of us in the audience and the meeting was rapidly called to order and then closed with an appeal to any parents who had not paid the donation to do so in order for the school to remain functional. Parents stood in groups whispering afterwards, shocked at the threat of shooting, making the enormous trauma and frightening reality of living in a country in a state of collapse very real for us all.

## 3% PASS RATE, SILOBELA, SHURUGWI: 2005

Speaking at a school in Shurugwi in February 2005 President Mugabe revealed the shocking facts about the state of education: "In Silobela they had a 3% pass rate. Here there was a pass rate of 8%. In other areas it is 6%."

## POCKET MONEY: 2005

My son's first year at a senior boarding school started in 2005. In the eight page, A5 Handbook for 'Parents and their Sons' containing information and instructions, it was obvious that Zimbabwe was already in a state of economic collapse. Inflation started that year at 133% in January and by

December it would be 585%. On page six of the handbook, in capital letters: "Your son may not have in his possession more than $20,000 in cash (the rest must be banked)."

Having spent most of my childhood receiving pocket money ranging from twenty five cents to one dollar a week, pocket money and savings was a tradition that I had continued with my own son, giving him five to ten dollars a week until he was about ten. To imagine, just three years later that a thirteen year old would have Z$20,000 pocket money was beyond comprehension, as was Zimbabwe's economic mayhem. As absurd as it may sound, at the time that I handed over the Z$20,000 pocket money, a single loaf of bread in Zimbabwe cost Z$3,500 so in reality I was only giving my son enough for five loaves of bread!

## SUPPLEMENTARY FEES AND TOP UPS: 2005 – 2008

School fees normally paid in advance at the beginning of the term for the following three months made it impossible for schools to meet budgetary requirements during the years of economic collapse. Hyper inflation and regular devaluations of the currency led to the need for supplementary fees or, as they became widely known, 'top ups.' Those two little words 'top-ups' were our worst nightmare as parents and we attended the meetings preparing for the worst, knowing we would have to find another big chunk of money, truck load of groceries or other forms of payment to keep our children in school.

In the last week of February 2006, six weeks into the first term of the year, the circular letter from the private senior school read: "We warned you that there was a strong possibility that we would have to ask for a Supplementary Fee during the course of the first term of 2006 if inflation were to rise higher than forecast. Unfortunately it is necessary to charge a supplementary fee of Z$20 million. .... This will bring the Lent Term fees up to Z$118 million. ... Our original budget was based on an assumption that inflation would average a little over 500% during the first term ... the Reserve Bank has predicted that inflation will peak at around 800% during March 2006."

Meetings and circulars outlining the required top ups became the norm and happened every school term. In late May 2007 two weeks after the second school term had started, the legal and political minefield had become far more complicated and now it wasn't just a question of money or goods, there was far more going on behind the scenes. The private school which was required to get approval from the government on their fee structure, had not had a response from the Ministry of Education. Despite a High Court order granted to the school ordering the Ministry of Education to respond to their fee structure application, submitted two months before, nothing had been heard from government and so the school were on their own. It was illegal to charge fees that had not been approved by government and so the schools had to find ways around the matter. In a letter to parents they told us the facts and what they required of us if the school was to remain functional:

"Food inflation as measured by a leading supermarket is 13,613%. A revised budget has therefore been drawn up for the Second Term based on the following fundamentals:

- We will do our best to pay staff salaries that are adequate to ensure their continued motivation and enthusiasm.
- We will maintain the quality of food provided to your children.
- We will maintain the fabric of the school."

They said they fully intended to comply with the Education Act regarding school fees but because they hadn't received a response from the Ministry they had decided to charge a "cost recovery deposit" and take the following actions:

- A provisional bill for the cost recovery deposit would be issued within a few days.
- Any amounts already paid would be deducted.
- A parents meeting would be called within a week when parents would be asked to approve the charging of the 'cost recovery deposit' and approve the school's application to the Ministry for the specified fees.

Eyebrows went up at the next sentence but again we needed to read between the lines if we wanted our children to keep having a school to go to. The sentence read: "You will also be asked to pass a resolution that, in the event that the Ministry does not approve the fee applied for, any balance of the cost recovery deposit should automatically be donated to the school." The word donation raised alarm bells, memories of the traumatic 2004 donation meeting at the junior school and the threatened shooting still fresh in my mind.

## THE EDUCATION BRAIN DRAIN: 2007

The Progressive Teachers Union of Zimbabwe (PTUZ) carried out an audit of teachers in Zimbabwe in 2007 and their findings were shocking. Between January and August 2007 15,000 teachers had left the country and by November 2007, the number had soared to 25,000.

"PTUZ secretary general, Raymond Majongwe, said the majority of teachers who quit had been absorbed in neighbouring countries such as Botswana, South Africa and Namibia, with many working as labourers at construction sites in South Africa, which is preparing to host the 2010 Soccer World Cup tournament. ... Both Minister of Education Aeneas Chigwedere and his permanent secretary Stephen Mahere were not immediately available for comment on the matter. However, Chigwedere last week told Parliament that Harare would approach its southern African neighbours to ask them to stop taking Zimbabwe's teachers.... Zimbabwe employs about 108,000 teachers but educationists say the country requires about 120,000 fully qualified teachers to ensure effective learning in schools. (Khumalo, N. 2007)

## BARTERING FOR SCHOOL FEES: APRIL 2008

Arriving at my son's senior school in the last week of the holidays I wanted to beat the crowds and pay the fees for the coming three month school term. It was the middle, winter term of the 2008 school year and the one in which he would be writing his mock O' levels, in preparation for the final examinations in November 2008. There were three main options offered for paying the school fees:

- Z$135 billion
- US$1,500
- GB£750

The Zimbabwe dollar amount of 135 billion was only valid for the next three days after which it would change to match the changing black market rate.

"Any other options?" I asked.

"People are paying in car tyres, fuel coupons, drums of fuel, even in cows," the Bursar said, "take your pick."

This was the bartering system for school fees in April 2008. Unbelievable, I thought, I couldn't make this up if I tried! Could it possibly get any worse? Yes!

Four months later, in August 2008, as the third and final term of the school year loomed, the dreaded O' Level term, I was back in the Bursar's office at the school. Instead of worrying about the subjects my son was writing for O' levels, whether he was studying enough or what results he may get, yet again the nightmare was paying the school fees.

"How will you be paying your son's fees?" the Bursar asked when I arrived at her office and sat down at the desk. I knew she wasn't referring to the normal ways people pay bills such as with cash, cheques or by bank transfers, so I asked her what the options were this time. I could feel my eyes widening and mouth beginning to drop open as the Bursar gave me the bizarre choices:

- 2000 litres worth of petrol or diesel coupons.
- Foreign currency (South African Rand, American Dollars or British Pounds) to the value of 2000 litres of fuel.
- Cash in Zimbabwe dollars but the price quoted was only valid for 8 hours. (Yes! Hours not days!)
- Meat: the school would accept a slaughtered and butchered cow, or pigs, or sheep or chickens; the quantities were subject to negotiation but would have to equal the value of 2000 litres of fuel.
- Tyres: new tyres to fit any of the schools vehicles: cars, minibuses or buses, equal to the value of 2000 litres of fuel.

"What about cheques in Zimbabwe dollars?" I asked.

Sorry, she said, these are not accepted, even if they are for double the required amount and even if they are bank certified cheques. By the time the cheques clear, which can be anything up to ten days, they are worth a fraction of the original amount due to hyper inflation. The government's official inflation rate had just been announced and was 11.2

million percent, an increase of nine million percent from the previous month.

## DIFFERENT PERSPECTIVES:
## GERARD'S STORY

There was a significant difference between private and government schools which was particularly apparent during Zimbabwe's economic collapse and years of hyper inflation. Government schools were crippled by low wages, big intakes, insufficient resources and inadequate funds for maintenance and improvements. Students were often from impoverished backgrounds, struggled to afford fees and uniforms and in Zimbabwe's years of crisis, they often arrived at school in the morning hungry. Government schools had strict controls over the fees that could be levied as these were handed down by Ministry directives and there were very few perks to encourage staff to stay.

For educators in government schools the lure of greener pastures, be they to private schools in Zimbabwe or to other countries, was significant. This all made for very different perspectives for educators in private and government schools. Gerard, an educator in a private school in Harare, described how three perks made a significant difference to teachers in private schools:

"In the 2005–2008 period I was employed by a Harare private school and one year we attended an educators conference in Modjadjiskloof, a small town in the Limpopo province of

South Africa. Whilst there various staff from various Zimbabwean schools were sharing their accounts of the difficulty of daily life 'back home'. As the accounts seemed to increase in drama with each new story, I looked around at my colleagues from my particular school and could see the same look of doubt on their faces. In private I confirmed that we all felt the others were exaggerating as the situation did not feel as bad as they were telling it. Given time I digested this apparent gap between their experience of daily life and ours. I realized a few key factors that took the sting out of life for us at my school:

A parent at our school was a dairy farmer and twice a week he would bring milk to the school when fetching his kids. On these days staff would bring their own containers and pay for milk off the back of his truck. Our school governing body Chairman worked for ZSR (Zimbabwe Sugar Refineries) and once a month would have a ton of sugar delivered to the school which we staff would purchase. Lobels Bread donated a hundred loaves of bread a week to the school, for the children, however we could not fairly divide and distribute this between the 400 plus learners in our school so the headmaster divided it instead amongst the staff."


## THE EIGHT HUNDRED BILLION DOLLAR SCHOOL SKIRT: 2008

Every day for nine days I queued with hundreds of others at my local bank in order to withdraw the maximum daily limit of one hundred billion dollars. I had promised an unemployed friend that I would buy her teenage daughter a new uniform skirt for school so that the other kids would stop teasing her about the tattered and painfully short one she was wearing. Where once there had been six school outfitters in our town, the ravages of economic collapse in 2008 had left us with only one shop selling school uniforms. Without any competition the prices are very high and it's a case of take it or leave it. The shop assistant told me the skirt was six hundred billion dollars but the price was going up every day. She said she wouldn't take a cheque and that I should keep checking on price changes.

On the black market a hundred billion dollars is worth the equivalent of just twenty British pence and yet this is the maximum amount we're allowed to draw out every day. After six working days when I'd drawn out the maximum daily allowance and had six hundred billion dollars in my hand, the price of the skirt had gone up to seven hundred and fifty billion dollars. By the seventh day, the price of the skirt had gone up to eight hundred billion dollars and my patience was wearing transparently thin. By the ninth day I had drawn out nine hundred billion dollars and at last I gained the upper hand because on that one day the price rises faltered, perhaps the manager or accountant had woken up late I thought! This was my lucky day. The skirt cost eight hundred and eleven billion dollars and I finally had enough cash in my hand. Who would have thought that something so simple as buying a plain, bottle green skirt would be such a nightmare? It seems so absurd that children are still required to wear school uniforms in a country where inflation is officially stated at two million, two hundred thousand percent.

When I gave my friend the precious parcel with a single bottle green school skirt for her daughter, her eyes filled with tears of gratitude. Her daughter also needed a pale blue blouse, a pair of white socks and a pair of black shoes but for now the crisis was over and the taunting by classmates would stop, thanks to the eight hundred billion dollar skirt.


**HOW THE SCHOOLS SURVIVED:  2005 - 2009**
**THE HEADMISTRESS' STORY**
"Schools compiled lists of items they needed, offering parents the option to pay their children's fees partly or wholly in goods. In private day schools where students were not receiving accommodation or meals, the items included:

- Toilet rolls
- Paint
- Bond paper (for printing and duplicating)
- Cleaning materials
- Dry food such as flour, sugar, rice, maize meal, pasta, tea, coffee, milk powder.
- Chickens
- Fuel coupons

In private boarding schools where hundreds of children lived on campus the need for food was immense and almost all groceries could be used to negotiate a value towards school fee payments. This included perishable, deliverable items such as milk, bread, vegetables, fruit and meat or dry goods and pantry items. There were also options for paying fees in vehicle spare parts, equipment and fuel.

In many schools each student was required to bring a specified number of fuel coupons per term in addition to their fees. Fuel coupons were usually for 20 litres of diesel or petrol, they had to be purchased in US dollars and became a very common method of payment for all sorts of things aside from fuel. Some people were paid their entire wages in fuel coupons which they could then trade or barter for food, cash or almost anything you could think of. Because fuel coupons did not lose their value, they became the most sought after form of payment.

Staff were given fuel coupons and food hampers at regular intervals to help them survive hyper inflation and repeated devaluations which had rendered salaries worthless. In the school holidays some of the head teachers would go to South Africa in the school bus, stock up on groceries in Polokwane, bring them back to Zimbabwe and use them to make up food hampers for the school staff.

In urban and rural government schools, in addition to paying monetary fees, parents were required to provide, per child enrolled at the school, some or all of the following items in specified quantities:

Cooking oil                     Salt
Soft drink concentrate          Candles
Sugar                           Tea bags

| Maize meal | Milk powder |
| Dried fish (kapenta) | Bricks and building materials |

Donations from parents, former students and well wishers kept many schools and institutions going and saved them from closing down. Donations of money, food items, vegetables and fruit were invaluable, often arriving unexpectedly as the country fell into deeper and deeper collapse. Whenever money came in from students' fees the rule for schools and institutions was the same as it was for individual and family budgets: spend the money straight away! Don't bank it! Store rooms, stock rooms and any available space was filled with mountains of stationery, hardware and maintenance items, cleaning products, hygiene products, sanitary items, dry and canned food and anything that was needed to keep the institution functional."

**THE UNIVERSITY STUDENT'S STORY:**
**OCTOBER 2008**

Standing in a huge bank queue I got talking to a young woman in front of me who told me she was a university student in Harare. She kept using the word 'pathetic' to describe conditions at UZ (University of Zimbabwe) saying there was no water on the university campus. Taps, pipes, geysers and cisterns are dry and in the residence hostels the toilets have been locked and sealed off for more than six months. "Everyone has to go off campus and collect their own water to use the toilet," she said. "It's pathetic I thought I was going to university to learn not to carry water. It's no wonder there's cholera everywhere." Our conversation was cut off as a bunch of Green Bombers (Youth Militia) tried to push in to the queue somewhere and all hell broke loose. A fairly orderly queue suddenly became a wild, angry mess as people surged forward and tempers rose and the university student's story was lost in the madness of everyday life.


## A MONTH IN SCHOOL DURING THE WHOLE YEAR.
## LILLIAN'S STORY: DECEMBER 2008

The academic year has just ended in Zimbabwe but for most families it has come as a non event. Parents whose children attend rural government schools have reached the point of utter despair after a year in which their children have had less than a month in the classroom. Lillian is 15 and this year should have finished the first half of her O' level syllabus but at the end of 52 weeks her school writing books have only got two or three pages of notes written in them. All year it's been one thing after another that has kept the classrooms closed: teachers on strike; elections; schools being used as polling booths; pre and post election violence and teachers fleeing the country to find work in the Diaspora.

In the last term of the year which began in September, Lillian's parents hoped that at last their daughter might be taught some lessons but by then, after four months of abductions, beatings and post election violence, all the teachers had fled. On the first week of term all the children arrived at the school but no teachers turned up. By the second week some children were still walking to school every day but the teachers strike had deepened. At the beginning of the third week Lillian came back from the school after a couple of hours and said that the classrooms were still locked, the Headmaster hadn't turned up and a caretaker told the children to try again next week.

At half term Lillian still hadn't seen her teacher, opened a single book or even set foot in her classroom. In despair her parents began looking for a place for Lillian at other schools. All the other rural government schools were in the same position: closed, no teachers and not offering any chance for a teenage girl to write her O' levels. Mission schools were still operating but because of the collapse of countless rural government schools, they were grossly over-subscribed. At one Mission school that Lillian's father went to, the Headmaster said he had been intimidated into enrolling eighty more students then they had facilities to cope with. These were the children of government and security personnel and others with connections in high places. The Headmaster had no choice but to agree to take them in despite the fact that he had run out of desks, chairs and text books and the teacher to pupil ratio was three times more than it should be.

Urban schools weren't much better: more students than places; collapsing infrastructure; decrepit equipment and a rapidly dwindling number of teachers. Lillian and her parents will accept any place at any school for the 2009 academic year. Even with cholera stalking the towns, raw sewage flowing in the streets and alleys of high density areas and no food in the shops; anything is better for Lillian than not being able to finish her schooling. If she cannot get some O' Levels, Lillian knows she is destined for a teenage marriage and a life of toil growing vegetables and trying to eke out a life engaged in subsistence agriculture in a dusty, primitive village.

## O LEVEL EXAM PASS RATE 1998 -2007

| | |
|---|---|
| 1998 | 14.58% |
| 1999 | 15.69% |
| 2000 | 13.38% |
| 2001 | 13.99% |
| 2002 | 13.80% |
| 2003 | 12.80% |
| 2004 | 10.20% |
| 2005 | 12.00% |
| 2006 | 14.20% |
| 2007 | 9.85% |

(Samukange, T. 2014)

## THE PLIGHT OF THE TEACHERS: 2008/2009

During a year-long strike from 2008 to 2009, teachers demanded higher salaries paid in US dollars. This strike led to nearly 94% of all rural schools closing and school attendance rates fell from 80% to 20 %. (UNICEF, 2009)

Teachers were one of the lowest paid professions in the 2000's, receiving the equivalent of US$10 for every three months of teaching. Their salaries in 2009 were as low as one US dollar a month (IRIN, 2013)

## LIFE AND DEATH PILLS:

### DIANA'S STORY: SEPTEMBER 2008

When I met Diana, a teacher at a nearby government junior school, she told me that her pay is presently Z$9,000 a month, equivalent to 50 British pence or 70 US cents. Diana is epileptic and her tablets cost Z$22,000 a month, more than double her entire monthly salary. "Without my son in South Africa helping me, I would be dead now," Diana told me and when I asked her what her son did in South Africa she laughed when she told me he worked in a garage pumping fuel. "Imagine, he earns more than me, and I'm a qualified teacher!"

## DIARY OF ABSURDITY:

### SALARIES IN VOUCHERS: FEBRUARY 2009

The Reserve Bank Governor has announced that civil servants are going to be paid part of their salaries in US dollar 'vouchers' which they'll be able to exchange, not for real bank notes, but for food at some shops which are yet to be identified. He didn't say if civil servants would be able to see doctors, access medicines, get on buses or pay for fuel and utilities with these US dollar vouchers. The balance of their salaries will be paid in Zimbabwe dollars which are now completely worthless. So while the rest of the country is starting to breathe again in the multiple currency explosion that has taken over in the last month, civil servants are still bottom of the heap and won't be getting any hard foreign currency: US dollars, Rand, Pula, Pounds.

**SHINY SUITS, DARK GLASSES AND US DOLLARS:**

**BOBBY'S STORY: FEBRUARY 2009**

Three weeks after government schools should have opened, children are still outside playing on the streets. Parents are desperate and will do anything to get their kids back into classrooms. Bobby told me told me what happened at the church mission school where his daughter is a pupil. The teachers and parents had a meeting, agreed that fees would be paid in foreign currency and teachers paid in US dollars and everything looked set. Uniforms were ironed, shoes shined, trunks packed and the school opened. The next day lessons started but two hours later a car drove up. Men in shiny black suits and dark glasses emerged and said they were CIO (Central Intelligence Organisation) and that they also needed foreign currency; they took all the US dollars that had been paid in fees and left the school with nothing, completely unable to function. A little while later the teachers were called to an emergency meeting. Before long the school bell rang, classrooms emptied and the teachers went home.

Bobby was desperate to get his daughter back onto her O' level syllabus and started asking around about other schools. His friend's child at another mission school said the teachers were offered one thousand South African Rand a month (100 US dollars) but refused to work for such a small amount, and

172

so no lessons were underway there either. Another parent whose son is at a rural government school said he'd paid the requested thirty US dollar school fees but no teachers turned up for work. Another said his teenage daughter came home with mud on her clothes and blisters on her hands. Teachers hadn't come to school so the headmaster gave all the kids manual gardening chores rather than let them go home. His daughter cried and she tried to get the mud stains off her dress and said all she wanted to do was go to lessons and learn for her O' Levels, not cut grass, pull out weeds and clear drains and paths around the school. Zimbabwe has an insatiable appetite for education and this is the hardest thing to be witnessing nearly thirty years after Independence.

## TALKING SHOES, PHONE BILLS AND GUAVAS: SANDRA'S STORY: MAY 2009.

By May 2009, despite the new 'unity' government, the new Education Minister David Coltart said: "Government coffers are bare." Undoing the damage done after five years of collapse wasn't going to be a quick fix. Promises of salary increases for teachers came from the international donor community and waiving school fees for the children of teachers, broke the strike that had been going on for months but it wasn't enough for teachers who couldn't even afford to get to work anymore.

"Clothes are a luxury," Sandra said when we talked about whether she was going to go back to work. "How can I stand in the classroom with these talking shoes?" she said, lifting her foot up to reveal the sole peeling away from the upper, flapping at every step she took. "I've glued it together so many times but it just falls apart every few days with the long walks to work." A qualified senior school teacher with twenty years experience, Sandra doesn't have a car, computer or a mobile phone. "I was thinking of going South to work for three months. Lots of my friends at school have been doing it: going to South Africa and working as cleaners, child minders, house workers or cooks. That way you get some extra money to bring back and help you survive for a few months."

The day after Sandra and I chatted was the first day of the new school term and two children were sitting in a tree picking guavas at the house next door.

"Hello," I said, "aren't you going to school today?"

Giggling and squirming, the boy finally answered: "no money." The fees that term were US$50 per child, a fortune if you're unemployed.


**THE IMPACT 2000-2010**

In the first decade of the 21st century, 45,000 out of 100,000 teachers in Zimbabwe left the profession. (Moore, Kriger & Raftopoulos, 2013)

A decade after the 2004-2009 collapse of Zimbabwe the O' level pass rate in 2018 was 31,2%, the country was clearly still paying the price of its government's negligence towards teachers and education. In 2018 when the collapse began all over again, teachers fled for greener pastures when the government converted all their savings and salaries from US dollars into Zimbabwe dollars. In the education sector Zimbabwe had yet again not learned from its own mistakes of just a decade before.

# CHAPTER 7
# LIFE WITHOUT ELECTRICITY

Flick a switch for lights, turn a tap on for water and lift a lid for the dustbin: the three critical everyday things people in urban areas take for granted and which industry and commerce depend on for production. When the utilities failed, everyone had to take control of their own needs. For a long time we asked: what's worse, no power or no water? As Zimbabwe's crisis deepened we soon found ways to live without continuous mains electricity and generated our own power. Going without electricity was an inconvenience for households, a huge expense for industry and commerce but we found ways around it; going without water was another matter altogether. Without a regular supply and a means to store water, everything ground to a halt and health hazards were rampant. Garbage removal, something people took for granted in urban areas, was the essential service we had to take into our own hands as local authorities failed. With an estimated 68% of Zimbabwe's population living in rural areas in 2008 and nearly a million others having come off invaded farms, a lot of people already knew how to cope without the three utilities of life but for the 'townies' it was a big learning curve that took quite a lot of getting used to.

## SURVIVAL RULES FOR ELECTRICITY CUTS AND OPTIONS FOR OTHER POWER SOURCES

- Always be prepared for power cuts. The worse the situation in the country gets, the longer the power cuts last.
- Don't bank on load shedding schedules. The power could come on at any time or stay off for much longer than announced.
- Always treat the mains electricity as live, even when it's off; never do any repairs without switching off the mains.
- Always get up in the middle of the night, or whenever the power comes back on, and plug in anything that needs recharging; don't wait till the morning because chances are the power will be off again.
- Wait a few minutes for power to stabilize when it comes back after a power cut to avoid damage to equipment from fluctuations and surges.
- Keep everything fully charged: batteries, phones, torches, computers.
- Buy rechargeable A3 and A4 batteries for portable devices; buy a couple of battery chargers so you can recharge numerous batteries at a time.
- Inverters are essential for changing direct current (DC) to alternating current (DC). Consult an expert to get the right size inverters and batteries to suit your appliances.

- 12 volt batteries are essential for storing power and using with inverters to run appliances and portable devices. Get expert advice to help you match your needs to your budget.
- Batteries need to be replaced regularly; add it to your budget and put a few dollars aside every month.
- Portable power banks for emergencies are invaluable for charging cell phones and other small devices; small power banks can fit in your pocket or briefcase.
- Solar power is essential. Get specialist help to get the best options out of your budget.
- The best advice for solar lights is that you can never have too many: torches, lamps, lanterns; fixed, portable, overhead and hand-held. Some portable lights also have dynamos with wind-up cranks which are helpful in emergencies.
- Get an electrician to do the wiring and installations all the way down from solar panels to batteries, inverters and appliances. The danger of overcharging batteries, acid leaks and exploding batteries mustn't be underestimated and charge controllers, well ventilated places and child proof barriers around batteries are essential.
- Generators are only as good as your ability to house them and run them safely outside. You have to be able to find, afford, carry and decant the fuel to run the generator and have somewhere to store the fuel safely. Generators need servicing on a regular basis

and in residential areas you need accommodating neighbours who will tolerate the noise of generators. Remember that while the generator is roaring you can't hear other noises so be very aware of your security.

- Invest in gas appliances if you can: a gas bottle with cooking ring, two plate gas cooker or gas stove, gas fridge. Invest in gas bottles, hoses and regulators that fit your appliances, store them safely and keep the gas bottles full all the time.

## ZIMBABWE'S POWER

Electricity in Zimbabwe is generated from Kariba Hydropower, Hwange coal-fired power, and three small thermal power plants. Erratic and severely limited electricity supplies, which took hold in the mid 1990's bought Zimbabwe close to a standstill in the early 2000's and the cocktail of neglect, corruption, lack of maintenance and unpaid imports, continue to haunt us two decades later. The Zimbabwe government loved to apportion blame on 'The West' and 'Sanctions' but the AFDB (African Development Bank) didn't hide the true facts in their report for the 2000-2010 decade:

"The domestic generation has been reduced owing to lack of regular maintenance and imports have been cut back because of the inability of Zimbabwe Electric Supply Authority (ZESA) to settle its bills regularly. Because electricity is fundamental to Zimbabwe's economic and social development, the persistent lack of adequate and reliable supply has resulted in significant losses to the economy. ... Over the last 10 years [2000-2010] Zimbabwe imported 29 percent of its power supply from the neighboring countries (with annual dependence on imports ranging from 21 percent to 42 percent). These supplies came mainly from Mozambique, Democratic Republic of Congo (DRC), Zambia, and South Africa." (AFDB, 2011)

According to the World Bank only 36% of Zimbabweans had access to electricity in 2008 and that number had only risen to 41% by 2018.


## THE SKEWED COST OF ELECTRICITY: 1996-97

The average electricity tariff was 2.6 US cents per kWh in 1996-97, while the fully loaded cost to cover operations and capital development programs was estimated at 6 US cents per kWh. (World Bank, 2010)


## THE DREADED FAULT

The very worst thing that can happen when it comes to electricity cuts is when your line has a fault and yours is one of only a few houses with a problem. At night you look out and see houses all around you with lights on while you and maybe a couple of neighbours are in darkness. In March 2006 it was my turn to go through this rite of passage in Zimbabwe's electricity crisis. I kept a record of the days that followed in the single phasing nightmare and more than once cursed my own frugal behaviour of stocking up on meat and perishable goods but it taught me a new survival rule : don't stock up on meat unless you've got back up freezer facilities.

## DIARY OF DISASTER: SINGLE PHASING FOR SIX DAYS: 2006
## FRIDAY 3 MARCH

At lunchtime the power went down to single phasing; I only noticed it when I plugged the TV in and it popped, banged and the plug and wires went black. I'd learnt over the years that low power was far more damaging to appliances than high voltage and so I ran around unplugging everything. The deep freeze was clicking and ticking, the fridge had already switched itself off and no other appliances were working. I switched off the geyser at the mains and tested the voltage: it was down to 180 and should be 220 and if I switched a light on it dropped to 130.

That night the geyser was still hot, so I was able to have a shower. I phoned ZESA four times between 3.00pm and 9.30pm that night and each time they said they were coming but they never arrived. Richie was home from school on an exit weekend and the poor lad had a dismal time: no hot water, no computer, no TV and I couldn't even send him back with clean and ironed clothes. I think he probably wished he'd stayed at school.

## SATURDAY 4 MARCH

By 10.00am all the hot water had gone and it was raining incessantly. This weather had been going on since Thursday:

mist, wind and temperatures down to 16 degrees. We had cold breakfast, cold lunch and cold supper. By 5.00 pm all the bread in the deep freeze had defrosted. The Kelly Kettle was put into service, working overtime outside, its smoky funnel fed with dry Msasa pods and twigs, making tea and coffee and later heating water to have a bucket bath. Repeated calls to ZESA yielded no assistance and just a growing list of excuses. Ours is the only house affected by the problem and we were very low on their fault fixing priority list.

## SUNDAY 5 MARCH

Boiled eggs for breakfast, made on the gas stove which is almost out of gas and keeps spluttering and going off all the time. I hadn't been able to fill the cylinder because there is no gas to buy anywhere. In the deep freeze things are looking bad. All the meat we've bought and saved through the food shortages is now at risk. The top layers have completely defrosted: chicken, sausages, mince and stewing steak. In the fridge all the milk is going sour. I am making repeated calls to ZESA  every four hours or so, so they don't forget me, hoping that maybe they'll  get so annoyed with me that they'll come and fix the fault, but they don't and every time I phone there's another excuse. It wouldn't be so bad if only they would tell me the truth; I fume and mutter and keep hoping. It's hard trying to stay positive and keep a sense of humour whilst squatting over a smoky fire trying to boil a kettle in the damp mist, rain and wind; eyes streaming, hair, hands and clothes stinking of smoke. Later I had a sponge down from a five litre bucket of smoky warm water heated outside.

## MONDAY 6 MARCH

Still no sign of ZESA. Foul weather, wind and rain continuing. Met a man outside his gate who said their house had power and if I wanted to use his stove, I would be welcome; I love the heart of ordinary people

## TUESDAY 7 MARCH

Again, ZESA technicians don't come all day and I phone the ZESA manager at home with a number someone's given us and read out the whole list of excuses that we've been given by ZESA over the past five days. Unbelievably a short while later a seven tonne truck churns up the hill with four men sitting across the front seat. They hoot at the gate and no one gets out the truck, but a window opens. They say they are from ZESA but it's too dark now, so they'll come and sort out the problem tomorrow. Why on earth did they bother I mutter; this excuse annoying me more than any of the others in the past five days. In the house the situation is bad: the meat in the deep freeze is lost as is the milk and veg in the fridge which now has its own colony of fruit flies.

## WEDNESDAY 8 MARCH

ZESA don't come all day but finally arrive to fix the fault at 8.00pm after another call to the Manager at home. The Manager said the fault wasn't recorded in the book and had never been written down in the last six days. This time the engineers do get out of their vehicle, put up a ladder and replace the porcelain insulator which has broken on their pole, working by the light of their car headlights. In less than an hour the repair has been done and the electricity comes back on, six days later.

After 35 phone calls and nine visits to the ZESA depot, these were the excuses from ZESA during the six day power cut:

- No diesel
- No engineers
- No spares
- Phone later when the Foreman is here
- Everyone's out on jobs
- Phone later when the engineers are here
- We're coming tonight
- We'll definitely be there later
- We are trying to source spares
- We're coming for sure but in daylight hours
- It's dark and engineers can't see
- We never received a report of your fault
- There are lots of faults books, maybe your fault is written in another book.

When Zimbabwe went into its second economic collapse a decade later in 2018/19, power cuts due to faults (usually in the form of exploded and burnt out transformers) would go on for two or three weeks, making the five or six day power cuts of 2006 seem like child's play!

### THE SKEWED COST OF ELECTRICITY: 2007
In 2007 it cost Zimbabwe Z$90 to produce a kilowatt of electricity but that same kilowatt was sold for Z$5.

### THE GREEN DATSUN AND THE 'DEAD FLEET' ADVENTURE: NOVEMBER 2007
With prolonged power cuts part of our life, sometimes for 12 but more often 18 hours a day, when the power does come on it is a race to get everything done because you never know how long it will last. After 30 hours without power I phoned ZESA at 7.00am in the morning on a sultry November day, hoping to be first on the list for attention. They said that there was a fault and that I should check later. By then I had learnt the most important lesson of survival and that was to complain to the service provider, often! The more you phoned the better; if you could get a person's name on the faults help line it was even more beneficial and if you recognized their voice and addressed them by name, even better still.

At 11.00am on that November day I phoned again to enquire about progress and was told they'd done nothing yet. "We've got the staff and the parts we need but we don't have a vehicle to come and fix the problem. Do you think you could help us?"

Half an hour later I picked up the Foreman, two electricians, a ladder and an extendable pole. I was the driver and our first stop was to unhook connections on one street and then go to the electricity sub-station a few kilometres away. As they switched off a line at the sub-station, we all heard a loud clunk and could see sparks on another line. Yikes! What had I let myself in for I thought, instinctively ducking at the sight of the sparks, which in retrospect was a pretty pointless reaction. What I had thought was going to be an hour of fetching, driving and dropping off, turned into a marathon. There was a problem at the sub-station and so back to the depot on the other side of town we went. Four more electricians were located, more spare parts, huge coils of cable a massive extending ladder and a pile of forms and paperwork.

Stopping behind a small green Datsun at the intersection with the main road I left a fair distance between us, very conscious of the huge ladder extending right out across my bonnet at the front and hanging well over the tail gate at the back of my pick-up truck. The lady in the green Datsun stalled and her car started slipping back towards us; the two men in the front of the truck with me were pushing back into their seats as we could all see where this was leading. Hasn't she seen me, I wondered and gave a couple of quick taps on the hooter to alert her and then held the hooter down as the Datsun slipped ever closer to my bonnet. With visions of the ladder going right through her back window I was now worried but had nowhere to go because there was someone behind me. At last I breathe a huge sigh relief as the Datsun roars into life, lets out a belch of black smoke and off she goes! With the Datsun zooming off in the other direction I cross the intersection and we head off back to the substation, the car full of chatter and nervous laughter from my passengers in the front and back.

From the sub-station I was directed deep into the high density suburbs where the roads are in a shocking state, huge potholes and gullies leaving  me driving on a footpath, straddling lines of maize cultivation on either side of the track, getting the electricians as close as possible to the place where the fault is. When I literally can't go any further everyone piles out, ladders, cables and spare parts are carried to the site and 30 minutes later the problem is fixed. Without power for 30 hours for a fault that took 30 minutes to fix.

Reloading the ladder and re-tracing our steps to switch on what had been switched off, I asked the question I asked everyone: so how are you surviving this situation in our country? As always, the flood gates opened, and we talked all the way back. The Foreman told me that they have a 'dead fleet' with only one vehicle left operating to cover the whole district stretching for scores of kilometres in all directions.

"We won't survive this rainy season without customer input," he says as I turn into the gates of the ZESA depot. There's a small tin hut at the entrance gate and the guys are sitting on upturned plastic crates eating sadza (maize porridge) and they wave as I drive in; not even a canteen for them to have their meals, how can this be 27 years after Independence I wonder, but say nothing. The internal driveway and roads are littered with potholes and as I go round the back for them to unload the ladder and cables from my truck I'm struck at how the place looks like a breakers yard: broken trucks, vans and huge lorries in various stages of disrepair everywhere, robbing parts from one vehicle to fix another. This is survival Zimbabwe style! And yet, despite it all, everyone is polite, courteous, friendly and very grateful that today I helped them do their job.

Many thousands of people benefitted from my midday adventures on that November morning and all it cost me was courtesy, a few litres of diesel and about thirty kilometres of traipsing backwards and forwards to fetch and carry and switch on and off. All in all, a lot of good lessons learned that day for surviving in a failed state, not the least of which was don't get too close to little green Datsuns.


## SURVIVAL RULES AND TIPS FOR KEEPING THINGS COLD
Prolonged power cuts or faults lasting days at a time led to a whole new level of learning and rules, hints and tips for keeping things cold.

- Don't open the freezer door. The longer you can keep the door shut the longer it will stay cold.
- Three quarter fill empty two litre plastic bottles with water and freeze them solid. Use them as ice blocks

in the deep freeze and they will help keep the freezer colder during long power cuts. (Empty milk bottles work well)

- Invest in ice bricks, freeze them and spread them around in the deep freeze to keep the temperature down.
- Put all the fresh milk in the deep freeze or a cold box packed with ice bricks when the power goes off and put the milk back in the fridge when the power comes back on to stop it going sour.
- Keep a Tupperware container in the fridge with frozen ice blocks in it to help keep the fridge temperature down during long power cuts. Refreeze the ice blocks when the power comes back on.
- Turn the fridge thermostat to its maximum so it gets very cold when the power is on and stays colder longer when the power goes off.
- Have a small cold box that you can use as a mini fridge during long power cuts. Put a small bottle of milk, a few veg and the items you intend to use in one day into the cold bag with frozen ice bricks to keep it cool; this saves you from having to open and close the fridge door and prolongs the life of other items in the fridge.

**THE DREADED DEEP FREEZE INSPECTION: OCTOBER 2007**
After three weeks of only getting electricity from 11.00pm to 4.00am every day in October 2007 (the hottest time of the

year), my deep freeze never got a chance to freeze solid and survive nineteen hours a day without power. Finally, the time came when I couldn't put it off anymore and knew I had to save what I could and deal with the rest to avoid contamination, bacteria and food poisoning.

First to go were all my precious berries; carefully collected wild berries from creeping white stemmed shrubs which grow on dusty roadsides, in thickets in the bush and in overgrown areas of the garden. I never managed to identify them, but they looked a bit like raspberries, and I took to calling them dusty berries because they only needed a little scratch of dust to grow and thrive in. The leaves are pale green on top and almost white underneath, and the stems are covered in vicious thorns making the dusty berries difficult and painful to pick but all the more precious when collected. Once I discovered how quickly and successfully the little red dusty berries froze, I collected them a few at a time, whenever I got there before the birds, and froze them in bags to have a few for breakfast every day. Sometimes when I had a bumper collection of dusty berries, I made them into the most delicious jam, and they became a much prized wild survival ingredient in my pantry and freezer. On the dreaded day of the freezer inspection the dusty berries had not survived the very lengthy power cuts. Being small and soft they were almost continually defrosted and when I saw little bubbles in the bags, from what was obviously fermenting fruit, I knew my precious dusty berries had to go.

Three packets of mince and three of stewing beef were right on the edge: completely defrosted and dripping blood and needed to be cooked immediately. They went straight into two big pots where they were cooked up with generous amounts of chilli and curry before being put into Tupperware containers to be used in the next couple of days. Three other packets of stewing beef were too far gone for people but were well cooked and labelled for dog food in the next few days. My motto was "if it's going green it's got to go" and sadly a couple of other items fit that category during the freezer inspection and so out they went.

It didn't matter how much we ranted and raved, moaned and complained, dug holes in the garden and threw precious food away, this was the reality of living in a country dictated entirely by politics, riddled with corruption and in a state of economic collapse. In October 2007 ZESA said it was costing Z$90 to produce a kilowatt of electricity and the government would only allow them to sell it for Z$5. They were making a loss of Z$85 on every kilowatt of electricity generated. ZESA were also importing power from South Africa in 2007, paying US 2 cents a kilowatt but only allowed to sell it at a tenth of that price. It was one of those absurd "Emperor's new clothes" situations where everyone except the government could see the problem, or if they could see it, they didn't deal with it in their never ending quest to retain popular votes.

With ongoing 19 hour a day power cuts, an empty deep freeze and no food left, survival got much harder in October 2007. This was the time when supermarkets were mostly empty and there was no food to buy. My friend Steve and I put our savings together and went on the hunt for gas to try and run a newly repaired gas deep freeze. A big heavy deep freeze with rusting bottom and big black cooling pipes coiled on the back of it we finally scraped together the fourteen million dollars we were told it would cost to fill a 20kg gas cylinder. Gas refilling in Marondera had stopped months ago and so the gas bottle had to be taken to Harare where it would be put in a queue with hundreds of other gas cylinders waiting to be filled. It took three days before our gas cylinder reached the front of the queue and was filled but by then the price had gone up to twenty six million dollars.

## DIARY OF ABSURDITY: 'MULTIPLY PRICES BY ONE MILLION DOLLARS': JULY 2008

A sign on the wall in the ZESA (electricity supplier) office this week read: 'Multiply prices on your statement by 1 million dollars.' Standing in the queue in the ZESA offices on a Monday morning, the line was moving painfully slowly. It was dark and quiet in the electricity suppliers building as ironically, absurdly, there was no electricity! This is a typical Monday in Zimbabwe: the electricity goes off before 5.00am and if we are lucky it will come back on in fifteen or sixteen hour's time, at around 9.00pm at night. It's not just residential areas which are without electricity; it's the entire town, all the businesses, two hospitals, ten schools and scores of factories. When I finally got to the front of the queue I explained to the teller that I haven't had a statement for four months so I don't know how much to pay. Electricity is billed by the unit and the meters are normally read and accounts hand delivered in the urban and residential areas every month.

"We are no longer sending statements," the teller says, "it's too expensive to print and deliver accounts."

"So how much do I owe?" I ask.

"I don't know," she responds. "The electricity is off so I can't check your account on the computer."

"How much shall I pay then?"

"Just pay what you think," she replies, "one or two hundred billion dollars will be enough for a private residence."

I hand over a hundred billion dollars and she writes me a receipt for 100,000 dollars. When I query the error on her receipt she points boredly at the sign on the wall and says: 'multiply by a million to get the right figure.' 100 billion dollars is the maximum amount of cash I am allowed to withdraw from the bank a day and it is worth about 30 US cents; this is the absurd face of life in a failed state.


**THE SKEWED COST OF ELECTRICITY: 2009**

"In 2009, the average end-user tariff for ZESA is estimated at 6.5 US cents per kWh, while the economic cost of service provision was estimated at 9.8 US cents per kWh." (World Bank, 2010)

## COOKING OPTIONS

Looking for cooking options that did not rely entirely on electricity or gas was crucial in Zimbabwe as the electricity crisis continued and both gas and paraffin were in short supply and very expensive. Some of the cooking options were dirty, smelly and messy, others were time consuming and hard work and they all required a lot more energy than flicking a switch on but learning to live like a pioneer in the 21$^{st}$ century was essential.

## BOIL THE KETTLE

The cardinal rule to keeping food on the table during Zimbabwe's eighteen hour a day power cuts was to boil the kettle and fill flasks with boiling water at every opportunity. Regardless of the time of day or night, whenever the electricity flicked on, run to the kettle. A flask of boiling water gives you a head-start for everything: a cup of tea, porridge, noodles, soup, vegetables and for those much needed hot water bottles in winter in Zimbabwe where windows aren't double glazed and there's no central heating

## THE HOT BOX

Making a Hot Box became a necessity when the electricity was off for eighteen hours every day, there was no gas to buy and no incentive to bend over a smoky fire outside in the cold winter wind. Once I had the right box and the right filling material, the Hot Box was a life saver and almost as good as a Slow Cooker, without the electricity of course.

In order to hold heat for as long as possible, I found a thick, heavy cardboard box which was big enough to hold one large pot in the centre. Using double layers of old winter pillowcases, so that you could wash the top one when there was spillage, and one large continental pillowcase, I filled them with the smallest kaylite balls I could find. It took a bit of time and lots of half cooked meals to work out that the smaller kaylite balls worked best, as opposed to chips or beans, because they packed in tightly and formed a very effective insulation that kept the heat in. I finally managed to get kaylite balls about the size of beads from freight packers who dealt with glassware and breakables, but they didn't believe me when I said I was going to use them for a home-made oven. Filling the pillowcases was a nightmare because the kaylite balls stuck to everything and seemed to make their own static electricity leaving me adorned with very annoying little white balls stuck on my hands, arms, clothes, hair and the furniture.

The next learning curve was not to overfill the pillowcases; you needed enough kaylite balls to have a nice deep bed on the bottom and sides of the box but not so much that the pillows were too rigid and prevented you from snuggling the pot into the padding and moulding the top pillow over the lid. The secret to the Hot Box was to always start with boiling ingredients and a hot pot. Bring it to the Boil was the rule; as soon as the food was boiling you nestle the pot into the pillows on the bottom and sides, snuggle another pillow over the top of the pot and then close the flaps of the box, putting something heavy on top to keep the heat in. Almost everything was possible in the Hot Box from rice to vegetables, stew, soup, porridge and pasta although the latter tended to stick together in a clump but worked well in a stew. Timing was as always, a bit hit and miss but it wasn't long before I could guesstimate how long things would take to cook and, best of all, nothing ever got burnt.

## THE PLANT STAND STOVE

There's nothing quite as back breaking as cooking over an open fire at ground level, not to mention leaving you grimy and smelling of smoke. Adapting a plant stand turned out to be the perfect waist high alternative to squatting in the dust to make breakfast lunch and supper. The wrought iron plant stand which once allowed colourful, cascading plants to be placed at two levels was ideal. On the bottom level a roof tile provided the fireplace: strong, heat resistant and easy to tip the ashes out. The upper level was converted into the stove top: a few pieces of wire tied on in a criss-cross pattern formed a grid strong enough to hold a pot or frying pan.

The plant stand stove worked beautifully and was fuelled almost entirely on hard dry Msasa pods and thick sticks of which I always had an abundant supply thanks to the big Msasa trees in my garden. There were of course disadvantages to cooking over an open fire, regardless of whether it was at ground level or waist high. Smoke was the main culprit leaving my fingers permanently stained yellow as if was a chain smoker, eyes red and hair sticky and wiry from the smoke. There were also numerous encounters with the inevitable errant flame that singed arm hairs and eyebrows, leaving me making my own Zimbabwean fashion statement more than a few times.

I soon learnt that I needed to be more inventive and cook simpler, quicker things to save time and reduce the amount of combustible material needed to feed the fire with. Another lesson I learnt very quickly was that it was imperative to keep the lid on the pot or pan all the time otherwise everything got infused with smoke, sprinkled with ash and garnished with sticks and leaves. Any prior appeal for eating smoked foods wore off very quickly after a few sessions of cooking outside over the open fire.

In July 2007 after days of snow in Johannesburg, the cold front moved up into Zimbabwe. As was the pattern it took about four days for the cold to arrive and when it did the attraction of the outside plant stand stove wore off very quickly. It was 2 degrees Celsius at 5.45 am on that particular July morning and not at all funny to be standing outside in the freezing cold trying to boil water for tea. If I hadn't previously exhausted my repertoire of colourful adjectives and swear words to attach to electricity suppliers, ZESA, this was the day I found more. My fingers were freezing, the Msasa pods didn't want to burn, thick frost lay across the garden and even the water in the bird bath was frozen and little blue Waxbills were skating across the surface.  It was a winter day such as we hadn't had for years and if it hadn't been so tough to survive, it would have been very beautiful. On that day of all days I realised how many wood chips, pods and sticks were needed just to boil a pot of water for tea. I decided that whoever had first coined the phrase: 'a watched pot never boils,' must surely have been cooking outside over a smoky winter fire with frozen ears, nose, fingers and toes.

Standing outside shivering in the cold in the winter of 2007 I gained a new respect for the millions of Zimbabweans living in un-electrified rural villages who had to cook on open wood fires every day of their lives, and who had never known the luxury of anything else. It is such a waste of energy to get energy that it makes you not want to eat at all.


## THE THREE LEGGED POT

The black, cast-iron, three legged pot was a regular at my outside cooking sessions. This was the ideal candidate to sit for hours over the coals on an open fire; perfect for anything that needed long, slow cooking time and would emerge completely undamaged by flames, soot and ash.

Never did I imagine that I would look back on outside cooking over a smoky fire with anything other than relief that I had survived it and managed to keep a meal on the table. With the passing of time my mind has allowed me to block out the exhaustion, stinging, watering eyes and smoky cough and replace it with nostalgia for early evening meals with a friend and my young teenage son sitting outside in the glorious orange glow of sunset. Avocado's picked from the tree in the garden, sliced or mashed onto home-made bread spread with home-made butter and accompanied by a bowl of hot mushroom soup ladled out of the black three legged pot on the fire. Surviving Zimbabwe's collapse had taught me so much more than just despair and anguish.


## THE KELLY KETTLE

The Kelly Kettle was my most treasured possession and the most frequently used item in my arsenal of equipment necessary for surviving the power cuts. I'd been given a Kellly Kettle years before by my sister and it was a neat thing to take along on picnics and outings in the bush, not to mention being a great talking point. Portable, light weight and requiring just a few bits of dry kindling, never did I imagine that Kelly would be a life saver when it came to surviving Zimbabwe's collapse in the late 2000s. Made of aluminium the Kelly is a cylindrical double skinned flask; you fill the outer skin with water (it takes about a litre and a half) and light a fire in the inner chamber of the flask. Also known as a Volcano Kettle, the Kelly sits on an aluminium base which you fill with paper, twigs, dry pods and small dry items of kindling. As the fire burns, the flames roar up the centre, heating the water in the outer chamber and expelling the smoke at the top. You feed the fire by dropping dry pods and twigs down the chimney until the water boils which takes four or five minutes. The outer water chamber has a spout whose mouth is blocked with a cork on a chain to prevent water spillage in transport and to stop dirt from contaminating the water chamber. You are supposed to take the cork out of the spout when you are boiling the water because if you don't the cork swells up with moisture and as the pressure builds up it is pushed out explosively, followed by a jet of boiling water scalding anything in its way. That was a lesson I learnt the hard way, nursing scalds on my arms and chest, but Kelly was still my best friend when there was no electricity.

## THE SOLAR COOKER

The solar cooker became my other best friend during the long, quiet days of no electricity. The best way to get energy without using energy came in the form of a parabolic solar cooker which arrived in the back of a friend's pick-up truck one bright sunny morning at the height of Zimbabwe's power cuts. I happened to be in the right place at the right time when solar cookers were being donated by a German NGO to an institution and there was one left over that was going begging. The large, shiny parabolic dish attached to a frame with adjustable settings to angle it to the sun depending on the time of day, and a grid in the centre on which to place your pot, was instantly put to use.

Getting the most effective heat from the solar cooker took a bit of practice and needed bright sunlight with no trees or shade in the way and no cloud interference. The trick with the positioning was tilting it to just the right angle so that the sun reflected off the curved sides of the solar cooker and aimed the brightest glare directly onto the base of the pot. It didn't take long to discover that the best pot to use was a black one as it retained the heat and the quickest lesson to learn was that you needed oven gloves as the pot got very hot very quickly and getting burnt was a reality.

Once you got the sun aimed at exactly the right place on the solar cooker you would see a bright white light in the bottom of the pot followed soon afterwards by little bubbles rising to the surface. Getting two litres of cold water to boil in less than ten minutes was the most rewarding achievement, particularly as it didn't need anything other than free, clean, bright sunlight of which Zimbabwe has in abundance almost all year round.

Before long I could cook almost anything on the solar cooker including porridge, soup, egg and bacon, toast, stew, pasta, chilli con carne, vegetables, rice and even managed to make flapjacks once. Burning was a problem if you didn't keep a close eye on the solar cooker and this wasn't restricted to just burning the food it also included burning and melting pot handles, knobs on lids, oven gloves, wooden spoons, plastic handles on ladles and spatulas and even, on one notorious occasion, a skirt hanging on the washing line. A pot of food had been taken off the solar cooker and as the angle of the sun changed the bright glare reflected from the solar cooker onto the washing line, much to the amusement of my young son Richie who thought it was hysterical to watch Mum's skirt smoking and starting to turn black! Richie discovered that it was the neatest trick to throw a handful of dry grass stems onto the grid of the solar cooker when it was in the full sunlight and the grass would catch fire almost immediately; this trick even surpassed popping ants and ticks with a magnifying glass on a bright sunny day. Burning from the solar cooker also extended to fingers, hands and eyes; wearing sunglasses to avoid being blinded by the glare was essential and a cheap pair of throw-away sunglasses always hung on a hook ready for solar cooking days.

## SOLAR COOKER FUDGE

Keeping up your morale in times of prolonged crisis and uncertainty is imperative. Solar cooker fudge was a little treat perfected outside and well worth putting on your sunglasses and sacrificing some of your precious hoarded sugar.

 2 cups white sugar

1/2 cup cocoa

1 cup milk

4 tbls butter

1 teaspoon vanilla extract

Grease an 8x8 inch square baking pan and put aside.

Put all the ingredients except the vanilla essence into a saucepan, put your sunglasses on and go outside to the solar cooler on a bright, sunny day. Stir to mix and then bring to the boil, stirring constantly.

Reduce heat by tipping the angle of the solar cooker slightly away from the direct sunlight and simmer; don't stir again. If you have a thermometer, cook until temperature of the fudge mixture reaches 238 Fahrenheit/ 114 Celsius. If you don't have a thermometer simmer until a drop of the mixture in a cup of cold water forms a soft ball (exactly like you do when making marmalade).

Remove from the solar cooker. Add the vanilla essence and beat with a wooden spoon until the fudge loses its sheen. Pour the fudge into the prepared baking pan and allow to cool. Mark into squares and cut it before it gets completely solid.

## AMAI SIMON AND THE GAS STOVE:
## GERARD'S STORY: 2007

Gas was the obvious option for cooking during eighteen hour a day power cuts but because all Zimbabwe's gas was imported and there was no foreign currency to import it, gas became almost impossible to find in the years of Zimbabwe's crisis and on the rare occasions when you did find a supply, it was fiercely expensive and out of reach of most people. That didn't stop the surprise arrival of a gas stove at Gerard's house in 2007:

"Our house had a huge kitchen. One day I got back from work to find a gas stove in the kitchen: four plates, an oven and eye-level grill. Outside a 19kg cylinder stands. The cook, amai Simon, [mother of Simon] said: "please may I keep this here? My house is too small."

"Of course, but how did you get it?" I asked.

Amai Simon told me that it was a trade between her and someone. This was common practice at the time. So I asked her how she would pay for the gas. Amai Simon has no idea what the gas will cost, so I point out that 19kg will cost her nearly 19 million Zim dollars, a million dollars a kg. Amai Simon blanches, this is well beyond her salary. "Please can you fill it, then I will cook for you when there are power cuts?" So a deal was struck but Amai Simon mostly wanted the stove to bake cakes to sell to raise money for her church. About a month after this a transformer near our home blew and there followed over 400 hours of power cut. God used Amai Simon to cover my family's cooking needs that month! "

## WATER

### SURVIVAL RULES FOR WATER SHORTAGES

- Store it because you never know when the taps will run dry.
- Buy lots of buckets, as many as you can afford and have space to store: 20 litres for storage; 10 litres for easy carrying and decanting; 200 litre plastic drums/dustbins.
- Buy dark plastic water containers which help inhibit the growth of algae.
- Always buy buckets with lids and always keep them on and firmly closed to prevent dust, litter and animal contamination and to stop mosquitoes from breeding in the water.
- Always boil your drinking water.
- Boreholes may seem the perfect solution but are dependent on a power source to pump the water.

Borehole water must be tested to be sure the water is safe to drink.

- If you have a well always keep it firmly sealed to prevent contamination and accidents. Test that your well water is safe for human consumption and if it isn't, it is perfect to use in the garden to keep fruit trees and veggie gardens going.
- Connect pipes to your gutters to collect rain water and store it in drums or channel it into wells being used for garden purposes.
- Build a stand and install a bulk water tank: 2000, 5000, 10,000 litres. Ensure the stand and tank is high enough to feed into your house water supply and make sure the tank has a lid to prevent it being contaminated by dirt or animals. Get a plumber to connect the tank into the mains and make sure to have a tap to close and open the tank and a non return valve to stop the water flowing back into the mains pipes.
- Separate your water into different colour containers for different uses: drinking, food preparation, washing up and laundry. Use laundry water for flushing the toilet and grey water from washing up for the garden.

**WATER SAVING TIPS**
- Showers only, no baths

- Lower the ball valve in the toilet cistern or put in a large water displacement item in the cistern so it doesn't need so much water to flush.
- Only flush the toilet two or three times a day or when necessary.
- Switch the tap off while you brush your teeth.
- Have a bowl in the kitchen sink to catch the water when you are washing hands or cleaning vegetables and use that water for the garden.
- Disconnect and remove hosepipes from all garden taps.
- Wash clothes and dishes by hand or set machines onto shorter programs to use less water.

## DIARY OF EXCUSES: DON'T SLEEP IN THE BATH: 2003

At a time when Local Council (Municipality) officials still bothered to respond to enquiries and complaints from residents, this is what they told me when I asked them why we'd had no water for some days and if this was as a result of water rationing:

- We are about to start water rationing
- In reality the water rationing hasn't actually started yet
- It (the water rationing) has psychologically started
- The water rationing should start on the 10th (in three days time)

- Don't take this phone call as an excuse to sleep in the bath

## THE POLITICIZATION OF WATER: 2005

Nothing was spared from political interference in Zimbabwe during its years of crisis and collapse, including water. Six weeks after Zimbabwe's 2005 elections in which the opposition  MDC won almost 40% of seats in parliament, ZANU PF issued a national directive to overturn the 1976 Water Act and bring municipal water authorities across the country under the control of ZINWA (Zimbabwe National Water Authority). It was a decision that caused widespread dismay: water rates went up, service disruptions became widespread, little or no attention was paid to infrastructure and revenues raised from consumers went to central government coffers. More than a decade later when reviewing the evidence surrounding the devastating 2008-09 cholera epidemic, researchers wrote:

"The decision to usurp municipal authority over water, which had been under the control of the MDC in many areas of opposition support (including Harare), had major implications: (1) it immediately deprived MDC-controlled city councils of an important source of revenue, which they had been using to fund civic projects and maintain infrastructure; (2) it provided the cash-strapped ZANU-PF regime with a new stream of revenue … ; and (3) it allowed the ZANU-PF to assume control of another essential element for life." (Cuneu, Sollom & Beyrer, 2017)

## DIARY OF NECESSITY: USING THE BATH AS AN EMERGENCY WATER RESERVOIR: 2008

Once a week, if I'm lucky and the municipal water comes on, I fill the bath from the tap and use this as an emergency reservoir for the days when the water doesn't come on at all. Dipping carefully into the bath so as not to disturb the nasty brown sediment, I flick out drowned mosquitoes before carefully filling bottles, jugs and bowls, careful not to spill even a drop. Every time I do this it helps to strengthen my determination to save up my dollars and get a water tank as soon as I can afford it.

## APPEALING FOR HEAVENLY INTERVENTION

Coming out of church on Sunday after having prayed fervently for an end to cruel, greedy, selfish leaders and crippling shortages, I had added a little selfish prayer that when I got home there may be electricity or water, both would have been considered nothing short of a miracle but there was no harm adding a P.S. prayer for that too! As if someone above was trying to tell me something, parked outside the church was a filthy dirty white Peugeot station wagon covered in red dust. Someone had written in the dust: "Wash me." Below, someone had added: "With what?" That said it all for the state of our country stuck in years of unresolved water shortages.

## HOME TREATMENT OF WATER

Days  without water, dry taps everywhere and when the municipal water did come on it was often filthy dirty with green slime on top and rusty brown sediment on the bottom which erupted with brown, slimy,  bubbles drifting up from time to time. Desperate people were digging shallow wells in the bush and on the roadsides and we always boiled every drop of water we got to try and keep diarrhoea, dysentery, typhoid and cholera away.  The recipe we all learned off by heart was how to treat unsafe water with bleach which kills germs and bacteria. The recipe and method was written out on a piece of paper and stuck on the wall above the dry taps in my kitchen: 1 teaspoon bleach into 20 litres of water. STIR. STAND (Leave overnight or in the shade for at least two hours before using.)


## GARBAGE

### YEARS WITHOUT GARBAGE COLLECTIONS

Fold it, wash it and squash it were the three critical things to do when it came to surviving long periods without refuse removal. Sort it, give it away, burn it or compost it became regular weekend chores and stopping contagious dumping was a full time task. Every morning and evening walking along the street outside your home picking up litter was a critical chore; mornings were the worst time because overnight, under cover of darkness, people had absolutely no shame and dumped their litter on your verge as they drove or walked past. There's nothing quite as disgusting as dealing with someone else's dumped garbage but I learnt the hard way that if I didn't deal with it immediately by the next day someone would have added to it and then someone else and so the problem grew bigger by the day. Before you knew it, you'd have stray dogs looking for scraps on your verge, with flies and rats hot on their heels and the pile getting bigger and bigger.

**DIARY OF SHAME: THE MAN IN THE SEWAGE SWAMP: 2008**
When I heard news that a new tip had been established where people could dispose of household garbage I set out on an investigative mission. Driving at a snail's pace along the sandy road which runs behind a local high school, the road was badly eroded; many sections with huge gullies creeping out into the road threatening to swallow up car wheels that strayed too close to the edge. I slammed on the brakes when suddenly a man lurched out of the overgrown, jungly bush on the roadside The grass and weeds were head high, taller than him, hanging over the road, brushing the windscreen and roof of the car.

The man at my window was filthy, his hair thick and matted and his clothes torn and ragged. I raised my hand and greeted him and he immediately responded by cupping his hands together and clapping in the traditional Zimbabwean greeting. The man obviously lived somewhere here, in the bush nearby. Eight or ten lines of small maize plants were growing in a little cleared patch of thick black mud and a stinking stream of sewerage was seeping out of an overflowing septic tank, running through the middle of his crop. The smell was foul and I couldn't imagine how he could survive this hell or how he wasn't sick.

A little further along the road I realised that this was the tip people were talking about but in fact it was just another illegal dumping place. Garbage was strewn in piles everywhere. It had been a year since there had been any refuse collection in the town and people were desperate to get rid of their waste; out of sight out of mind was obviously their solution. The image of a starving, filthy man emerging from the bush and seeing sewerage running through his maize plants was a graphic, damning indictment of a country whose management had collapsed at every level.

## CELEBRATING THE RETURN OF THE DUSTBIN TRUCK: 2011

For the first time in over two years the dustbin truck came today. Unexpected and without any warning, not even hooting or trying to attract the attention of residents, there were suddenly dogs barking all over the neighbourhood and a distant roaring of an engine, signalling the return of the dustbin truck. It all began at 06.30am on the 22nd of November 2011, two years after the complete collapse of Zimbabwe's economy between 2005 and 2008. Unbelievably it had taken this long for new Councillors in the local authority to wade through the politics, corruption, nepotism, finger pointing, excuses and ghost workers and actually resume service.

Where do you start after two years without any dustbin collections? Absolutely determined not to dump my litter in the bush or on the side of the road, which had become the national past time, I had become a master of the art of sorting, cleaning, stacking and storing household rubbish. One woman's junk is another woman's treasure became my mantra and then it was just a question of finding out who wanted what. Paper waste was easy: primary and junior schools always wanted empty cereal boxes, toilet rolls and strips of corrugated cardboard; vets needed old newspapers, towels and anything that could be used for bedding in their kennels; doctors and hospitals always wanted magazines for their waiting rooms so that left things like labels from tins, jars and bottles  which either went into the burning pile or got buried in the compost.

Everything degradable and not edible or suitable for chickens or birds, from vegetable scraps and peels to eggshells and tea bags, went on the compost heap. I learned that roses, orchids and fruit trees loved banana peels and every morning would share out the remnants from the standard fruit salad supper of the evening before and give them to the fruit trees whose annual harvests saved my life when there was no food to buy. Plastic bags and packets were used, washed and re-used until they were falling apart and then were folded, flattened and stored in bigger bags, boxes and sacks, tucked away wherever there was space, waiting for the momentous day when the dustbin truck returned. Empty drink tins (very few and far between in my house!) were rinsed, squashed and then given to the charities who collected them; they recovered the small aluminium ring pull tags and sold them and then flattened the cans for sale also. Empty glass bottles always found a home; they were returned to supermarkets or given to bottle buyers; empty jam jars were always in huge demand by the countless women who made and sold pickles, preserves, jam and marmalade. Then there was everything else and after two years it had piled up in a mountain: light bulbs, empty tins, broken glass, batteries, hard plastic items, wire and metal.

The 50kg sack in the metal dustbin was so full and heavy that I couldn't even move it, let alone lift it out of the bin to drag to the gate. Luckily, we heard the dogs barking in every direction and were alerted to the momentous reappearance of the dustbin truck. Two of us hoisted the sack out of the bin and dragged it out to the road and I ran back inside and frantically started collecting up piles of flattened plastic bags and bottles that had been stashed away waiting for just this day. I gathered up enough to fill another 50kg sack in a few minutes and by then the dustbin truck was getting near. I dragged the second bag outside to the gate and went back to the storeroom for a third.

It was like a street festival out on the road. Whole families were gathering outside their gates. With smiles and exclamations of disbelief, we watched the truck come lumbering up the hill, its engine roaring and straining, exhaust belching black smoke. We were all still in our night clothes: dressing gowns, T shirts, shorts and track suits; waving and calling out to each other in delight at the first collection of our dustbins in over two years. The dustbin men were dour and silent. They didn't greet us, smile or offer any comment about where they'd been for the last two years or what they'd been doing with our monthly refuse removal payments and most of us didn't say anything because all we wanted was for them to take all this rubbish away and make sure they came back again every week.

Two hours later and long after the dustbin truck had gone, I had filled the 50kg sack in the outside dustbin again as bit by bit I cleared some of the piles of stashed folded, washed and squashed garbage from the garden shed, storeroom and even under the kitchen sink. Inevitably the dustbin truck didn't come back for another month but by now I'd had years of practice at folding, squashing, rinsing, burning, composting and filling bags; this was another lesson in how to survive a failed State.

# CHAPTER 8

# FUEL, PLANES AND WITCHCRAFT

## FUEL HINTS, TIPS AND THINGS YOU NEED

- Buy good quality 10 or 20 litre metal jerry cans (olive green are the standard colour for fuel). Bear in mind that when decanting, the jerry can has to be higher than the tank and a 10 litre jerry can is easier to lift to a height.
- 200 litre drums for bulk storage
- Reinforced siphon pipe with ball nozzle for decanting
- Filter or sieve to use when decanting fuel from drums and jerry cans to catch flecks of rust, grit and dirt (old stockings work well in an emergency).
- A safe, cool, ventilated place to store fuel
- Buy it when you see it and keep your tank full all the time.
- If you travel by road outside the country always fill up before you get to the border on your return
- When looking for fuel be prepared with all forms of payment methods: coupons, cash, debit cards, mobile phone banking
- Always be ready to join a  fuel queue at any time of day or night

Fuel, regardless of the form, for cars, buses, trains or planes, was in such critically short supply that everything came close to a standstill during Zimbabwe's years of collapse. When you live in a landlocked country and are entirely dependent on fuel imports, once your country runs out of money to pay for supplies, fuel shortages are inevitable. The worse the state of the economy gets, the worse the shortages are. Zimbabwe has been plagued by fuel shortages on and off since the late 1990s and although there were some periods of time when you could just drive in to a fuel station and fill up, queuing was always the red flag indicating a problem in the Ministry of Finance. The rule to live by was if you see a queue you fill up and stock up.

Queuing for fuel often involved many hours of waiting and was usually on the back of a rumour of an imminent delivery or even if someone had seen a tanker heading towards town. More times than I care to remember I would be leaving home at 4.00 am to go and get in a fuel queue with a flask of tea and a packet of sandwiches and considered myself lucky if I got home with a full tank by lunch time. Fuel queues became places of much social interaction as we sat nose to tail, unmoving for hours at a time. Often we would get out and talk to people in the queue, share a cool drink or snack and push each other's cars a few inches forward when the queue started moving to save starting the engine. That was when the drama started, when they started serving the fuel. Some fuel stations would offer a chance for pensioners to go to the front of the queues, but usually it was a case of first come first serve. Often it was a case of the first to the pump head was the first to get fuel, regardless of how they got there, because of the hordes of queue jumpers who pushed in. Queue jumpers were the bane of our lives and were completely unstoppable at those filling stations where the queues were not controlled and the pump attendants took bribes. The queue jumpers were often black market fuel dealers who would walk to the pump head and get jerry cans filled, lots and lots of jerry cans; others came in trucks and lorries with their 200 litre drums, pushed in front of you and then you had no option but to wait while their drums were filled. Unable to move, hemmed in with vehicles in front, behind and usually alongside you also, fuel queues were often not for the feint hearted!

Then there were the political queue jumpers and there was a never ending stream of them: well padded men in smart suits, wearing gaudy gold watches and dark glasses, pointy shiny shoes emerging from equally shiny luxury vehicles with government number plates: MPs, Councillors, VIPs and big wigs; cars and trucks with logos of the ruling political party stuck on doors and bumpers, army trucks, police and prison trucks, and always they came with numerous drums to fill up. There was nothing more likely to cause you to scream and swear at your windscreen than queuing for five hours and reaching the front of the queue only to see all the political queue jumpers in action, driving in the 'out' at the fuel station, blocking all other traffic until their vehicles and drums were filled.

Fuel coupons were issued by some fuel companies in the 2000's and became a very valuable commodity. You bought them in advance, paid in foreign currency, and handed them in at the filling station in exchange for fuel. Often the filling stations would only serve coupon holders or sometimes there would be a separate, shorter queue for coupon holders and best of all was the fact that the coupons never lost their value, regardless of hyper inflation, because they were denominated in litres not Zimbabwe dollars. When hyper inflation reached its peak in 2008, people were being paid their wages in fuel coupons; you could swop them for cash, pay school fees and even buy some commodities with them simply using the exchange rate on the day that you swopped the 20 litre fuel coupon. The accepted value of a fuel coupon was usually around US$1 a litre making the conversion into millions, billions, trillions and quadrillions very simple!

As the years of fuel shortages continued and the queues got longer and slower as less and less supplies came into the country, jerry cans and drums to store fuel in became very valuable commodities. Storing fuel in plastic containers wasn't safe and most filling stations weren't allowed to fill plastic containers and so we saved our dollars and bought jerry cans. When the fuel crisis was at its height you could expect to pay US$60 for a twenty litre jerry can and US$200 for an empty drum. A second hand market for drums and jerry cans soon sprang up, often a risky purchase because of the risk of contamination and rust in the containers.

Spending so many hours in fuel queues became a really good way to catch up on reading and paperwork and I never left home without a few newspapers, a book or my notebook where drafts of many articles were composed and articles in many newspapers read. It was ironic that I was reading articles about the world 'going green' while we were sitting in fuel queues hoping desperately to go anywhere: to school or work, doctor or dentist or just looking for food. We weren't calculating our carbon footprint on the globe, we were talking about sore feet and our human footprints on the hard African ground as we walked to work and school trying to survive the collapse of Zimbabwe.

## MIKE AND THE MINI BUS

There was never a shortage of stories from the fuel queues; knowing if they were true was another matter, a friend related this one:

"At a time when the fuel queues were huge and going round the block and into the distance, Mike had been in the queue for several hours. He was getting near the front when the queue stopped moving. After a while Mike got out his car to go and see what the problem was. A police officer had stopped the queue and was directing his own minibuses (his private sideline business) to go to the pump first. This was too much for Mike, he'd been there for hours, was hot, tired and hungry and an altercation with the policeman ensued. Mike hit the cop and knocked him over and was promptly arrested and taken to the police station. Mike admitted guilt, paid a fine and was allowed to leave. When Mike got back to the fuel queue all the other drivers got out of their cars and started clapping. Mike then discovered that his car, which, in the heat of the argument he'd left open with the keys in the ignition, had been filled up and parked on the side."

## BRAAIS AND POETRY IN THE FUEL QUEUES: PENNY'S STORY

"Fuel queues were one of my most challenging memories of the 2005-2008 years. My mother, who normally never arose before 9.00am and made no public appearances before 12.00 mid day, would appear bleary eyed to join a fuel queue at 5.00am. She flatly refused to be treated any different from the rest of the people in the queue and wouldn't accept pensioner's privileges and go to the front, nor would she let anyone else queue for her. I remember taking a bacon and egg roll to her many a time and more often than not she would get to the pumps only to discover they had run out of fuel. I remember seeing groups of people in the fuel queue unpacking a braai and passing the beers around whilst waiting, it was quite festive. When I waited in petrol queues some of my best letters and poetry were created as I watched life going on around me."

## GERARD'S STORY: 2007

Offering his memories of fuel queues, Gerard wrote this insightful story illustrating how adaptable people had become and how children were learning in their own way about survival in a country in a state of collapse; this was something many of us hadn't noticed as parents because we were too busy trying to keep our families safe and food on the table.

"Visiting South Africa on holiday, I stopped at a fuel station with no cars on the forecourt; "do you have fuel?" I asked a pump attendant. He seemed stunned by the question; I informed him that no queue back in Zimbabwe meant no fuel. On that same holiday, we stopped at a road-side cafe for food and I asked the kids "what would you like to drink?"

My then six year old daughter answered: "Cream Soda, please, and if they don't have that then Coke and if they don't have Coke, then a Fanta. I still have a photo I took of my daughter playing with her toy cars - all the cars were in a straight line - when I asked her what was going on, she sounded surprised: "It's a fuel queue!"

**PETROL INSTEAD OF DIESEL:**
**TREVOR'S TALE**

"Used to driving a small petrol car that was very fuel efficient and ran on the smell of an oil rag I was taking my cousin back to the airport but using a bigger vehicle. Seeing a filling station with a very small queue I thought this must be Christmas! This was my lucky day for sure, no queue and a tank that needed topping up; I pulled in straight away knowing I'd have plenty of time to fill up and get to the airport in good time. Getting to the pump the attendant put the nozzle in and the fuel started gushing in. Fortunately my cousin walked past and said the fuel smelled like petrol. At that moment I realized that I hadn't been thinking and had filled the diesel car with petrol. The tank had to be removed and drained and filled with diesel and we raced to the airport arriving just in time. "

## THE WHEELCHAIR IN THE QUEUE

"Barbara was in a long fuel queue that was moving very slowly and she'd been there for a long time. After some hours her husband who had mobility problems and was in a battery powered wheel chair came to join her; he had driven all the way from the Retirement Home where they lived about a kilometer away. They sat patiently waiting in the queue and to their surprise the manager of the garage came out to see them. He said that they wouldn't get any fuel that day because they were too far back in the queue and the underground tanks were almost empty. The manager took their phone number and told them to go home, promising to call and tell them when they could come and get fuel without queuing, which he did."

## THE MAGIC WAND: DIESEL FROM A ROCK: 2006 - 2010

While Zimbabwe was almost at a standstill due to fuel shortages and people spent days sitting in fuel queues, an outrageous story of witchcraft and spells started making news in 2006. It was a bizarre story which unbelievably managed to fool a number of top government officials and would forever be remembered as 'Diesel From a Rock.'

A spirit medium, also known as a witch doctor, Rotina Mavhunga found an abandoned fuel tank in the bush in Chinhoyi and came up with a plan for fame and fortune at a time when Zimbabwe had the highest inflation rate in the world and was in a state of economic crisis. Buying diesel from truckers going though Chinhoyi on their way to and from

Zambia, Mavhunga decanted the diesel into the tank she'd found, attached a pipe to the tank and hid it in the rocks in the Maningwa hills on Highlands Farm.

News soon spread that Mavhunga, also known as Nomatter Tagarira, could make diesel flow from rocks and people started going in large numbers to her 'shrine' to see the apparent miracle and maybe get the chance to buy a few litres of diesel at the same time. At a secret signal to her accomplice hiding in the rocks above, Mavhunga would appear to cast a spell, strike a boulder with her staff and diesel would start pouring down the side of the rock.

As the miracle story gathered momentum, Mavhunga summoned top government officials to come and witness her 'discovery,' claiming she was possessed by ancestral spirits who wanted to help Zimbabwe get over the chronic fuel shortages. We sat back and shook our heads in disbelief when we heard that President Mugabe had raised the issue in a Cabinet meeting and then proceeded to dispatch a 'Task Force' to investigate the claims of pure diesel that was apparently gushing out of a rock in the hot dusty hills in Chinhoyi. Included in the Task Force were three top government officials: State Security Minister Didymus Mutasa, Defence Minister Sydney Sekeramayi and Home Affairs Minister Kembo Mohadi.

Naturally where the Ministers went the news crews and security officials followed and so the story was exposed for all to see. In disbelief we shook our heads even harder at the photographs in the press of our country's senior ministers

223

sitting barefoot on the ground, shoes removed at the request of Mavhunga as a sign of respect. Photographs taken by NewsDay newspaper showed a group of security ministers who were captioned as: "gasping in delighted amazement as the woman known as "the diesel nganga" (spirit medium) gestured at a fountain of fuel."

Zimbabwe's three top Ministers of Defence, Security and Home Affairs reported back to President Mugabe that Rotina Mavhunga was indeed able to produce diesel from a rock. We couldn't believe that they had been hoodwinked and things rapidly went from being bizarre to downright ridiculous. Mavhunga became a national sensation and people started flocking to the Maningwa hills to witness this magic wand miracle for themselves. It was as good as any children's fairy story as you could imagine, diesel pouring out of a rock at the touch of the magic wand! Mavhunga demanded and received two cattle, three buffalos and Z$5 billion from the government for her discovery and as a "thank you" for rescuing the nation crippled by fuel shortages. The accounts of Peter Tafira, an eyewitness who lived near the spirit medium, were later revealed in a NewsDay article:

"Every powerful man came to this area except former President Robert Mugabe. She [Mavhunga] came with her people including the police and went up the mountain. They then told us that there is something special in the mountain and that they wanted to hold their rituals in it. The next moment the mountain was surrounded by people including government officials, who waited to pounce on the "duty-free" diesel for resale. A [Zimbabwe] flag was hoisted and the number and type of vehicles parked here was shocking.' According to Tafira, trouble began when the bigwigs sought to commercialize the ancestors' gift to the people. 'Trucks arrived to fetch the diesel and Mavhunga was against that. She told them that the diesel was for the people from the ancestors, hence it was for free.'" (NewsDay, 2014)

The next thing we heard was that President Mugabe was to send another team out to the rocks spewing diesel to investigate further. The second investigative team included the Minister of Energy and Power Development, Retired Lieutenant-General Mike Nyambuya, Science and Technology Minister Olivia Muchena, and Minister of Mines Amos Midzi. They discovered the obvious scam and Mavhunga went on the run. The diesel from a rock farce had finally come to an end, making a mockery of Zimbabwe's most senior leaders.

Three years later in September 2010 Mavhunga was finally apprehended and arrested. At the trial Judge Ignatius Mugova said: "The state channeled immense resources towards the 'diesel project.' Many vehicles and, at times, helicopters were used in a "wild goose chase" to secure large volumes of the "magic" fuel. Such a prank cannot be condoned in this court."

Rotina Mavhunga was convicted of defrauding the State and supplying false information to government officials. She served her sentence and was released in March 2012.

## TRAVEL, TOURISM AND COLLAPSING AIRLINES

One of the first casualties of a country in collapse is tourism and for owners and employees in the industry it becomes impossibly difficult to survive as guests stop arriving. Tourism was Zimbabwe's third largest earner of foreign exchange after tobacco and gold but that all changed when the country deteriorated into prolonged periods of human rights abuses, unpredictable outbreaks of political violence, hyper inflation and economic collapse. There is nothing quite as effective as instability and unpredictability in a country to kill travel and tourism. Shortages of fuel and money compound the situation a hundred fold. Local tourism in Zimbabwe contracted because people simply couldn't afford to travel as they focused on surviving hyper inflation, finding fuel and importing food because supermarkets were empty. All of these issues also had to be overcome by people trying to stay afloat in the tourism and hospitality industry.

International tourism to Zimbabwe reduced dramatically when domestic air travel collapsed; tourists simply couldn't get to holiday destinations unless they chartered private planes, making Zimbabwe a very expensive destination. Tourist arrivals to Zimbabwe shrank from 2.24 million people in 1999 to 1.27 million in 2004, a drop of almost fifty percent leaving earnings they raised for the economy following suit.

The demise of Air Zimbabwe had been going on for many years and Zimbabwe's economic collapse in the early 2000's simply hastened their downfall. In 1985 Air Zimbabwe had five

Boeing 707s, seven Viscounts and almost 1,500 employees. Their domestic flights went from Harare to seven internal destinations: Buffalo Range, Bulawayo, Gweru, Hwange, Kariba, Masvingo and Victoria Falls, all of which helped develop Zimbabwe into a tourist's paradise. Throughout the 1980s and 1990s everyday Air Zimbabwe serviced the main tourist triangle: Kariba, Hwange and Victoria Falls on flights that were almost always full. Leaving Harare in the morning as flight UM 228 and returning in the afternoon as UM 229, Air Zimbabwe was the lifeblood of tourism. Happy, satisfied tourists stood in the sun at remote little airports around the country, cameras and hearts full of wonderful memories and bags full of curios: carvings, sculptures, paintings, beadwork, hand-made clothing and tableware that supported the downstream income from tourism for many thousands of ordinary Zimbabweans. The knock-on effects of the losses caused by the collapse of Air Zimbabwe were like a big ripple in a small pond and there was nowhere to hide.

Writing in the Standard newspaper in 2005 Kumbirai Mafunda summed it up perfectly when he put a dollar value on the scale of the collapse of tourism: "a plethora of self-inflicted misfortunes has resulted in the shrinkage of earnings from US$770 million in 1990 to US$152 million in 2004." This 'shrinkage' left tourist resorts all over the country struggling to stay open. Resorts, hotels, B&Bs, cottages, lodges and conference venues offered off peak and mid-week specials, family booking reductions, special offers, free activities and reduced rates but as time passed more and more places were forced to put staff on three and then two day weeks, laying others off completely and many eventually had to close altogether.

A decade later, in their 2018 book Mawere and Marongwe wrote about the impact on Zimbabwe's tourism industry of the FTLRP (Fast Track Land Reform Programme) which began in 2000 in the form of land invasions and the compulsory acquisition by government of privately owned commercial farms, and continued for much of the following two decades.

"Average hotel occupancy fell from 57% in 1999 to 34% in 2006 which was complemented by a fall of bed occupancy from 42% in 1999 to 25% in 2000. … According to the ZTA (2009) several lodges and hotels like the Inn on Ruparara, Nyanga Village Inn, Chizarira Wilderness Lodge and Anglers Rest, among others, closed operations due to substantial decline in tourist arrivals in the country. However to those who endured there were massive retrenchments of labour force and a wide deterioration of services.

"In 2017, a decade after Zimbabwe's first collapse and a year before the second crisis began, an average occupancy of 48% was recorded (ZTA report 2017) which was still below that of 1999 which was 56%. This shows an indication of the deteriorating situation in the tourism industry in Zimbabwe. This stagnant growth is attributable to the impact of the FTLRP which had far reaching negative effects on the economic, political and social environment in Zimbabwe." (Mawere & Marongwe, 2018)

Attracting tourists became almost impossible when Zimbabwe was making international headlines every day for all the wrong reasons: violence, brutality, human rights abuses, lawlessness, widespread hunger and more. Some tourist resorts, B&B's and Guest Lodges survived thanks to the arrival of international NGO's, media organizations and their staff who had come to Zimbabwe to feed the starving, document human rights abuses, conduct investigations and lobby for political reforms; a sad indictment on the attractions of Zimbabwe.

As Zimbabwe started to slide into its second collapse a decade later, an article in the Herald newspaper revealed that when domestic air travel stopped "traffic at Kariba airport declined from a peak of around 14,000 arrivals in 1999 to around 3,000 in 2018."

By March 2018 Air Zimbabwe was only flying to two internal destinations from Harare: Bulawayo and Victoria Falls (previously they went to eight centres); they only went to two regional/intercontinental destinations: South Africa and Tanzania (previously: they went to ten African countries) and they no longer travelled to any international countries (previously they went to seven international destinations).

Zimbabwe hadn't learned that if you want tourists to spend their precious holiday dollars in your country you had to have good governance and economic stability; you had to supply the industry with necessary foreign currency to pay for vital imports such as fuel and spare parts and if you wanted to keep your flagship airline flying you had to stop corruption.

## AIR ZIMBABWE PASSENGER NUMBERS: 2005

Passenger numbers on Air Zimbabwe fall from 1 million in 1999 to 23,000 in 2005.

## AIR ZIMBABWE AIR FARES NOTICE: MARCH 2006

Public notice: "Air Zimbabwe fares will be denominated in US dollars with effect from March 2006." (This was three years before the introduction of multi-currency systems in Zimbabwe)

## AIR FARES INCREASE 200-500%: OCTOBER 2006

Air Zimbabwe fares increase between 200% and 500%; prices have to be converted and paid in US dollars.

- Harare to London return:
  old price Z$385,300; new price Z$1.8 million
- Harare to Johannesburg return:
  old price Z$99,830; new price Z$340,000
- Harare to Bulawayo return:
  old price Z$52,000; new price Z$190,000
- Harare to Victoria Falls return:

  old price Z$68,500; new price Z$260,000

## PRICE CONTROLS AND AIR FARES: FEBRUARY 2008

Despite the spiralling collapse of the economy the government's National Incomes and Pricing Commission pegged air fares at absurd rates that even their own Air Zimbabwe could not adhere to them. "Service providers such as the national airline Air Zimbabwe have also defied the pricing commission by pegging a return ticket for the Harare-Bulawayo route at Z$381,850,000 instead of the gazetted price of Z$229,400,000. The Commission said a one way ticket to London was Z$2,864,700,000 (2.8 billion) but Air Zimbabwe is charging Z$4,479,750,0009 [4.4 billion) plus US$100 departure tax." (The Zimbabwean, 2008)


## PRICE CONTROLS AND HOTELS: FEBRUARY 2008

When the Zimbabwe government extended price controls into the tourism and hospitality industry, owners had two choices: abide by the government's sub economic prices and go bankrupt or ignore them. Most did the latter: "A room at Meikles [Hotel] costs Z$273,000,000 [273 million] instead of the Z$55,000,000 [55 million] stipulated by the NIPC (National Incomes and Pricing Commission). Other hotels like Rainbow Tourism Group have also ignored the NIPC's recommended prices for rooms and meals." (The Zimbabwe Independent, 2008)

## FARMHOUSE CHRISTMAS LUNCH:
## STEVE'S STORY 2007

"In 2007, struggling with fuel shortages, power cuts and empty supermarket shelves the annual family get together at Christmas came up for discussion. It was going to be hard work with all the shortages and family coming from different parts of Zimbabwe and from South Africa to cater for. We talked about it and phoned around but all the prices we got from restaurants in Harare were outrageously expensive and so a day in the country at Malwatte Farmhouse Restaurant sounded like the perfect option. Beautiful lawns and rose gardens where the kids could run around, gorgeous shady Msasa and Acacia trees so we could sit outside; it sounded like the perfect Christmas venue for our group of ten people.

I took a drive out to Malwatte to have a look at their Christmas menu and see if it was affordable and if we could get a booking. It all sounded perfect; they said they would be open, they could fit our group of ten in and the menu looked great: a seafood starter, ham, turkey or beef for the main course with fresh veg from their garden and Christmas pudding and ice cream for dessert. I thought we'd struck gold so made the booking and everyone was happy with the plan. A week before Christmas I phoned Malwatte to check that everything was still OK and they were a bit vague; for a moment I got the feeling that they'd forgotten but after a short chat everything seemed fine and it was all systems go again; they wrote my name down and I said we'd be there about midday.

We arrived in two very full vehicles and ten of us climbed out at Malwatte; the grandkids immediately went running off into the garden, playing hide and seek and catchers between the rose bushes and round the herb garden. We sat outside under a beautiful blue sky and hot sun and had pre lunch drinks which were limited to a choice of either beer or gin and tonic and took an awful long time to arrive; there were quite a few other guests around and they obviously didn't have enough staff on duty to meet everyone's needs. Someone commented on the fact that there was a lot of smoke coming from somewhere behind the restaurant and someone else joked that they must be cooking our Christmas lunch outside on an open fire as there was no electricity. That comment caused much laughter especially as by then we were all getting into a nice festive mood. The grandkids were still rushing around like crazy and getting filthy dirty, diverting back to the table every now and again to have a gulp of Fanta which was the only soft drink available.

Eventually we were called to a table under a long, thatched, open gazebo across the other side of the lawn but it wasn't long before we had a problem. There were bees everywhere: under the thatch, coming in from outside, crowding around a dripping tap nearby and going crazy around sticky Fanta and beer glasses. It wasn't long before we decided that this wasn't going to work, someone was going to get stung and so we asked if we could be seated inside. No problem, the waiter said, swatting bees away as he loaded our glasses onto a tray and all ten of us traipsed inside. While we waited for a couple of tables to be put together a bit of a ruckus ensued and we watched as another waiter went outside towards the gazebo carrying a tin of fly spray and started spraying the bees. That was definitely not a good idea and it sent the bees into a frenzy and the waiter into a panic of arms and legs akimbo as he tried to get away from very angry bees.

This was turning into a Christmas lunch to remember! The menus were brought and handed round but there seemed to be quite a few missing things: the starter wasn't available anymore, there was no turkey after all but there was ham and beef and veg from the garden. No problem, we bought the grandkids a couple of packets of potato crisps as they were starving by now and ordered another round of drinks and then we waited and waited.

When the Christmas lunch came it was suspect to say the least: everything smelled of smoke, the ham was a suspicious deep red colour which at first glance looked raw but proved to actually have been deep fried to the point of no return and the beef was black on the outside and very raw in the centre. The veggies had been boiled to death but the chips were nice, albeit not really traditional Christmas fare. When the waiter came to collect our plates very little had been eaten and he asked if everything had been alright. Someone managed to stop giggling and told him that actually it hadn't been alright at all and before we knew it the manager arrived at the table proffering a bottle of whisky by way of apology. On the House, he said, apologizing profusely for the cooking "challenges" encountered over an open fire out the back.

The whisky drinkers in the group sampled the bottle and decided it was definitely not conventional whisky and had probably been produced from a still under a tree out the back, probably alongside the open cooking fire which might explain a lot about the state of our meal too! The dessert came and you can't really go wrong with ice cream and chocolate sauce, not sure what happened to the Christmas pud and no one bothered to ask but all the plates were licked clean.

Coffee was ordered, it arrived after a long wait but it had a very strange taste. The water had been boiled in the sadza (maize meal) pot and tasted and smelled very strongly of sadza. Cathy saved the day inviting us all to her home for more coffee and Christmas cake in her garden with lots more giggles and roars of laughter as the meal was discussed and the very memorable Christmas day dissected. Despite everything that had gone wrong this was one of the happiest Christmas days and one we'd never forget."

**THE QUINTILLION DOLLAR LUNCH: 2008**

In late 2008 it was a rare treat to go out to lunch with friends. Most places had closed because they couldn't get basic supplies and those that were still open were fiercely expensive. Three of us were having lunch together and we decided to spoil ourselves. The waiter arrived and asked us if we'd like a drink before lunch. With his pen poised I asked for a gin and tonic while my friends ordered a vodka and Coke and a glass of wine.

"Sorry we haven't got wine," the waiter said.

"OK I'll also have a vodka and coke then."

"Ah no, we haven't got any vodka."

"OK we'll all have gin and tonics then."

The waiter dutifully wrote down three gin and tonics and came back ten minutes later with an empty tray and the unsurprising statement: "We don't have gin."

Rather than ask for any other drinks I asked what they did have available.

The answer and choices were easy: "Pilsner, Coke and Fanta!" the waiter declared with a beaming smile.

A little while later the menu appeared and again we went through the charade.

"One cheese and mushroom omelet and salad, one quiche and salad, one toasted ham and cheese sandwich and chips."

Again, sorry: no mushrooms, no quiche, no ham, no cheese, no bread.

"OK so what do you have that we can order?"

We ended up with one Coke, two Fantas, one pork chop, two quarter chickens and three chips.

The bill came to 108 quadrillion dollars.

And the lesson was learnt: ask what they've got, not what you want: an important lesson in survival in Zimbabwe.

# CHAPTER 9
# WORK, SUPER POPS AND PENSIONS

## THE FLOOD TIDE OF ZIMBABWE'S SKILLS

In 2005 in a study by the SIRDC (Scientific and Industrial Research and Development Centre) in Harare, it was reported that close to 500,000 of Zimbabwe's "professional cream" had left in recent years to work abroad. The SIRDC noted that the figure could be a "gross under-estimation" of the real number of Zimbabwean workers in the Diaspora. At that time, in 2005, it was estimated there were between 3.5 and 4.5 million Zimbabweans in exile in South Africa, legally and illegally; political and economic migrants fleeing a country in collapse. Countless thousands were literally running for their lives: fleeing political violence, torture and brutality, escaping persecution and extreme harassment. Many bore the physical scars: bruised, bloodied and with broken bones; many more carried the mental and emotional scars: deeply traumatized, plagued by horrors, nightmares and memories of what had happened to them. Between 2000 and 2009 millions left as economic migrants, either to start their lives again permanently in other countries or in timeless transit by necessity so that they could send money home to support their families in Zimbabwe. In July 2005 estimates were that 3,000 to 4,000 people were crossing into South Africa every single day; in the years that followed the numbers grew with each fresh outbreak of political turmoil and economic collapse It was a flood tide and for people just trying to make a living, it was little wonder:

| Inflation | January | December |
|---|---|---|
| 2005 | 133% | 585% |
| 2006 | 613% | 1281% |
| 2007 | 1593% | 66,000% |
| 2008 | 100,580% | 79,6 billion% |

South Africa was only one destination of many but because it was the most developed country on our borders it was often the first choice: near enough to be able to go home easily, far enough away to be safe. The flood tide spread far and wide, across continents and oceans and it seemed that everywhere you went there were Zimbabweans and always they were delighted to see you, to talk, shake hands in the Zimbabwean way, reminisce, laugh and to tell you how much they loved Zimbabwe, the country they couldn't survive in.

Staying or going was always on our minds and whatever each of us decided to do, and why, was the hardest choice of our lives. Two decades later, trying not to remember, not to think about it, has become a necessity for mental survival for most people. It only needs a few stories to paint this painful picture of deciding to stay or go.

## THE PLIGHT OF PENSIONERS: 2004
Pensioners in Zimbabwe were already in dire straits by 2004 when savings were being constantly eroded by inflation and

people had resorted to selling their homes and assets in order to survive. Pensioners who should have been able to look to their families for help couldn't because their children had lost jobs, been evicted from farms, been laid off as businesses collapsed and were struggling to survive themselves. Many adult children of pensioners had already made the painful decision to leave the country and start again. A standard level government civil service pension for retired teachers, nurses, office workers and countless others in mid 2004 was Z$42,311 per month; it looked like a fortune on paper but when put next to a list of basic expenses at the time, it was a death sentence.

Basic expenses May 2004

- Poverty datum line, per month          Z$980,000
- Inflation:                             505%

Services (monthly)

- Rent (one bed cottage)                 Z$60,000
- Electricity (1 geyser, 1 stove, lights)  Z$40,000
- Water (minimum 15 cubic meters)        Z$40,000
- Rates & municipal charges              Z$50,000
- Telephone                              Z$40,000
- Medical aid (insurance)                Z$90,000

Medical costs

- Consultation with doctor               Z$50,000
- Consultation with dentist              Z$60,000
- Month supply of blood pressure pills   Z$20,000
- 5day course non-specific generic antibiotic  Z$25,000
- Anti inflammatory pills (20)           Z$60,000

| Basic groceries | Quantity | Price in Z$ |
|---|---|---|
| • Bread | one loaf | 3,000 |
| • Pasta | 500g | 5,300 |
| • Eggs | one dozen | 6,500 |
| • Flour | 2kgs | 7,000 |
| • Milk | one litre | 2,500 |
| • Margarine | 500g | 4,400 |
| • Cheese | 300g | 14,000 |
| • Instant coffee | one jar | 12,000 |
| • Tea bags | 100 | 5,000 |
| • Jam | 500g | 6,000 |
| • Sugar | 2kgs | 4,000 |
| • Peanut butter | 500g | 8,000 |
| • Oats | 500g | 4,000 |
| • Toothpaste | 100ml | 10,000 |
| • Oil | 2 litres | 21,000 |
| • Soap | one bar | 4,000 |
| • Rice | 2kgs | 7,000 |
| • Chicken | 1kg | 24,000 |
| • Soup | 1 packet | 2,000 |
| • Mince | 400g | 7,500 |
| • Toilet rolls | 4 rolls | 3,600 |
| • Detergent | 400g | 5,000 |

**FROM A NISSAN SUNNY TO A MERCEDES:**
**PAUL'S STORY: 2005**

In 2005 after the March elections another brain drain took place from Zimbabwe. Paul, an auditor in Harare, looked at the strange things that constituted his everyday life in Zimbabwe and made the decision to join the exodus.

"By 2005 I was a millionaire in Zim dollars and used to get a salary increase every month. To survive the electricity cuts I had a gas stove and shower. My gas showers used to be quick in and out affairs, reminding me of our school days and I always made sure I had a spare gas bottle for emergencies. I drove an old Mini to save on fuel so I wouldn't have to spend so much time sitting in fuel queues. If I had any money left at the end of the month I knew I'd had a bad month.

I was an auditor and lived in a garden flat. I bought my first car in 2003 and had to sell it a year later to pay for repairs and then I bought a cheaper car. Having a car in good condition was an asset if you worked for the right firm as you could claim mileage and that helped a lot on the financial side. When we went to see clients the team would share a car or use the staff mini-bus. Partners at the accounting firm used to drive Nissan Sunny's but because money was losing value so fast they upgraded to a Mercedes and a Land Rover Freelander, quite a status jump!

I remember flying to Victoria Falls from Harare in March 2005 and was so shocked that the ground below was bare but there hadn't been a drought. Then I realized that the bare land we were flying over on the route to Victoria Falls used to be prime farm land for growing crops but that had all come to an end with the land grabs. When the results of the 2005 elections came out, and were clearly rigged, I got a one-way ticket to London. About three months after I got to England the London bus bombings happened and I wondered if I'd jumped from the frying pan into the fire. I came to England with just my clothes and slept in my sister's lounge for about three months and got a job as a barman."

## SUPER POPS AND THE TERRIFYING MACHINE THAT MADE THEM: 2007

Fly by night operations were the new normal in Zimbabwe in 2007 as everyone from producers to consumers tried to find ways to survive. Bottle stores would appear from nowhere and just as quickly disappear; butcheries opened in obscure areas, receiving suspicious carcasses from even more suspicious abattoirs; and strange 'factories' with very dubious health and safety standards started producing one hit wonders.

The latest one hit wonder factory in my hometown reminded me of a bakery I'd been into in Mozambique a couple of years before. Standing in the baking sun a group of women in colourful wraps waited patiently outside the door of a small, grey building. One by one they went in and emerged with round loaves of newly baked bread, hot from the oven. The smell was intoxicating and when it was my turn to go in, I couldn't believe my eyes. A brick oven stood in the middle of the room, a woman sat on a chair near the doorway and one man with a long handled wooden implement with a flat oblong paddle on the end manned the oven. The heat pouring out of the oven almost took your breath away, instantly drenching you in sweat. The bread was ready and being unloaded from built-in shelves in the oven. The man pushed the wooden paddle into the oven, scooped up two loaves at a time, swung round and slipped the bread onto the concrete floor. At first, I thought he must have dropped the bread by mistake but there was no mistake as again and again the paddle went into the oven, scooped up the bread and deposited it onto the floor. You told the woman at the door how many loaves you wanted, she took your money, you bent down and picked your bread up off the floor and that was all there was to it. No need for cooling racks, trays, tables or serving counters, just an oven, a long wooden paddle and two people: one to make and unload the bread and one to collect the money.

Shopping Mozambique style came to Marondera in the form of the Super Pops factory. The difference from the bakery in Mozambique was the fact that Super Pops were being made in an enormous empty warehouse where machines and dozens of people had once worked, before the economic collapse. Outside the warehouse in the overgrown car park a shop owner from a town 100km away was pacing up and down, cursing, muttering, shouting into his cell phone and angrily pointing at his empty seven tonne truck. When I greeted him, he immediately launched into the reason for his rage. He had ordered one thousand bulk packs, each containing twenty packets of Super Pops, and his order wasn't ready; it wasn't even half ready because the electricity had gone off and they couldn't do the 'firing' and couldn't use the bag sealing machine.

There were about twenty people in the huge empty warehouse, eight men and twelve women, the latter sitting on their wraps on the concrete floor. After a round of greetings and hand clapping, I asked the man who seemed to be in charge if he could show me how the Super Pops were made. He was delighted to do so and immediately took me on a guided tour which basically consisted of one machine and a line of 50kg bags of maize waiting to be popped.

The machine, so innocent looking at first glance, so utterly terrifying when you saw it working. was about the size of a small grinding mill. There was a smallish cylindrical barrel into which they put one bucket (20kg) of maize kernels. One cup of water was added, 'to get pressure,' the man said, and then the hinged lid of the barrel was closed.

Underneath the barrel, about ten to fifteen centimetres away, were half a dozen electric heating elements. That part was really scary because neither the naked wires nor the heating elements were protected in any way, no insulation tape or conduits, no bars or cage surrounding the hazard. If someone bumped into the machine there was no doubt they would get seriously burnt, or worse. Mounted onto the frame of the machine was a pressure gauge on which all the numbers had completely worn off. The glass cover that used to protect the sensor and numbers on the circular gauge had gone and there was a hand drawn blue line on the bent, battered gauge.

The young guy showing me round proudly explained everything, beaming delightedly at every question and laughing at every expression of shock and horror I made at the incredibly dangerous nature of it all, not to mention the antiquated, unprotected machine and the naked, exposed wires snaking across the floor! Then he showed me the trigger and I wanted to run, or be sick, or both!

A long steel pole called the 'trigger' was leaning up against the wall. I mentally did a run through of the process so far: maize pips into the barrel, add a cup of water, switch on the heating elements, the pressure builds up and when the marker reaches the blue line on the gauge, the trigger is used to open a small flap of the barrel which lets air in, releases the pressure and then all hell breaks loose as 20kg of maize seeds explode into huge mountains of popcorn.

In the Super Pop factory the evidence of exploding maize kernels was everywhere. My young guide grinned widely and showed me a pile of shattered tin sheets that had been on the roof of the warehouse. I looked up and sure enough there were a number of roof sheets missing overhead and the bright blue sky was clearly visible through the natural skylights. The youngster said the maize had exploded 'late' and in the wrong direction and had literally broken the sheets of tin roofing above. He pointed to the wall in front of the machine and I saw that it was peppered with pock marks that looked like bullet holes; they had been made by the exploding popcorn he told me. It seemed there should have been some sort of an angled shield attached to the barrel to force the exploding popcorn to be channelled into a collecting area, but there was no sign of a shield or a collecting area. The youngster said that if you stood in the line of the exploding popcorn, the force would kill you and I was very glad there was no electricity at the time as it all sounded very unpredictable.

When all the kernels had popped and the machine and heating elements were switched off, it was time for the harvest. The popcorn lies in heaps all over the floor wherever it landed after the explosion and then the women move in, sweep it up with little grass hand brooms, scoop it into buckets and then pack it by hand into the small 50 gram bags. The Super Pops packet says that the contents are salted but there's no sign of salt here and nothing covering the floor where the popcorn lies. There is no sign of the bags being weighed either: Zimbabwean standards and guesswork at its best! The women aren't wearing any protective clothing, not even plastic gloves and are literally picking the popcorn up off the floor that we are all walking on.

At this point in my guided tour the electricity still hasn't come back on (thank goodness for that I think) so they can't use the bag sealing machine but the women have made their own, using candles. Sitting on the concrete floor, surrounded by popcorn and bags the women hold the bags over the naked candle flames which melts the plastic and they press the edges together, burning their fingers and sealing the bags all in one go. Finally, my guide gave me the numbers and this explained why Super Pops had almost become our staple diet in Zimbabwe. Each 20kg bucket of seed maize produced 1,000 bags of popcorn. Each bag of Super Pops costs Z$35,000 and the vendors and street sellers sell it for Z$70,000 to Z$100,000 a bag.

The demand for Super Pops was massive in 2007, regardless of how it was made and the non-existent health and safety standards. Everywhere you went people always had a packet of Super Pops on hand in the days when there was no food to buy in the shops. It had become our staple diet: for breakfast in place of cereals, at lunch in place of sandwiches; in our children's break and lunch boxes at school and to snack on walking home from work.

At the end of the tour I thanked my guide, said goodbye to the women sitting on the floor and went to the car. About to start reversing, the young guide who had shown me around ran up to the car window and gave me four packets of Super Pops. "Free for you!" he said smiling. I thanked him again and passed out a handful of peppermints in exchange for what had been a fascinating half hour of Zimbabwean ingenuity: survival at its best.

**MIRRORED SUNGLASSES AND HOME-MADE STOCK FEED: HELEN'S STORY: 2008**

A shiny pick-up truck pulled into Helen's run-down dairy farm, one of the very few that have survived the government's land grabs. Stock feed for the cows had been impossible to get for months, hoarded stockpiles have been depleted and the milk production had dropped from 1,800 litres to 250 litres a day. Helen ordered and paid up front for cotton seedcake from one of the hundreds of door to door black market dealers who seem to be running the country in 2008. That was the last Helen saw of them, or her money. Helen lost fourteen of her dairy cows to starvation in three months and had lost count of how many calves had died in the same period of time. She had sold others that were losing condition to butchers and was now in a last-ditch desperate effort to save the stronger cows.

"2008 is truly the worst time ever. We've had two calves born in the last two days and I just look at them and think: Oh hell, another two mouths to feed. And the calves are heifers too; it's usually a time to rejoice but not now."

News travels fast of the approaching collapse of a business and the vultures were circling, looking for cheap deals, but despite her desperation Helen told the man behind the mirrored sunglasses in his shiny new pick-up truck to go away: she lost everything to them once and isn't making the same mistake again. Every day Helen scours the bush, looking for food to keep her cows alive. She sends the farm hands out far and wide looking for Acacia trees where they sweep up the dry, brown pods that have fallen to the ground and bring them home in empty grain sacks. The pods are chopped up in a mill along with grass, pea-hay left over from the winter crop and dry maize stalks left from last season. These are the survival rations to keep the remaining dairy cows alive. Not the same as the high protein dairy supplement Helen used to buy but a return to the old ways and hoping that change comes soon.

## LITTLE WHITE STICKERS AND HOME-MADE SOAP: MANDY'S STORY

In September 2002 I wrote in a Letter From Zimbabwe, the story of the impending eviction of a farming family in Arcturus. This is an extract from that letter called 'Little white sticker':

"This week I have had many desperate emails from farming friends who have been forced out of their homes in the past few days and are desperately looking for somewhere to stay. One friend told me that they were ordered out of their home by a senior politician who has now claimed five farms in the area. The farmer and his family were given 12 hours to pack up and get out. They do not know where to go, have no plans in place but knew that they had to get out or risk being put in prison - or worse. They went into a mad flurry of activity and when everything was piled up outside on the lawn Mandy's husband suggested she go around and stick white labels on the boxes and items that were the most important so that they would be easily identifiable when they found somewhere to live.

Mandy walked around looking at the contents of her life strewn on the lawn and with the help of Albert, one of the farm workers, stuck little white labels on her most treasured possessions.

When she had finished, Albert picked up the roll of stickers and stuck a little white label onto his chest showing that he wanted to come too and should not be forgotten. Mandy started to cry, she and her family have endured so very much in the last 30 months and in her words, they have been trashed and looted and are now booted." (Buckle,C. 2002)

Mandy Retzlaff and her family not only survived that horrific time but went on to rescue and relocate scores of horses from Zimbabwe's invaded farms to Mozambique where they later started Mozambique Horse Safaris in Vilankulos. Mandy's book, "One Hundred and Four Horses" tells that incredible story of courage and survival, but there was something else she turned her hand to along the way, making soap. Many weird and wonderful, strange and dangerous experiments later Mandy perfected soap making, and this is her recipe, in her words:

"This is a simple recipe with not much fuss.

Tools: A pair of glasses. A pair of gloves. A stainless steel or enamel pot. A stick blender. A rubber spatula and a scale. Caustic soda and oil. We use coconut oil.

Step 1: Put on your gloves and your glasses. This is the most dangerous part of soap making. You need 360 gms of caustic soda bought from a hardware store. At this stage caustic soda is dangerous so you need to take care. Once you have measured your caustic soda you need to add 650gms of mineral water. Stir well with a spoon and stand back as the fumes are caustic and it heats up. Put it in a safe place to cool.

Step 2: Now put your enamel pot on the scale make sure it's on zero and add 1800 gms coconut oil, if your coconut oil is solid you will need to heat it on the stove. Once the caustic soda is cooled you need to pour it carefully into the oil and mix with a spoon.

Step 3: Get your stick blender and blend the mixture until it's creamy white and resembles custard. You can now add 20mls of your favourite essential oil to give your soap a fragrance. You can also add a few tablespoons of olive oil or castor oil. Your soap is now ready to place in moulds which can be bought on line. The silicone ones are the best as it is easy to get the soaps out.

Allow a couple hours for the soaps to harden and then leave them for two weeks. The caustic soda leaves the soap and the byproduct of oil and caustic soda is glycerine. This is what makes your soap so much better."


**JOBS AND SALARIES: FEBRUARY 2008**
Finding and keeping a job in times of hyper inflation when there is 90% unemployment and companies are closing every week, is almost impossible. Getting a job with an NGO (Non-Governmental Organization) was always the first prize and the best advice you could give anyone but, like so many other things, it was much easier said than done. Although the number of international NGOs operating in a country in crisis

increase significantly as the humanitarian situation deteriorates, they often bring their own staff with them but there is always a need for drivers, transporters, translators and people on the ground with comprehensive knowledge of local conditions. The biggest attraction of getting work with an NGO, particularly an international one, is the salary which is often paid in US dollars and holds its value despite hyper inflation conditions.

In February 2008 a human resources survey conducted by the Organizational Excellence Consultancy exposed the differences between local and NGO salaries. Junior managers employed locally were earning between Z$8 and Z$10 billion a month while Chief Executives were getting Z$20 billion a month. Meanwhile in the NGO sector Directors were earning in the region of US$2,500 a month which translated to Z$37.5 billion, almost double that of their local counterparts.


## TRUNKS OF MONEY AND BAGS OF HIDDEN MEAT: SALLY'S STORY: 2007/2008

"The downward spiral started to accelerate when we were having to transport trunk loads of 'local money' [Zimbabwe dollars/Bearers Cheques] to downtown Harare within the hour that we received them in order to secure an agreed rate of exchange for foreign currency. This was to ensure our local orders/earnings as a textile manufacturer held value. Thankfully we were also exporters to South Africa and Germany, so a large portion of our income was in forex [foreign exchange]. This allowed us to pay for our inputs, keep the factory going and secure two hundred plus jobs. However basic commodities were fast disappearing, if not totally gone from supermarket shelves so our next task was to pay the workers in groceries as their wages would not even buy them a bag of mealie meal even if it was available to buy.

I remember ordering pallets of cooking oil, mealie meal, sugar, salt, matches, candles, green soap, washing powder, beans and dried fish from South Africa and having it transported to us in Harare after having organised one of our South African customer's to pay for the commodities on our behalf. Every Friday the workers would line up, not outside the paymaster's office but outside the storeroom to receive their food parcel in lieu of worthless Zimbabwe dollar Bearer Cheques.

As one of the management team I was paid a portion of my wage in forex. This allowed me to purchase items from across the border and from the black market that were no longer available in the supermarkets. My family, three sisters and their six children were only earning worthless money so had no means of obtaining any groceries. Every month, under cover of darkness in order to avoid the numerous police road blocks, I would travel to a farm some kilometres out of Harare to pay a farmer in "real" money for a slaughtered pig and cow. This valuable protein was pre-cut and wrapped in grain sacks for me to collect. These bags of meat would then be hidden under black plastic sheets in the back of my car hopefully to remain undetected if I was stopped and searched by the police on my way back to and across Harare as I distributed my valuable cargo to my siblings. We lived under the threat of the new law that did not allow anyone to transport or be in possession of basic commodities, especially mealie meal and meat. Any commodities found in vehicles would be confiscated and the "culprit" fined heavily for "hoarding." Amazingly we survived this crazy time."

## COWS THAT PURRED WITH JOY:
## THE DAIRY FARMER'S STORY 2008

"As a dairy farmer we were heavily dependent on stock feed purchases. 2007/8 was a poor rainfall season so we really needed supplies. In May 2008 I ordered my usual seven tons of cottonseed meal, a high protein ingredient of our home made dairy feed. I paid almost a million dollars (Zim dollars as we had no access to US dollars at that time) for the load. It was everything we had in the bank and no way to earn more without the food for the cows. It was never delivered. They said we hadn't paid. I checked at the bank and the deposit had gone through. We waited. We tried going to their depot but it was a back yard business. We asked the contact and chased all over with empty bags for the feed.

By the end of June we were unable to feed decent food to the animals. By the middle of July the cows were hungry. By the end of July they started lying down and dying. The calves died because we had no milk for them. Every day another cow or two would die. I started putting the cows in a paddock near the river. We should have been producing 25 litres from each of sixty cows, maybe more because they were all fresh in milk, it should have been a bumper season. In reality we were only getting 40 litres of milk from about thirty cows over two days. We milked them but there was no milk; the ones that gave nothing were dried off; others died and the numbers diminished. Despite our milk production crashing to just 40 litres every two days the tankers would still come and collect (for which I am still grateful.)

At the end of July we planted a quick growing vigorous type of forage sorghum. When you could hold a handful of the plant we cut it and fed it. At the end of a month it was knee height and we fed it. We watered a small paddock with a pathetic amount of water and kept the cows in there, the ones we were trying to milk. By November the feed cribs were full of bundles of rich green forage. Did you know that cows can purr with joy? These did.

And so the corner was turned. The most horrifying days of my life were over. And in the April of the next year those cows which were just dumped at the river started calving. And then the real miracle took place. In an industry which levels out at 50% replacement heifers, these cows came in with 90% heifers. By 2011, when we had to leave the farm I had my full normal complement of producing cows in milk. I drive my dairy herd now…. I had sold the cows and bought a new car."

## WILD FRUIT, UNDERGROUND HONEY AND FOOD FOR PAY: ADRIAN'S STORY: 2008

"I was fit back then, having shed 50kg over a three-year period of dieting and training unwaveringly. But my fruit bowl was empty, and I dared not complain as my employer was my brother. I did not want to add to his troubles. It was tough enough in the construction industry already, nothing held value for long anymore and he constantly had to think out of the box to keep his staff fed and provided for; he constantly had to think about how he was going to keep them alive.

One of my responsibilities was to travel 20km down an atrocious road to a farm where the telephones did not work and cell phone signal did not reach. It was here that I would have to consult the owner in private and negotiate to purchase maize meal. Within a day or two a delivery would arrive before sunrise. We would offload it at speed into one of the storerooms onto wooden pallets so that it was hidden from view, as though we were drug dealers. The maize meal was one component of the worker's pay. Shop shelves were empty and the chances of finding Rat Kill to stop rodents from consuming the precious food was unlikely and so we would ask the workers to take their maize meal home as soon as possible. We negotiated for ex-factory cooking oil and did the same thing. We engaged businesses who specialized in importing pallets of groceries for the rest of the items: soap, candles, matches, salt, sugar, peanut butter, jam etc. I recall much soya product being included to help with protein intake.

This was the worker's pay because the Zimbabwe dollar bank notes were worthless.

I often wondered what nutrition was going to sustain my endless cycling and jogging, but there was absolutely no chance that I would have stopped training after having made such achievements. The paths that bore my daily training were strewn with worthless bank notes often alongside discarded condoms. Even the vagrants, Zimbabwe boasts many, would not attempt to pick the notes up. I even recall fistfuls of notes being thrown out of car windows at the traffic lights in Harare for the begging children to pick up but even they did not want the useless currency.

Old bank notes were continually being replaced with new notes bearing more zeros. When this took place, the police would be out in full force at road blocks searching vehicles for old notes. At work we had to import calculators that could accommodate all the zeros. Price labels no longer featured in the shops and there was increasingly less reason to go to the shops at all as the shelves became totally bare. Zimbabwe had introduced price controls. Rather than selling products at a loss, shop owners chose not to restock at all.

I continued to train but took to the bush tracks so that I could pick wild fruits at every opportunity. One of the few affordable things was a barbequed cob of green maize. A work colleague once brought me a handful of green beans that she had grown. That night, whilst steaming them, it occurred to me that had it not been for these green beans there would have been nothing on my table. I walked through to the dining room table and sat down. Then my eye caught the fruit bowl, it was swollen with muzhanje fruit (Mahobohobo/Uapaca Kirkiana). My tears welled up as I realized that the gardener had gone out into the bush and picked these for his family and me. Never once did he come to me to complain of the unbearable circumstances. He would get up early in the morning and dig up underground honey, a job that requires immense physical strength. He only ever asked that he may store this source of sugar in my fridge which he would find devoid of anything else.

My brother had reason to make a visit to the home of one of my office colleagues and what he found lead him to later investigate my fridge. He called me into his office the following day and with tears rolling down his face apologized for being so focused on keeping the business going. From that day on my own pay became a weekly box of fruit and vegetables and some meat that was negotiated from the same farm the supplied the maize meal. Me, my precious dog and cat were going to be okay. The construction workers were okay. Many were okay but the entire population was impacted by this period in our history. We are reaping the bitter harvest still, eleven years later. Businesses are bombarded by requests for donations. That generation whose lives were dedicated to the establishment and smooth running of an efficient country, those who once responsibly accrued pensions to avoid been societal burdens, were left bereft of their savings and now require donations to see out the remainder of their days."

## MANUFACTURING CAPACITY 2006-2009

## PERCENTAGE OF ESTABLISHMENTS WORKING AT FULL CAPACITY – BY SUB SECTOR: 2006-2009

| Sub-Sectors | 2006 | 2007 | 2008 | 2009 |
|---|---|---|---|---|
| Foodstuffs | 29 | 7 | 0 | 7 |
| Drinks & Tobacco | 18 | 9 | 0 | 8 |
| Textiles | 38 | 25 | 13 | 14 |
| Leather & Footwear | 29 | 14 | 14 | 0 |
| Wood & Furniture | 14 | 14 | 0 | 0 |
| Paper & Printing | 36 | 18 | 0 | 0 |
| Chemicals | 25 | 10 | 5 | 0 |
| Non-Metallic Minerals | 50 | 0 | 0 | 0 |
| Metals & Metallic Products | 18 | 14 | 10 | 4 |
| Transport Equipment | 33 | 22 | 0 | 0 |
| Other Manufacturing | 14 | 14 | 13 | 29 |
| All Manufacturing | 27 | 13 | 5 | 5 |

(Source: ZIMSTAT Business Tendency Survey, 2006-2009)

## MANUFACTURING CAPACITY DROPS TO 10%: FEBRUARY 2008

In February 2008, the CZI (Confederation of Zimbabwe Industries) President, Callistus Jokonya, said that the manufacturing capacity had collapsed to around 10%. "Several companies are producing at levels lower than that. To be honest with you, if we find a company producing at 10%, it is rather pleasing at the moment. ... No one will produce at a loss. It is wrong to label businesses which are not producing as being unpatriotic. ...The CZI and ZNCC [Zimbabwe National Chamber of Commerce] estimate that 80% of all products in shops and supermarkets are imported goods as local manufacturers are yet to recover from last year's price blitz." (Chikwanda, C. Zimbabwe Independent, 2008)

## FALLING THROUGH THE CRACKS: PENSIONERS 2004-2009

In the worst years of Zimbabwe's 2004-2009 crisis the only help for pensioners came from small, private charitable groups; there was no aid at all from a government that had no money. Quietly and discreetly volunteers looked for, persuaded and cajoled donors; mobilized people to collect and deliver food, toiletries and funds to help pensioners pay their rent and utilities, buy medicines, food and other essentials and survive a crisis which no one could have prepared for and over which they had no control.

"There but for the grace of God go I," was a phrase often on our lips and in our hearts when we found pensioners living in shacks, sheds, garages and store-rooms because they couldn't afford the rent of cottages or flats. Pensioners who owned their own homes and had been forced to sell them to survive hyper inflation and were still left destitute. People whose life savings of multiple thousands and even millions were reduced to a few cents as the currency was repeatedly devalued. It was a time of such madness that a four bed-roomed house on an acre of land was worth the same as half a kilogram of bacon in mid 2008.

There were pensioners whose electricity and water had been disconnected for non-payment. Men and women in their seventies and eighties eating once a day or even once every second day; cooking over open fires, storing rain water in buckets for washing and bathing and living in conditions of indescribable hardship and squalor. People who couldn't afford soap, washing powder or basic toiletries. People whose glasses were held together with tape and putty, whose dentures were broken, who needed hearing aids, walking sticks and wheelchairs. Everywhere you looked there were elderly people falling through the cracks of our failed State.

There were countless elderly people in dire need of medical attention in situations that were horrifying and belonged in the dark ages. People with open wounds and abscesses crimson with infection and festering with bacteria. Men with advanced, untreated prostate problems, clothes and bedding saturated with urine; women with open, suppurating tumours on their breasts. There were pensioners halving and quartering their blood pressure pills and other medicines to make them last longer. People who were left weak, dizzy, disorientated and confused after stopping their life sustaining drugs for diabetes, heart conditions, cancer and countless other illnesses because they couldn't afford them. There were many who had not been able to survive the collapse of Zimbabwe and tragic stories of those who resorted to suicide.

The hardest reality about the plight of pensioners in Zimbabwe's repeated cycles of collapse was that families who would normally have helped their elderly relations had themselves been forced to leave the country when they lost their jobs, savings and assets in the financial crashes. It took those younger families years to re-establish themselves in other countries, get jobs, find places to live and get their children into school. The long established system of the younger generation stepping in to help their elders fell apart.

**TEN TRILLION DOLLAR LOAF OF BREAD:**
**JOHN'S STORY: JANUARY 2009**
"When I got my January 2009 pay slip the ink was so faint that I could barely read it but when I held it up to the sunlight the words said it all for the state of things: 'Six zeros have been removed from this notice due to space constraints.' As a middle manager I earned 14 trillion dollars a month, 7.6 trillion dollars had been deducted for tax and other compulsory government levy's leaving me with a net monthly income of 6.7 trillion dollars. A loaf of bread on the day I got my January 2009 salary was 10 trillion Zimbabwe dollars, (equivalent to 1 US dollar) and was more than my entire monthly salary. It's pointless even going to work anymore but I know that if I quit I'll never get another job in our collapsed country."

## THE BANK ACCOUNTANT'S STORY:
## MAY 2009

"So many companies are struggling to stay open and many are only working only two or three days a week. Our bank is barely functional since the US dollarization of the Zimbabwean economy. Although we all needed the economy to recover with the US dollar, the effect on the banks is huge and my hours, as a senior bank accountant, have been cut to just two days a week. No one trusts banks anymore and after losing everything people aren't depositing money or using savings accounts. It's a familiar pattern that we've become used to under the Zanu PF government: it starts with extended shut-downs around public holidays, giving us long weekends for example and then it becomes forced leave, and then reduced working hours. None of us know if our jobs are safe or for how long. Everyone thinks that because we work in banks we are rich but we are like everyone else and have the same responsibilities as them."


**PENSIONS TIPS**
- Don't save local currency
- Don't invest in pyramid/Ponzi schemes
- Don't sell your house unless you have to and then only sell in foreign currency
- Don't save in government investment schemes
- Use international pension schemes that will protect you from currency collapses
- Don't keep all your savings in one account

- If the economy starts to crash, cash in your local currency pension; buy stable foreign currency and invest in assets which maintain their value and can be sold later

## EIGHT MILLION FOR HALF AN EGG:
## ROB'S STORY: JULY 2008

Banks have started taking six zeros off our accounts because their computers' accounting systems can't cope with all the digits now. Ever since Mr Mugabe was controversially sworn in for his 6th term as President prices moved up into hundreds of billions and calculations went into trillions. The banks haven't made the removal of zeros common knowledge, or even common practice, and unless you fight your way to the front of the hundreds queuing in the banks everyday and actually ask how much money you've really got in your account you are none the wiser: maybe they've taken off six zeros, or maybe they haven't! One day your bank statement will show you having a billion dollars (nine zeros) and the next day it may have dropped to a thousand dollars; if you are able to ask them they say "just add six zeros."

At 82 years old Rob hadn't eaten for two days when I met him and he had no food at home because all his money seemed to have disappeared from the bank. The eight trillion dollars that he had, had suddenly plummeted to eight million dollars and it wasn't enough to buy anything at all, not even one single fresh egg. "My life savings are gone; my pension's worthless," he said and he was in the same boat as ten million

Zimbabweans whose government had failed them, completely and utterly.

## HOME-MADE SOUP AND 'CONSTANT' PUDDING: ANTON'S STORY: 2005-2008

"When inflation went out of control, as the Warden of a Retirement Home. I sent out emails to as many addresses as I could lay my hands on, explaining the situation we were facing. The response was incredible and we started getting help from all quarters. Relatives of residents in the Diaspora were one of the main targets, and most responded favorably. The rate of exchange between Zimbabwe dollars and US dollars or British Pounds was enormous: in 2005 US$1 was worth Z$10,000; in 2006 it was worth Z$100,000; in 2007 it was worth Z$4,000,000; and in 2008 (after thirteen zeroes had been removed from the currency) US$1 was worth Z$700,000,000,000 (seven hundred billion dollars!) By 2007 £25 was enough to support one pensioner's accommodation and three meals a day for a month. At the time of severe food shortages, when there was nothing on the shelves of the shops, a decision was made at committee level to dispense with the catering company and do the catering ourselves. We were feeding about seventy residents at the time. Although this gave us added stress, there is no doubt that the benefits outweighed the headaches.

The menu for three meals a day was certainly not the most exciting, but it was nourishing and wholesome. Availability and cost dictated what we could provide. Breakfast generally consisted of porridge, an 'eggy dish,' toast and tea. Bacon was out of the question except on vary rare occasions. The main meal was at midday, and wasn't always with meat, followed by dessert, usually instant pudding (we had a very good supplier at affordable cost). This became known as 'constant pudding' because we had it so often! Supper was always a wholesome 'home-made' soup with bread. We somehow always managed a roast for Sunday lunch.

Donations in the form of fresh produce came in on a regular basis from local producers. One farmer who still managed to run a beef herd, used to donate an ox on a fairly regular basis. Strict control of stock in our storerooms was administered, thanks to my late wife and resident volunteers. Truck loads of donations came in from South African donors for retirement homes all over the country. External funding helped incredibly in that it enabled us to import pallets of groceries from South Africa; this consisted mostly of canned goods such as tinned fruit, fish, vegetables and baked beans and dried goods with bulk cater-pack quantities of flour, rice, sugar, pasta, cereals, oats, soup powder, salt, soya and dry beans. Cleaning products, essential for maintaining health and hygiene in a large residential setting were vital and these also came in bulk on pallets from South Africa. These included such things as washing up liquid, surface cleaner, toilet cleaner, polish and soap.

Power cuts were a big concern particularly when it came to preserving all the food in the fridges and freezers and just when we needed it most we were assisted by the donation of a generator. With 200 litres of diesel a month we were able to run four deep freezers and the cold room on the generator in times of lengthy power cuts. Cooking was done on a wood fire outside using dead wood collected around the large and well treed complex or coal that we bought. The food always tasted of smoke but we were just thankful to be able to keep food on the table all throughout the years of collapse.

Maintaining the large workforce necessary for daily operations in the home was a continual concern. Wage negotiations were ongoing throughout the years of Zimbabwe's 2004-2009 crisis with approximately sixty five staff members in security, maintenance, catering and frail care departments. By 2007 we were paying all the staff on a fortnightly basis to try and cushion them from the ravages of hyper inflation and in 2008 we were paying small amounts of foreign currency whenever we could. Donations often came from the most unexpected sources, but without the kind assistance of donations, large and small, I really do not know how we could have survived. A lot of small donations actually added up to a great deal. How did we survive? In a nutshell: Only by the Grace of God."


**DIARY NOTES:**
**TWELVE FUNERALS, IN MEMORY OF SAM: 2010**
By the end of winter 2010, I had been to twelve funerals. All were of pensioners. Six were expected and two inevitable, but four were of men and women who shouldn't have gone so

soon and who died as a direct result of the dire state of Zimbabwe.

One of the funerals was for Sam, a seventy year old widower who kept very much to himself. When I first came across Sam, he was living on virtually nothing. Pitifully thin and weak, his pantry had a couple of unlabelled tins on the shelf, a bag of maize meal on the floor and a small heap of sweet potatoes which he'd grown in the garden. Sam had turned his fridge off because he couldn't afford to pay the electricity bill anymore and his cottage was stark and bare as he had sold everything he could in order to survive. Emergency food parcels were arranged, each one received with tears and humility, but I often saw the look of shame in Sam's eyes; shame that he had come to this.

For two days after Sam passed away, we were actually contemplating a pauper's burial because no relations could be found. There was talk of a cousin in New Zealand, but she could not be traced. Someone thought there may have been a stepdaughter in America but that search also yielded nothing. Sam had worked in the Railways; his pension had stopped coming five years ago when the economy collapsed and his savings had been lost to hyper inflation.  Every day that passed without a decision being made on how to pay for Sam's burial, the mortuary costs were rising until finally a benefactor paid for this one last dignified act for an old railway man. There were only four of us at the graveside and as the coffin was lowered, I threw in a flower and whispered: "No more worries now Sam."

## THE POLICEMAN'S PENSION:
## JOHNNY: 2009- 2019

Johnny joined the BSAP (British South Africa Police) in 1970 when he was 17 years old. He stayed in the police force until 2000 ('when this nonsense started' he said). In 2009 his pension, after 30 years of service in ZRP (Zimbabwe Republic Police), was US$38 a month. A decade later when the Zimbabwe government converted all bank accounts, salaries and pensions to Zimbabwe dollars, Johnny's US$38 pension was converted to Z$38 a month, enough at the time to buy two loaves of bread and a year later enough to buy half of one loaf of bread.

## NSSA PENSIONS AND THE 95 MILLION DOLLAR FRAUD: 2019

Zimbabwe introduced the National Social Security Authority in 1989 requiring employers and employees in all formal sectors to pay equal contributions to the authority to a total of 7% of basic monthly salary to fund pension payments and accident prevention and workers compensation schemes. NSSA soon became the goose that laid the golden egg, but not for the contributors. Riddled with corruption scandals relating to housing schemes, building purchases, improper tenders, luxury vehicles, air tickets and more, NSSA officials got very rich while contributors received miniscule pensions. NSSA pensions were eroded to the point of being completely worthless during the years of hyper inflation from 2003-2009 and again a decade later in Zimbabwe's next economic collapse when it cost more to travel to the bank to collect your NSSA pension than the value of the pension itself. The scandal of all scandals was exposed in 2019 when a forensic audit of NSSA exposed US$95 million worth of corrupt activities and implicated the Minister of Tourism who was arrested and still awaiting trial a year later.

In November 2019 NSSA was paying pensioners, who had contributed for thirty years, Z$200. It wasn't enough to pay rent, see the doctor, get an antibiotic or buy a week's groceries, but it could get you six apples.

## THE AFTERMATH:
## 2009 AND INTO THE SECOND COLLAPSE OF 2019/2020

When Zimbabwe stabilized in 2009 by entering into a coalition government, the entire nation was on its knees. A quarter of the population were living and working outside the country; we were a nation deeply traumatized by a decade of political violence, ravaged by hunger disease and absolute destitution. Everyone had to start again: bank accounts were empty, shop shelves were bare, pensions and savings were lost. Tendai Biti from the political opposition, MDC, took over as the Minister of Finance and managed to rapidly stabilize the economy by introducing what was called "a basket" of currencies that could be used in the country, the main ones being the US dollar and South African Rand. Everyone who could, went into a work frenzy, trying to restore some of their losses but for pensioners it was too late because they had no way of restoring lost life savings, investments and pensions. All the safety nets that people had put in place over the decades of their working lives to ensure independent financial security when they retired ,were lost during the first collapse of Zimbabwe between 2000 and 2009: savings were gone, pensions rendered worthless, investments devalued to zero, assets and properties sold to survive, farms and land seized by government. A decade later, in the second collapse of Zimbabwe, the same calamity hit the next generation of workers and pensioners when the government converted US dollars to Zimbabwe dollars which in the first year lost 95% of their value. Again pensions, savings and investments were lost, a calamity confounded by hyper inflation close to 1000% by the middle of 2020.

# CHAPTER 10
# OX DRAWN AMBULANCES

Coping with the collapse of Zimbabwe's health care sector was the hardest of all issues to deal with during the years of crisis. While President Mugabe and most senior government leaders travelled to South Africa, the UK, China, India and other countries for medical treatment, back at home we struggled to find and afford even basic antibiotics and over the counter pain killers. People requiring specialist treatments, procedures and surgeries, and who could afford it, went to South Africa and India for medical care. Meanwhile people who couldn't afford to travel had to take their own bedding and food to hospital, provide or pay for the medicines and equipment medical staff needed to treat them, from disposable gloves and bandages to plaster of Paris, splints, syringes, needles and everything in between.

Our families and friends in the great Zimbabwean Diaspora provided vital support to help keep us alive and healthy from 2004-2009. Boxes, parcels and packets flooded my post box for years with over the counter pain killers, basic medications, asthma pumps, water pills, statins, heart tablets, blood pressure medicines. In tightly packed boxes came vitamins, glasses, hearing aid batteries, plasters, antiseptic, gloves, syringes and more. Parcels came from the UK and USA, Canada and Europe, lovingly packed, gratefully received and always shared far and wide to people in remote rural villages, hospice workers, small clinics, retirement homes, childrens homes and more. Nothing was ever wasted and everything always found a home from a packet of plasters to a tube of toothpaste, a strip of Paracetamol to a much needed asthma pump.

Small church groups and charities in the UK, USA, Canada and Europe became a lifeline for vulnerable people in Zimbabwe, sending containers packed with supplies and equipment. The government did not waste a single opportunity to charge punitive taxes on these life saving donations, causing us to hang our heads in shame at their greed in our time of need. International organizations worked tirelessly in all medical sectors from making sure people had access to clean water, to assisting with issues relating to malaria, TB, HIV, malnutrition, cholera, child care, maternity and others.

Despite our desperate situation, everywhere there were heroes, local and foreign: at remote run down hospitals, in ill equipped clinics, at Mission hospitals, tucked away in small suburban houses in our towns and cities and under the trees in rural villages. There were doctors who waived their fees, specialists, anaesthetists, surgeons and so many more who either gave their services for free or charged the bare minimum. Without them the casualties from Zimbabwe's years of crisis would have been far greater. I hope that one day all those dedicated heroes will get the recognition they deserve; without them we would not have been able to survive Zimbabwe.

## HINTS AND TIPS

- Boil all drinking water.
- Wash all fresh produce.
- Learn how to make rehydration solution and always have ingredients available.
- Keep a good stock of everyday medicines and First Aid items in your cupboard.
- Buy prescription medicines in bulk, check for the longest expiry dates.
- Get prescriptions from your doctor and ask friends and family to buy stocks outside the  country.
- Use a runner to buy and bring medicines from neighbouring countries.
- Maintain your medical aid (insurance) at all costs.
- Get international medical insurance if you can; ask family outside the country to assist.
- Stay as healthy as you can; take vitamin supplements especially during periods of poor diet.
- Grow and eat as much fresh produce as you can, especially fruit, vegetables, eggs and milk.

## LIFE EXPECTANCY 1980 AND 2004

1980:        59.7 years
2004:        33.9 years
(World Bank; *UNDP)*

## THE FRIGHTENING FACTS OF OX DRAWN AMBULANCES: 2004

As Zimbabwe's growing food insecurity, collapsing commercial agriculture, economic and political turmoil and a gathering brain drain took hold, a catastrophe of immense proportions was unfolding in 2004 in the country's health sector. The head of the WFP (World Food Programme), James Morris, who was also the special envoy for humanitarian needs in southern Africa, was quoted in the international medical journal, The Lancet, saying he was "personally overwhelmed" by the crisis in Zimbabwe. Morris "scrapped a planned visit [to Zimbabwe] in June after being told that no government officials had time to see him. The trip was meant to assess the "triple threat of food insecurity, weakened capacity for governance and AIDS." (The Lancet, 2004)

In July 2004 Zimbabwe's Ministry of Health and Child Welfare asked for and received nine ox drawn ambulances from UNICEF (The United Nations Children's Fund). With a top speed of 10 miles a day, ox drawn ambulances made international news, earning yet more ridicule for Zimbabwe and highlighting the collapse of the health sector. Comments in a BBC report and other sources watching Zimbabwe exposed our dire situation:

"We are going back to the stone ages," MDC spokesman Paul Themba Nyathi said. "The gains made over the last twenty years to address maternal mortality, especially to provide emergency obstetric care services, are at risk of being lost," Dr

Juan Ortiz, Chief of the Health, Nutrition and Environment Section at Unicef. (BBC, 2004)

"In 2004 only 3.4 percent of the structures that were targeted for spraying [for malaria] were actually sprayed. The malaria control teams not only lacked insecticides, but also couldn't obtain the fuel that they required to drive into the malarial areas." (Tren, Ncube, Urbach & Bate, 2007)

UNAIDS estimated that Zimbabwe had one of the world's highest HIV prevalence rates at 24.6% and nearly one million AIDS orphans. (The Lancet, 2004)

In 2004 Zimbabwe had only six ordinary doctors for every 10,000 patients. The University of Zimbabwe was training 80 doctors a year but most of them emigrated as soon as they were qualified. (UNDP, 2004)


## WE DON'T WANT YOUR TENTS:
## DESTRUCTION, HIV ORPHANS AND TB: 2005.

In the winter of 2005, shortly before Zimbabwe's elections, authorities launched Operation Murambatsvina (translated as Clear the Filth), a widespread clearance of 'informal settlements' across the country, using bulldozers to raze people's homes and businesses to the ground. The UN Secretary General sent a special envoy, Anna Tibaijuka on a fact finding mission to Zimbabwe and she found that approximately 700,000 people had been left homeless. Human Rights Watch reported that: "Operation Murambatsvina had disproportionately affected women, children, foreign-born persons, and people with HIV/AIDS, who are the more vulnerable groups in society. The government refused subsequent United Nations offers to erect temporary tents or more permanent homes, claiming they were un-African." (Freedom House, 2006)

The HIV/AIDS crisis went on to become a focus of concern in 2005. Between July and September 2005 the price of Antiretrovirals in pharmacies increased from Z$450,000 to Z$1.2 million (US$17 to US$46) for a month's supply. (Plus News) The UNICEF Executive Director, Carol Bellamy, gave the grim numbers of Zimbabwe's children infected and affected by HIV: "Some 110 Zimbabweans under the age of 15 will become infected with HIV/AIDS today. Another 110 will be infected tomorrow, 110 more the day after that." UNICEF revealed that "one in five Zimbabwean children are now orphans; a child dies every 15 minutes due to HIV/AIDS in Zimbabwe; 160,000 children will experience the death of a parent in 2005". (IRIN) TB was also taking a heavy toll in Zimbabwe as the country's crisis escalated with mortality increasing by 189 percent, from 45 deaths per 100,000 persons in 1990 to 130 deaths per 100,000 in 2005. (WHO, 2005)

## BANANA LEAVES FOR COLOSTOMY BAGS: 2006

As Zimbabwe's collapse escalated, the impact on health services was unbelievable; decades of development and improvement were lost and we had resorted to the most primitive measures to survive. "At Chidamoyo Christian

Hospital about five hours drive from Harare, the staff have learnt to make do with very little. Bicycle handlebars are used to make a traction bar for a broken arm and banana leaves for a colostomy bag. Intravenous bags double as Foley catheter bags and, when available, Foley catheters also serve as chest tubes. Almost everything, including bags and gloves, is sterilized in pressure cookers, heated over an open fire and reused." (Tren, Ncube, Urbach & Bate, 2007)

## NURSES, DOCTORS AND HOSPITALS: 2006
In 2006 Zimbabwe's health care sector was in virtual collapse and it was estimated that over 40,000 Zimbabwean trained nurses were working outside the country. WHO statistics showed there was only one doctor for every 10,000 people in the country and Zimbabwe's Ministry of Health statistics revealed that fewer than one in four posts for doctors in government facilities was occupied and that four out of five district hospitals had no doctors at all. (WHO; SW Radio Africa; Zimbabwe Ministry of Health ,2006)

## THE COST OF CARE: JANUARY 2006
- General practitioner (consult) $864,000
- General surgery, specialist (consult) $1.1 million
- Physicians, paediatricians, neurosurgeons (consult) $2.1 million
- Chest X-ray $2.9 million
- Hospital, private, per day $8.87 million

- Single ward per day $7.98 million
- 2-bed ward per day $4 million
- General ward per day $3.68 million
- Casualty $1.8 million
- Delivering room $4.6 million
- General anaesthetics per min $129.400
  (The Herald, 2006)

## DIARY NOTES: MILLION DOLLAR ANTISEPTIC: 2007

Trying to stop a cut on my leg from going septic, I searched high and low for a simple tube of antiseptic ointment. How could something so simple be so hard to find? Will I ever come to terms with the extent of this collapse I wonder? Finally, I found and bought a 30 gram tube of Betadine antiseptic ointment and the price was Z$1,359,000. Printed on the bottom of the till slip were the words: Have a nice Day!

## DOG MEDICINE FOR PEOPLE: 2007

Desperately trying to find Phenobarbitone for a man who suffered with epileptic seizures, we scoured the pharmacies and hospitals but there were no tablets to be found anywhere. Chatting to a friend one day she said she had used Phenobarbitone to control seizures in her dog and may have a few left in the back of her desk drawer. While she rummaged, the light bulb came on: vets! Sure enough a couple of phone calls were made and we found a vet who dispensed phenobarb for dogs and they were exactly the same as those used for people. Problem solved and my epileptic friend was saved by a vet, the tablets coming in a packet with the words 'For Animal Use Only' printed across the top!

## RED CROSS: ZIMBABWE LIKE A 'WAR SITUATION': 2007

Speaking at a one day workshop on Human Rights at the National University of Science and Technology (NUST) in Bulawayo, the ICRC communication delegate for Southern Africa, Sebastian Brack, said the health delivery crisis had reached "war situation" levels and could no longer be ignored if lives were to be saved. "This is not our mandate as ours is mainly in armed conflicts. We are trying to convince Geneva that there is need for ICRC to increase its presence in Zimbabwe and help the suffering citizens deprived of good health." (NUST, 2007)

## 100 MILLION DOLLAR CONSULTATION FEES: FEBRUARY 2008

The NIPC (National Incomes and Pricing Commission) stated that government  hospitals are supposed to charge Z$10 million for a consultation but in reality, most medical institutions are charging anywhere between Z$35 million and Z$100 million.

## HOME-MADE UROSTOMY BAGS:
## LYLE'S STORY.  WINTER 2008

When Lyle heard I was making a trip to Harare he asked if he could have a lift as he needed to see his urologist. We both needed to be in roughly the same area and set off in good time to make Lyle's appointment. It was a beautiful winter's day, clear blue sky and bright warm sun so I was more than happy to sit in the sun in the car reading a book while Lyle went inside for his appointment. He was gone for about thirty minutes, very quick for a specialist I thought, and he was very quiet when he got back in the car.

"Everything OK?" I asked. Lyle nodded but I wasn't so sure, A bit later in the morning after a few more stops I asked Lyle if he needed anything as I wanted to pop into a supermarket on the off-chance that I might be able to get a loaf of bread. It was very unlikely as bread was like gold these days, along with almost everything else, but worth the chance. Lyle passed me a few bank notes asked me to get him some supermarket shopping bags.

"I've got loads of used shopping bags if you want?" I offered but Lyle said he wanted new, clean bags.

Emerging with no bread but a dozen new supermarket shopping bags, we headed home. We chatted for a while as I drove along in the sun and then Lyle told me what had happened. Recently recovering from extensive bladder surgery Lyle had a urostomy and desperately needed some urostomy bags. He had tried everywhere in our home town but there were none anywhere and after his brief meeting with the specialist this morning, the doctor had shown him how to improvise with a supermarket shopping bag, taping it securely onto the stoma with Elastoplast and preventing irritation on his skin with Vaseline. As Lyle talked, I was glad I had my sunglasses on so he wouldn't see the tears in my eyes. How low could we go?

## MULTIPLY PRICES BY ONE MILLION: 2008

Buying a month's worth of blood pressure medicine at Greensview Pharmacy the till slip read: Enalapril 10mg: $71,000. But in fact, I paid Z$71 billion because at the bottom of the till slip it said: Multiply Prices by ZW$1 M. (One million)

## TRILLION DOLLAR ANTIBIOTIC: JULY 2008

After a chronic gum infection which left two teeth being extracted, the doctor said the cause was very likely the result of inadequate diet and vitamin K deficiency (vitamin K helps the blood to clot) so I was given a prescription for a common penicillin based antibiotic which I needed to take in large doses, 1,000 mg three times a day, for two weeks and ordered to eat as much fruit and vegetables as I could to boost my system.

With a face swollen like a hamster with full pouches, the hunt for the antibiotic began. The first three pharmacies I went to didn't have the common antibiotic in stock and in fact had very few medicines at all. The fourth pharmacy said they did have the antibiotic but the price was two trillion dollars. The pharmacy wouldn't take a cheque, saying it was cash or nothing. Doing the sums in my head left me with this absurd situation: the daily cash withdrawal limit from the bank was one hundred billion dollars (about 40 US cents) a day; this meant I would have to stand in a bank queue for twenty working days in a row before I had withdrawn enough of my own money to buy the antibiotic, assuming the price remained the same, which of course it wouldn't. Looking for an urgent solution I phoned another pharmacy and they said they did have the antibiotic but it was Z$1.6 trillion. When I arrived at the pharmacy an hour later the price had gone up and was now Z$3 trillion. The only way to get round this nightmare was to find someone who would give me a few US dollars which opened doors everywhere and made anything possible, including a simple penicillin antibiotic.

**LIFE AND DEATH BLOOD PRESSURE PILLS:**
**MARGE'S STORY. JULY 2008**
Because inflation was well over one and a half billion percent all shops and businesses had completely stopped accepting cheques by early 2008. By the time a cheque was deposited and cleared by a bank it was worth a fraction of its original value and so without cash and without cheques we faced each day with exhaustion and fear, wondering how long we would be able to survive this. For people on life preserving medication, this disastrous cash regime imposed by the Reserve Bank of ridiculously small daily withdrawal limits, has literally turned into a matter of life and death. Queuing for ninety minutes to withdraw her maximum daily limit of cash, 72 year old Marge said that the maximum one hundred billion dollar withdrawal that she was allowed only enabled her to buy three single blood pressure pills. "I'm supposed to take

one a day," she said but I knew she would join the hundreds of thousands of others who were halving or quartering their tablets to make them last longer.

## HOME-MADE COUGH SYRUP: WINTER 2008

As we stood in queues for bread, money, sugar or bank notes, we swopped recipes for home made remedies, this one for cough syrup did the rounds in winter and worked beautifully:

Peel and chop an onion into small pieces and put into a small, clean glass or jar.

Pour 2 tablespoons of honey over the chopped onion or use brown sugar if you don't have honey.

Cover the container and leave to stand for 12 -24 hours.

Drain off the liquid that has gathered into a separate container and take a spoonful two or three times a day.

## OUTPATIENTS:
## FRANK'S STORY. AUGUST 2008

Frank got to the hospital early, an hour before the Outpatients department opened. There were already forty people ahead of him standing in a winding line and the queue was growing every minute. When the doors opened at 8.00am there were about 200 people waiting to see the Outpatient pharmacist to collect life preserving medication on repeat prescriptions for conditions such as high blood pressure, asthma, HIV/AIDS, epilepsy and diabetes. Many of the faces in the queue were familiar because they had all been coming here for over a week in the desperate hope of getting their medicines from the outpatient pharmacy. Even though the pharmacy doors were open, nothing happened for an hour and there was no explanation for the delay but at 9.00am the pharmacist finally appeared and he went quickly down the line looking at people's open case-record books. That was the fancy name for the little school exercise books that everyone had to buy themselves and then produce every time they went to the hospital where nurses and doctors would scribble illegible comments and hand write prescriptions in the exercise books which you then presented at the pharmacy to get the drugs.

Down the line the pharmacist went: "Nothing, nothing, nothing," he repeated as he looked at the books being held open by the patients. The pharmacist at this big, provincial, teaching hospital had none of the drugs needed by any of the waiting patients: no antiretrovirals for HIV, no insulin for diabetics, no blood pressure pills, nothing for asthma, nothing for epilepsy.

"You're wasting time here," he said "go and try somewhere else, we've got nothing." The hospital had no drugs on hand; no stocks on order, no money, no budget and no idea when there may be a change in the situation. In a few minutes the 200 strong queue had dispersed. The pharmacist offered to write referral letters for people to take to chemists in South Africa, Zambia, Botswana or Mozambique and said he was sorry but there was nothing else he could do. Frank watched a woman sitting on a wooden bench crying; he tried to comfort her but she was inconsolable. "I'm going to die," she whispered. She, Frank and everyone else in the queue were in the same desperate situation.


## HOME-MADE FRIDGE MAGNET: OCTOBER 2008
REHYDRATE :
6 teaspoons sugar
Half teaspoon salt
1 litre water.
MIX and DRINK...DRINK...DRINK.


## BAD WATER AND RAW WHEAT:
## GILL'S STORY. NOVEMBER 2008
When Gill said she had severe stomach pains and cramp I feared the worst. She'd just come back from a few days away and my first thought was cholera. Just last week Medicines Sans Frontiers warned that a million people in Harare alone were currently at risk. The bacterial disease is spreading fast and although it's worst in densely populated areas of Harare, now it's also being recorded in many places around the country. I wrote down the rehydration mixture for Gill and gave her a jam jar of sugar because there was none to buy in any of our empty shops.

This cholera outbreak's been like a ticking bomb waiting to go off for ages: urban water supplies have virtually collapsed; frequent water cuts, no maintenance, broken pipes and no chemicals to treat raw water. Everyone's been forced to collect water from wherever they can and boreholes and wells on private land are in huge demand. Morning and evening there are scores of people lining up in the suburbs with 20 litre containers outside urban residences where owners are allowing them to get water. Shallow wells are being dug on any available open ground: in fields, on roadsides and even next to cemeteries. The water from these wells and other unprotected pools is suspicious to say the least and we just hope that everyone's boiling their water.

When I saw Gill again yesterday it was a huge relief to hear that she was on the mend. She said she'd bought a small bag of raw wheat from some women who had been scavenging for grains on the roadside after a bag had fallen off a truck and this was most likely what had caused her illness. Seeing people picking up grain on roadsides from tuck spillage had become a familiar sight in 2008. Health risks were everywhere at this stage of Zimbabwe's collapse and it was terrifying to see the smallest ailment becoming a matter of life and death.

## ONE FAMILY'S STORY: NOVEMBER 2008

Oscar, in his thirties, living in a small town on the other side of Harare has only been able to find work two nights a week as a security guard. Oscar used to work on a farm, in charge of the cattle: dipping, dosing, vaccinating, branding, castrating, de-horning. He knew how to put ear tags in, check hooves and clean wounds, load and unload cattle trucks, mix and measure the winter feed, monitor the salt licks and mineral blocks and he had loved his work. All that stopped with farm invasions: his job, his home and his lifestyle all gone. Oscar doesn't get paid in money but in food on his part time security job: a meal when he arrives at work in the evening and another in the morning before he knocks off. It's only a small plate of *sadza* (maize meal porridge) but it fills his stomach and he knows how lucky he is to get it. On the other five days of the week Oscar survives on the vegetables growing in his garden, wild fruits that he gathers in the bush and on flying ants that he catches on anthills early in the morning and after its been raining. His wife is terminally ill with HIV/AIDS, they can't get or afford the antiretrovirals and now she's is in bed most of the time, barely able to walk and too weak to do anything for herself. Oscar knows that he's watching her die and that she's nearing the end but there's absolutely nothing he can do to help her.

Disaster struck five days ago when Oscar's 19 year old nephew and wife and their six month old baby came for a visit. Leaving the baby with Oscar, the young couple said they had to run an errand and would be back in a couple of hours. They never came back. Oscar found a small bag of baby clothes stuffed in a bush near his house, proof enough that the parents weren't coming back for their child. A dying wife, a six month old abandoned baby, two nights a week working for food. How can he can go on?

## DIARY OF DEATH: CHOLERA. 2008 AND 2009

When the rains came in November 2008 the cholera outbreak which had been surfacing on and off since about June 2008 went into full swing. The ancient disease, known as the 'blue death' because of the colour your skin turns as you lose so much body fluid, is caused by the Vibrio Cholerea bacteria spread through food or water contaminated by faeces of infected people. Breakdown of municipal water supply, lack of garbage collections and blocked sewers, all these services that we pay our local municipal councils to provide, are to blame for this tragedy. These are my diary entries from that terrible time.

## 4 NOVEMBER 2008

'Cook it, Peel it, Boil it …or Forget it. '

This is the slogan we're all trying to keep in our minds and live by every day to keep ourselves free of cholera. We are boiling everything and trying to avoid all hand contact with other people as this cholera is spreading faster and further every day. 9,000 confirmed cases now, 50 yesterday alone and they say that 360 people have died but we all think the real number is much higher as people simply aren't making it to the hospitals, clinics and health centres, which have no drugs, no gloves and often no staff.

## 18 NOVEMBER 2008

The government are down-playing the spread and impact of cholera but last week even the Herald (State controlled newspaper) published a photo of a truck carrying dead bodies (cholera victims) for mass burial. Next was the news from the Master of the High Court that the Courts had been closed for two days because there was no water in the building.

Parliament was adjourned after sitting for just one day because there was no water for hand basins or toilets.

## 24 NOVEMBER 2008

No one knows how many people have died so far but some estimates are of more than 250 deaths. The Chairman of Doctors for Human Rights said that 100 people had died in Harare's high density suburb of Budiriro. CHRA (Combined Harare Ratepayers Association) have issued an alert that the State have sealed off two cholera control centres (Beatrice Infectious Diseases and Budiriro Polyclinic) from the independent media and NGOs and are down-playing the death toll.

## 26 NOVEMBER 2008

Cholera patients making it to our collapsing health facilities are having to buy their own gloves, syringes and drips. Relations of cholera victims who have passed away say there is a dramatic increase in the demand for graves. Lines of newly covered graves stretch out in row after row in the cemeteries. First HIV/Aids, then hunger, now cholera. God help Zimbabwe.

## 4 DECEMBER 2008

Deputy Minister of Water says there are only enough water treatment chemicals in the country to last 12 weeks. UNICEF are distributing 360,000 litres of water a day in Harare and handing out soap and buckets. Failed state for sure when the international community have to come and give us buckets, soap and clean water. Shame on Zim.

## 12 DECEMBER 2008

We are hanging our heads after Minister of Information, Sikhanyiso Ndlovu, blames the cholera outbreak on the UK saying it's a "serious biological-chemical weapon" attack. "Cholera is a calculated, racist, terrorist attack on Zimbabwe by the unrepentant former colonial power, which has enlisted support from its American and Western allies so that they can invade the country."

## 17 DECEMBER 2008

The UN has announced an escalation in fatalities with almost 1,000 confirmed deaths. Cholera cases are now being reported in all 10 of Zimbabwe's provinces.

## 5 JANUARY 2009

It's been almost impossible to get an update on the cholera situation over the Christmas and New Year break with facts and figures as elusive as ever from our own authorities. Why are they trying to hide this tragedy? The WHO (World Health Organization) released figures on the 1st of January: 30,000 diagnosed cases of cholera and 1,564 recorded deaths.

## MID JANUARY 2009

It's getting scarier by the day; 8,500 new cases of cholera are being reported every week. OXFAM says the high mortality rate is because people are "seriously weakened by hunger, HIV and AIDS."

## LATE JANUARY 2009

Not many people are talking about cholera now because it's become such a sensitive political issue because it's exposing the health disasters that we're facing every day. Government hospitals are not functional, there are no drugs, equipment, food or linen and the nurses and doctors who haven't left the country are on strike. Medical personnel say they won't go back to work until they get their salaries in US dollars. Government doctors in Harare are earning the equivalent of 32 US cents a month, YES, a month; it's an outrage.

## JULY 2009

Huge relief! The cholera outbreak is finally over but we've paid such a heavy price for bad water, bad sanitation, collapsing health facilities and bad management: all adding up to a cocktail of death. The official figures are 98,596 cholera cases and 4,369 deaths; many people believe the death toll was far higher than this as people just died at home.

## CHOLERA: THE AFTERMATH

"In December 2008, in response to the [cholera] epidemic, Physicians for Human Rights dispatched an emergency delegation to Zimbabwe to investigate the country's health infrastructure and to document possible ongoing human rights abuses. The organization's investigation revealed multiple such abuses as well as the true scale and scope of the epidemic. These findings have been supported by other reports. Most critically, ZANU-PF's loss of municipal elections in Zimbabwe in 2005 led party leaders to refuse to fund municipal budgets for cities where it had been defeated, including in Harare, the capital. These retaliatory cuts led to a cessation of water purification for the city and eventually, the redirection of raw human sewage into the city's main reservoir. A breakdown in the most basic elements of water and sanitation infrastructure underpinned the cholera epidemic in Zimbabwe." (Cuneo, Sollom & Beyrer, 2017)

## DON'T GET SICK: JUNE 2009

I knew I'd done some serious damage to my arm when I tripped and fell on a concrete step in my garden last week. The pain was extreme and it took me a few minutes before I could get up. Not much to see, no pools of blood or extruding bones just grazed knees and hands but an arm that started swelling up almost immediately. After I'd pulled myself together I tried to get some help. Not so easy! The land line phone wasn't working again and the mobile phone had no signal, again. For some weird reason when the electricity goes off the mobile phone signal disappears too and you can't make calls or send text messages.

Nothing to do but wait for help, I laid a luke warm 'cold pack' on my elbow and cursed the daily sixteen hour power cuts which had left everything in the fridge and freezer slowly getting warmer, including my emergency cold pack. Six hours later I made it into the doctor's office. A hasty examination, comment on the degree of pain and swelling and the Doc said I needed an X Ray as it seemed probable I had a broken bone in my elbow.

The X Ray machine at the local government hospital wasn't working so I headed to a private hospital. The Radiographer had to be phoned and then collected from his home in an ambulance as there are no other hospital vehicles in working order anymore. A shocking up-front cash payment of US$50 was needed even though I have medical insurance. Back to the doctor's rooms and it was a US$20 consultation fee to be told I'd broken the tip of my radius right at the elbow. US$10 for 30 pain killers and then the prospect of a possible surgery in a week's time. Not a comforting thought because the charges of all medical and surgical procedures are in the thousands of US dollars: anaesthetists, assistants, surgeons, hospital charges, equipment. Thankfully I was able to avoid the surgery and every day afterwards I woke up and said to myself: don't get sick.

## 50% VACANCY RATE IN PUBLIC HEALTH SECTOR: 2009-2013

Lack of staff for medical education training, and high drop-out rates in public sector health care posts have resulted in vacancy rates of over 50% for doctors, midwives, laboratory, and environmental health staff. (Global health workforce alliance, 2013)

## GOVERNMENT DOCTORS AND NURSES IN ZIMBABWE: 2010

"There are 1.6 physicians and 7.2 nurses for every 10,000 people." (Zimbabwe Ministry of Health, 2010)

## LIFE EXPECTANCY IN ZIMBABWE 1960-2015

| | |
|---|---|
| 1960 | 53 |
| 1965 | 55 |
| 1970 | 56 |
| 1975 | 57 |
| 1980 | 59 |
| 1985 | 61 |
| 1990 | 58 |
| 1995 | 50 |
| 2000 | 44 |
| 2005 | 43 |
| 2010 | 50 |
| 2015 | 50 |

(United Nations)

## 16,000 NURSES FIRED:  APRIL 2018

A decade after cholera ravaged Zimbabwe and with little change in the governance of the country, the health sector in Zimbabwe was in a state of near collapse: doctors and nurses barely able to survive on their wages, chronic shortages of staff, equipment, specialists and medication. In April 2018 Vice President Chiwenga fired 16,000 nurses who had gone on strike for better wages, working conditions and unpaid allowances dating back eight years. The Nurses Association

(Zina) responded to the firing of their members and the statement that had been made by the Vice President:

"The nurses dismissed as 'misleading' [claims] that the government had addressed their concerns. Our grievances which relate to poor and dangerous working conditions, which threaten our health and affects the discharge of our duties, remain un-addressed," they said. "The $17,144,446 referred to by the Vice-President in his press statement as having been transferred to the Ministry of Health relates to arrear allowances dating back to 2010. It is in no way related to our current demands that triggered the collective job action." (IOL, 2018)

## DOCTORS STRIKE AND ABDUCTION: SEPTEMBER 2019

As Zimbabwe's second collapse gathered pace in late 2019, the crisis in the health sector was immense. Very little had been done by the government to aid the recovery of the sector since the 2004-2009 collapse. In September 2019 horror unfolded:

"Dr Peter Magombeyi, President of the Zimbabwe Hospital Doctors Association alerted colleagues that three unidentified men were forcibly taking him away from his home that fateful night of Saturday 14th September. A doctor with ZADHR (Zimbabwe Association of Doctors for Human Rights) said: "Our homes and workplaces are no longer safe. We don't know who will be taken next so we will not go to work until our safety is guaranteed. Right now, we are vulnerable." The day after the disappearance of Dr Magombeyi doctors protested with placards outside Parirenyatwa hospital in Harare. "Every doctor in this country should withdraw their services until he is released." A junior doctor in Zimbabwe currently earns around Z$1400 a month made up of Z$400 basic salary and Z$1000 'on call allowance.' Z$1400 is equivalent at the time of writing to around US$88 and getting less and less by the day as the value of the Zimbabwe dollar continues to decline." (Buckle, 2019)

"19 September 2019, Dr Peter Magombeyi, a medical doctor was found alive and disoriented, dumped about 33 km out of Harare in Nyabira. Dr Magombeyi was abducted on the night of 14 September 2019. He said he was held in a basement where he was tortured. There are fears that he was injected with an unknown substance by his abductors. The government accused him of faking the abduction and tried to prevent him from seeking medical treatment outside the country. (Amnesty International, 2019)

## DOCTORS FIRED: DECEMBER 2019

The government fired 435 of Zimbabwe's 524 Junior Doctors who were on strike. The doctors said they were incapacitated and can't afford to get to work and when they do, there is a chronic shortage of medication and equipment leaving them unable to treat their patients. Zimbabwe has 1,600 public sector doctors composed of 524 junior doctors, 818 middle level doctors and 220 consultants. Junior doctors are currently earning the equivalent of US$80 a month (US$2.60 a day).

In December 2019, three months before Zimbabwe and the world would be caught up in the Covid 19 Pandemic, there was only one hospital doctor for every 8,000 to 10,000 people in the country.

# CHAPTER 11

# COFFINS, GRAVES AND SCAMS

## COLLAPSING COFFINS: 2000

Not long after the start of land invasions in 2000, regular sources of agricultural income dried up as invaders claimed parts of our farms for themselves, one field at a time, regardless of what was being produced there at the time, driving us to increasingly strange ways of making a few dollars. When Micky, a neighbouring farmer, decided to fell some of his pine trees, before the land invaders grabbed the property and claimed the valuable timber for themselves, there were a lot of offcuts from the planking machines. The offcuts turned out to be the ideal length and width for making small items of furniture and the elderly tenant renting a cottage on Micky's farm said he could 'turn his hand' to almost anything and he happily took all the offcuts to see what he could 'knock up'. The first thing I knew about the plan that was being hatched was when Micky popped in and asked me if I'd be prepared to sell a few home-made wooden items for a small commission in my Trading Store on the roadside corner of my farm. I said I would and arranged a time to go and look at what items were being made from the pine offcuts.

Micky always gave everyone a nickname that either suited their character or because he could never remember their real name. I was never sure what my designated nickname was, but perhaps that was just as well. Micky had given the tenant in his cottage the nickname 'Bismarck,' due to some seafaring story that had got his attention, and I arrived one afternoon to find Bismarck hard at work at a makeshift work bench he had made and placed under a big shady tree. The smell of newly cut Pine was heady and fresh and there were deep piles of pine shavings under and around the work bench. It took a while to get Bismarck's attention; he had goggles on and was wearing a strange thick wooly hat with fold down ear muffs apparently to shield himself from the noise of the electric saw he was using to cut planks into measured lengths. While Bismarck stripped off his protective gear and brushed the pine shavings off himself, I glanced around and was surprised to see a long and fairly narrow box leaning up against a tree.

"Is it some sort of a tool storage box?" I asked.

"It's a coffin!" Bismarck responded, "I think they'll sell like hot cakes."

"A coffin!" I exclaimed in disbelief. This was the last thing I'd expected to see Bismarck making with Micky's pine tree offcuts. I had assumed it was going to be stools or tables or storage boxes, not coffins. Bismarck looked at me and I looked at him; the realization had just sunk in: he wanted me to sell coffins in my Trading Store. Lost for words for a moment I approached the long box for a closer look; something wasn't quite right and it struck me straight away. I was only five foot four and the box was slightly shorter than me.

"It's a bit short isn't it? I'd have to bend my knees to fit in there!"

Bismarck went red and I decided it wasn't the right time to make a comment about the dimensions of the box so I kept quiet. Bismarck muttered about this being the first experimental coffin so that he could get the shape and lid design and then thankfully Micky arrived so I didn't have to say anymore and we went off to have tea. Over a lengthy tea I grudgingly agreed that there probably would be a demand for coffins in view of the fact that almost 34% of the population was estimated to be HIV positive and statistics indicated that 3,000 people were dying a week from HIV Aids. It was a massive mortality rate but regardless of the facts, I still wasn't happy about selling coffins but reluctantly agreed, insisting that the quality and dimensions had to be a hundred percent right before I'd put them in my Trading Store.

In the days that followed I cleared a space in the stockroom of the store and broached the idea to the store keeper who immediately said she wasn't happy about it and wouldn't handle the coffins herself. I wasn't at all surprised and so we arranged that someone else would be called to deal with coffin sales. I made a couple of signs advertising coffins for sale and when everything was ready I recruited a couple of farm workers to help and we went down to Bismarck's cottage. Bismark wasn't home but had left a note saying the coffin was ready to go. It looked good, clean and professional, so we loaded it into the back of my truck and off we went.

Unloading the coffin at the store I took the lid off so it was quite obvious to the gathered spectators that I didn't have a body in there and we carried it into the stock room. Standing around the coffin I did wonder if it was going to be strong enough, the bottom didn't look as substantial as I thought it should. A great babble of laughing and exclamations erupted when I said I thought we needed to test the strength of the coffin. Naturally no one volunteered to get in, including me, so I suggested we use a few crates of coke bottles in the coffin and lift it up to see if the bottom was strong enough. On second thoughts I decided we should use crates of empty coke bottles, just in case, and that we should put some padding on the cement floor underneath, also just in case. Two crates, one at each end of the coffin was fine; a third crate in the middle caused an ominous creaking noise and the bottom sagged a bit but when the fourth crate was added, sure enough the bottom of the coffin fell out completely. Great shouts and exclamations of disbelief and laughter filled my little trading store and tears streamed down our faces as we watched empty cokes bottles rolling away in all directions. If a coffin couldn't hold four crates of empty coke bottles there was no way it could hold a human body.

That was it! No more conversation. I knew without a doubt that coffin selling wasn't for me and that Bismarck would have to make a few dollars with his carpentry venture somewhere else. We immediately loaded the collapsing coffin back into the truck and took it back to Bismarck. A few days later a message came from Bismarck: he'd found something more profitable than coffins to make. I didn't ask and he didn't offer any more details and that was the end of that survival plan.

## AFTER HOURS COFFINS: 2000-2004

For a number of years after I moved into town after being evicted from the farm, I would receive mysterious phone calls at all hours of the night and over the weekends. After the extreme trauma of war veterans and farm evictions, phone calls in the middle of the night were always un-nerving. Were there war veterans at the gate? Was a neighbour in trouble? Did I have to get out in a hurry? Who had been hurt? All were questions that instantly came to mind.

"Hello," I'd mutter incoherently, breathlessly into the phone, heart pounding, still in the fog of sleep in the middle of the night. There was almost always a lot of background noise on these night time calls: voices, crying, wailing and it was always hard to understand what the caller was saying. Often the only distinguishable words sounded like 'coughing,' and 'price.' Eventually, as the sleep cleared from my head and my brain came into focus, I realised that night-time callers were asking for coffins and the noise in the background was of grieving family members and gathering mourners.

It turned out that the previous occupant of my house had been a sales rep for a local undertaker and this phone number was listed in the phone book as an after-hours undertaker's number. Despite numerous calls and even a couple of visits to the undertaker to explain that I was getting all these night time and weekend calls from grieving relatives wanting coffins, the calls continued for a very long time until the after hours listing in the telephone directory was removed. Until that happened, I got the correct after hours number for the undertakers and propped it up against the phone by my bed. The last thing I saw when I went to sleep at night and the first thing I saw when I woke up in the morning were the words: COFFINS: phone 1234.

## FROM MUSHROOMS TO COFFINS: 2007

On the main road to Harare the sign at Mukuti Store that used to read, 'Bennetts Mushrooms' has gone. It's been replaced with one that read: 'Destiny coffins and caskets.' This was adaptability in a country in collapse but also the very sad reality that we were no longer producing food for the living but containers for the dead.

## HOME-MADE COFFINS, BURIAL ORDER FUEL SCAMS AND GRAVE ROBBERS: 2007

By the end of 2007, when Zimbabwe's inflation rate was sixty six thousand percent, undertakers reported that their coffin sales were declining. This wasn't because less people were dying, quite the opposite in fact, but now people had resorted to making their own coffins due to the severe economic conditions. In February 2007 a standard, plain wooden box coffin cost Z$1 billion while a lined casket was a minimum of Z$5 billion. There were many stories of people making their own coffins using doors and shelves that they removed from the brackets, frames and hinges in their houses and then used curtains as room dividers inside instead of doors. Many hospitals stopped offering mortuary facilities because people would abandon their dying relatives at hospitals and never return because they couldn't afford coffins and burial costs.

In 2007 it cost Z$300 million to hire a bus to take mourners to the Granville Cemetery fifteen kilometres from the centre of Harare and that was only possible when the funeral parlours could get fuel for the hearse and the bus to transport mourners. Fuel shortages had almost bought the country to a standstill with huge queues of stationary vehicles outside every filling station. A special fuel allowance was made available for undertakers with the requirement that a Burial Order be produced in order for fuel to be purchased. Burial Orders were only provided at government offices but very soon there were far more Burial Orders than people dying and there were also numerous Burial Orders for the same person. It hadn't taken long for one Burial Order to be photocopied multiple times and these were then used at numerous different filling stations by people desperate for fuel. As soon as that scam came to light a new rule was introduced and fuel would only be sold if there was an original Burial Order; photocopies were not allowed. In the blink of an eye that requirement generated its own scam too: one nicely printed form, someone at a desk under a tree with good handwriting, one rubber stamp and some red stamp pad ink and off we go again to the filling station.

Cremations had stopped being a guaranteed option at the only crematorium in Harare from as early as 2003 because there was often no gas to operate the furnace and by 2007 gas fired cremations stopped altogether. Gas was imported but wood wasn't and so the next option came from Mutare, on the eastern border of the country where wood fired cremations were undertaken. This wasn't as easy a solution as it sounded because of the distances involved; relations not only had to provide fuel to move the body of their loved one to Mutare but also had to provide firewood for the cremation. A call to the local undertaker was bizarre in the extreme as they would tell you exactly how many litres of fuel (diesel or petrol) they needed to transport the body to Mutare and also how much firewood, measured in cords, was required for the cremation.

Burials were the first choice for most people but at the end of 2007 the cost of a grave site in a municipal cemetery was Z$112 million. In what they called a 'cost cutting measure,' Municipalities no longer dug the grave to the required six foot depth. Instead they had a wrought iron frame which was laid onto the grave site as a marker; one man with a shovel literally skimmed off the top six inches and went home. It was then up to the relations of the deceased to dig the rest of the grave to the regulation six feet or pay someone to do it for them. The municipality's cost cutting exercise became a source of income for unemployed teenagers who said they could make Z$20 million a day deepening graves for mourning relations who had arrived to bury their relation only to find just a scratch in the ground.

Helping a friend make the arrangements for the burial of her husband, four men were recruited for the job of digging the grave. The Municipality provided the wrought iron template to demarcate the length and width of the grave and we provided the picks and shovels. Returning to collect the men who had dug the grave some hours later, a family member was met by a municipal employee who had wandered over to the site.

"Is no-one staying to watch the grave overnight?" he asked. The question was met with incredulity and blank stares. "If someone doesn't stay here to guard the newly dug grave, you will probably find it has been taken by tomorrow morning," the council worker said.

"Taken! The grave will be taken?" I exclaimed in disbelief at the absurdity of it all. Apparently there was such a high demand for graves and such extreme levels of poverty that some desperate people had resorted to burying their relations at night in graves that had been dug for other people. The council worker said that time and time again the hearse and mourners would arrive at the cemetery only to find the grave had already been occupied by someone else: buried, covered over and filled up.

The following day on a cold and windy afternoon we stood around the graveside as our friend was laid to rest. It was a short service attended by about twenty people. There were times when we strained to hear the prayers of the Anglican Priest as his words were blown away on the wind. Half a dozen young men were holding a memorial headstone-laying ceremony at the grave of their loved one a few metres away. They sang in quiet harmony and their voices swept across our little service. Our friend's coffin was lowered into the hard red soil accompanied by our tears and the sound of the soulful voices of African harmony a few graves away. As hard as we tried to survive Zimbabwe, the pain was always with us.

At the end of the brief service as people drifted away, the ugly reality had to be discussed again. Preventing grave robbers was another nightmare to contend with. Seeing lights flickering in cemeteries at night had become a regular, disturbing occurrence. Youngsters tasked with deepening graves would arrive early in the morning to find that newly filled graves had been unearthed and the coffins removed, leaving behind the occupant without the coffin. Cleaned, brushed and polished, lined caskets were worthZ$5 billion. The only way around this horror was concrete and relatives would pour concrete over newly buried caskets and stand watch at the gravesite over night while the concrete dried. Nothing was sacred in Zimbabwe now, not even death.

# CHAPTER 12

# SILENCING VOICES

**BE PREPARED**

From 2004 to 2009 the topic of conversation was always about where people would go and what they would do if the situation got so bad that they needed to get out of Zimbabwe in a hurry. An estimated four million people in our population of ten million had already left the country in the first five years of the new millennium. Some had applied for asylum in New Zealand, Australia, the United Kingdom, South Africa and the United States of America (among others) and they had packed their bags and gone. Many had left with nothing more than two suitcases, their farms and homes trashed, their rural village homes burnt, their family members tortured and traumatized in waves of horrific political violence. Others had got visas and gone to live and work in countries in the region, particularly South Africa, Zambia, Mozambique, Botswana and Namibia, while others had gone further afield and were in Nigeria and Angola. Perhaps the majority of people who left went in buses, kombis or on foot to the border nearest to them to get out at any cost: political and economic refugees who crawled under and climbed over barbed and razor wire fences. Many had no documentation at all; they moved at night, crossed raging, crocodile infested rivers, braving wild animals, dodging armed officials who may catch them, imprison them or send them back to Zimbabwe.

## EMERGENCY EXIT PLANS

My emergency exit plans had started years before during the invasion of our farm in 2000. Always ready to run at a moment's notice if the farm invaders got violent or decided to evict you from your own home with very little warning. In those frightening days the running away emergency kit consisted of things you would need if you had to run for your life in the middle of the night, escaping out the back door: backpack, passport, ID, money, jeans, jacket, running shoes, and torch.

Between the years 2004 and 2009 most people had emergency exit plans which included any or all of these things:

- Always keep the car full of fuel and have enough jerry cans of fuel to get to the nearest border.
- Pack one briefcase or rucksack containing all your family's personal records and documentation: passports, ID's, certificates, title deeds, medical records, bank cards, cash.
- Always have a backpack ready with essential clothing, medicine, torch, phone numbers and personal items and leave it in one central cupboard with a jacket, pair of jeans, good walking shoes and a warm top.
- A trunk with emergency food and medicines to last up to a week. This included items such as tea bags, coffee, pasta, tins, milk powder, packet soup, lentils, biscuits, soya mince, rice, sugar, dried beans, peanut butter, nuts, dried fruit, oats, flour.

Then there was the essential equipment which included a bucket, picnic set of crockery and cutlery, at least twenty litres of water; a small gas bottle, cooking ring, pot, pan and kettle. On the medical and hygiene side of the trunk was toilet paper, soap, toothpaste, pain killers, antiseptic, bandages and First Aid kit. Other emergency supplies included bedding, sleeping bags, pillows and blankets. In the vehicle you needed: driving licence, insurance papers, log book and registration; tool box, tyre pump, chain, padlocks, rope and a big roll of duct tape which could be used to make any repair of almost anything you can think of!

There were naturally always people who thought emergency plans were absurd and that the situation would never get that bad but for farmers and people working on farms, people lived on the edge for years; from 2000 to 2009 and beyond, always at the mercy of a lawless mob (often drugged, drunk and armed) and with no protection available from police, the courts or the authorities. At the height of Zimbabwe's collapse in June 2008, instability escalated in most parts of the country leaving thousands of people on the run, getting away from political violence which erupted before, between and after the two contested elections in the middle of the year. In late June 2008 the British Embassy sent out this notice to British citizens permanently resident in Zimbabwe:

British Embassy Travel advice: "25 June 2008. Travel advice for Zimbabwe has been updated to advise against all travel in Zimbabwe. We are also advising all British Nationals resident in Zimbabwe to review their security arrangements and ensure they have their own contingency plan in place to leave at short notice. In the event of a significant deterioration in the security situation, the consular assistance we will be able to provide will be severely limited.  You should make your own judgements about whether to remain in the current situation. A number of British Nationals have decided to leave the country at this time."

The advice was far from being comforting and in plain English translated to mean: 'you're on your own,' and so we all looked at our emergency exit plans with a more critical eye.

## SCHOOL SECURITY NOTICE: 2008

A week after the 2008 elections, Zimbabwe was on a knife edge. It had taken the electoral commission five weeks to count, verify and announce less than two and half million votes. During those five weeks a brutal campaign of violence and retribution by the ruling party and their supporters had left twenty people dead, hundreds injured and thousands homeless or on the run from the violent perpetrators.  April and May 2008 were times when the temptation to leave the country was very high. One week after schools re-opened for the winter term in May 2008, a short, 'stay calm,' newsletter came from my son's boarding school. It read:  'As far as the safety of your sons is concerned, we have introduced Security Procedures at school that will help us in the event of civil disorder.'

The fact that the words Security Procedures had been given capital letters were indication enough for the older school Mums like me, that the school took this issue very seriously and in its own strange way, the words gave comfort. The lesson here for surviving times of uncertainty, fear and mayhem was to stay calm and try not to panic. It was a lesson often easier said than done.


## RADIO: THE GREAT WALL OF THE AIRWAVES: 2000- 2014

The State will inevitably find ways to block information streams and silence voices of dissent when a country is in collapse, particularly when the government is intent on maintaining the illusion that nothing is wrong. When the first collapse of Zimbabwe started in 2000 we relied mainly on broadcast information in the form of independent radio. This came from three main, independent sources, each broadcasting for one or two hours a day, mainly early in the morning or evening: *Short Wave Radio Africa* (SW Radio Africa) broadcasting from London began in 2001. *Radio Voice of the People* (VOP) broadcasting via Radio Netherlands began in 2002. *Voice of America Studio 7* (*VOA Studio 7*) broadcasting from USA began in 2003.

As we learned the frequencies to look for and the times of the broadcasts, we also had to find ways of keeping our radios on during lengthy power cuts. Batteries, solar panels, inverters and wind up radios all became vital pieces of equipment in order to stay informed. As fast as we learned how to stay informed, the government learned to jam radio signals. By

2005 the State had found ways to jam independent radio broadcasts, initially of *SW Radio Africa* and soon after of VOP and *VOA Studio 7* as well. Reporters Without Borders highlighted the issue in 2006:

"According to sources in Zimbabwe, the jamming of Zimbabwean exile radio stations began after a group of Chinese technicians arrived in Harare in January 2005 under a trade accord between China and Zimbabwe. Housed at the Sheraton Hotel for three months, they reportedly carried out a number of installations including a radio jamming system using a ZBC transmitter in Gweru, in the centre of the country, and the ZBC Pockets Hill broadcasting centre in Highlands, a suburb of Harare. These illegal practices, which violate international regulations governing telecommunications, are one of the specialties of the Chinese government. Jamming is standard practice in China, especially the jamming of Tibetan radio stations and foreign radio stations beaming programmes to the west of the country. A Reporters Without Borders release described this policy as the "Great Wall of the airwaves." (Reporters Without Borders)

*SW Radio Africa* began broadcasting from London in 2001. Founded by veteran Zimbabwean broadcaster Gerry Jackson whose *Capitol Radio* had come under attack and then been closed down by Zimbabwean authorities in October 2000, *SW Radio Africa* was staffed and run by exiled Zimbabweans. Jamming of *SW Radio Africa's* broadcasts began in February 2005, a few weeks before parliamentary elections were to take place in Zimbabwe. Almost as soon as their nightly bulletins began the voices would be drowned out by a loud electronic noise making the reports completely inaudible. Unbelievably the Zimbabwe government even commented on the jamming of *SW Radio Africa*: "Zimbabwean presidential spokesman George Charamba publicly hailed the interference on 29 March [2005] while refusing to acknowledge that the government was responsible. "If the Zimbabwe government is jamming *SW Radio Africa*, kudos to them," he said. "If they are not and do not have the equipment (to jam), then it is time they look for that equipment." (Reporters Without Borders)

In 2006 the International Press Institute (IPI) Director Johan Fritz commented on the jamming of *SW Radio Africa*: "Having brought the independent press to its knees, it now seems that the Zimbabwean government is determined to do the same with independent radio stations, both inside and outside the country." (IPI)

*VOA Studio 7's* programmes for Zimbabwe began in 2003, were broadcast from America and produced by exiled Zimbabweans. Jamming of the *VOA Studio 7* radio broadcasts to Zimbabwe began in 2005 but were mainly limited to medium wave frequencies. In June 2005 an official with Zimbabwe's Central Intelligence Organization (CIO) told a South African based news site, *Zim Online*, and speaking on condition of anonymity: "There has been marked improvement on trying to block the US propaganda from reaching us since the beginning of this month. The team is now aiming to look for ways to completely block the signal coming via a transmitter in Botswana." Reporters Without Borders called the jamming 'sabotaging" and said: "*Voice of America* (VOA) have become the latest target of the jamming carried out by the Harare government with Chinese complicity. This new case of jamming shows how the Zimbabwean government despises its own people, blocking their ears to the news outlets it dislikes." (Reporters Without Borders)

VOP (*Voice of the People*) was created in June 2000 by former employees of the state-owned Zimbabwe Broadcasting Corporation (ZBC) with help from the Soros foundation and a Dutch NGO. Based in Zimbabwe, VOP began broadcasting in 2002 and came under repeated attack by authorities. Police raided their studio in Harare on 4 July 2002 and took away equipment. It was subsequently the target of a bombing on 29 August 2002 which destroyed the entire studio and all the equipment. In September 2005 VOP broadcasts were jammed by the same electronic noise as VOA and *SW Radio Africa*. In December 2005 VOP staff were detained and charged with practicing journalism without permission from the government controlled Media and Information Commission.

Of the three independent radio stations that broadcast through the years of Zimbabwe's first collapse, *SW Radio Africa* had a special place in my heart. From the time when my Marondera farm was invaded in 2000 I always had my radio tuned to whichever programme on ZBC Gerry Jackson was presenting, playing the music of my youth. One afternoon I was in the farm store working alongside Jane, the farm

Storekeeper, when the men who had invaded the farm and were squatting in the field outside my house, came into the store. Their taunts, insults and harassment started immediately and Jane kept coming near me and whispering: "just stay quiet, say nothing;" I guess she could see my face turning red, my hands shaking, my eyes shining with tears. I turned the radio volume up, Gerry Jackson was playing Led Zeppelin's "Stairway to Heaven" and for a few minutes it helped me forget the ugly present filled with trauma and fear. Next on Gerry's playlist was Jethro Tull's "Farm on the Freeway" and two decades later the lingering flute and heartfelt lyrics still haunt me, remind me, and bring tears to my eyes for everything that was lost: for my family and for Zimbabwe:

*"Nine miles of two-strand topped with barbed wire*

*Laid by the father for the son.*

*Good shelter down there on the valley floor,*

*Down by where the sweet stream run.*

*Now they might give me compensation*

*That's not what I'm chasing. I was a rich man before yesterday.*

*Now all I have got is a cheque and a pickup truck.*

*I left my farm on the freeway."*

(Jethro Tull: Farm on the Freeway)

When *SW Radio Africa* stopped broadcasting in August 2014 because of financial constraints, it left a great void in the lives of those of us still trying to stay informed and to stand up and speak out against tyranny and oppression. MISA paid this fitting tribute to the voices of courage and hope that had *supported* Zimbabwe throughout the darkest years of our country's collapse:

"MISA-Zimbabwe bemoans the closure of the pioneer shortwave radio station, *SW Radio Africa,* after 13 years of affording Zimbabweans, particularly those residing in marginalized rural communities, access to diverse views and opinions. … The history and evolution of the Zimbabwean media would not be accurately told if the station's immense contribution during the closure of private daily newspapers were to be omitted especially at a time when the majority of Zimbabweans were left at the mercy of the dominant state-controlled media. …Between 2003 and 2010, *SW Radio Africa* together with other exiled radio stations such as *Voice of the People, VOA Studio 7* and online publications, became the most prominent sources of news and views alternative to those churned out by the state media and in the process establishing a huge following among Zimbabweans. …The untimely closure of the station has dealt a blow to marginalized rural communities that 34 years after independence, still do not receive transmission of the mainstream public and private radio stations that broadcast in the country on Frequency Modulation (FM)." (MISA)

On the 11th August 2014 *BBC World Service Africa* Editor Richard Hamilton described *SW Radio Africa's* final news bulletin as tinged with sadness. "Although the Zimbabwean government jammed some of its short wave broadcasts, *SW Radio Africa* still had its loyal listeners - estimated at one point at around one million, he says. "We are gone so our voice is completely gone," Ms. Jackson told the BBC." (BBC)

## TELEVISION AND THE BRIEF LIFE OF JOY TV: 1998-2002

Zimbabwe only has one television station: ZBC (Zimbabwe Broadcasting Corporation) which is State controlled, has no independent editorial content, very little international news and is little more than a government mouthpiece. Funded by licence fees and advertising, ZBC is free to air leaving many people with limited financial resources no other option but to watch ZBC TV. During the years of Zimbabwe's collapse, starting from land invasions in 2000 and ongoing to the present day, ZBC presented a view which was totally disconnected from the reality on the ground in our collapsing country; there was often little or no coverage at all of political violence, attacks on opposition members and supporters or any voices of dissent.

For a brief period lasting less than four years Joy TV emerged on our airwaves. Founded by James Makamba, Joy TV opened in July 1998. Broadcasting for a few hours a night, Joy TV provided a breath of fresh air to Zimbabwe's airwaves and to our disbelief and delight their programming even included a nightly BBC news bulletin at 9.00pm. For the first time

Zimbabweans could see genuine, unbiased news, but it didn't last long. On the 1st May 2002, the BBC news bulletin disappeared from Joy TV. The Media Institute of Southern Africa, MISA, reported the event:

"A Joy TV official, who talked to MISA's Zimbabwean chapter (MISA-Zimbabwe) on condition of anonymity, said that the television station was instructed to censor the BBC news bulletins. However, the BBC policy says that their news bulletins must be shown as they are, and failing this the bulletins must not be shown at all. The official told MISA-Zimbabwe that the management chose to do away with the news rather than risk having the station's lease agreement cancelled." (MISA 2002)

At the end of May 2002 Joy TV disappeared from Zimbabwe's airwaves altogether after having its licence revoked by the Zimbabwe government. Pambazuka News reported on the end of the short life span of Joy TV: "Joy TV, started in July 1998, closed down on 31 May 2002, bringing down the curtain on Zimbabwe's botched experiment with broadcasting diversity and carrying the same dream down with it. Joy TV closed down after a lease agreement it had with the Zimbabwe Broadcasting Corporation was cancelled on the grounds that it violated the Broadcasting Services Act, which was enacted in 2001. The short but eventful life of Joy TV faced stern challenges especially direct interference from the government. This manifested itself in a "direct" order for the station to drop the BBC news bulletin it broadcast every day. Joy TV was also never allowed to flight local news except musicals and apolitical documentaries. " (Pambazuka News, 2002)

## VPNS AND BLOCKING THE INTERNET: 2018

Little did we know that the crude tactics of State officials in 2004-2009 of banning newspapers,  arresting journalists, reporters and photographers, bombing printing presses, listening in on phone calls, jamming short wave radio frequencies, cutting phone links and blacking out TV broadcasts, things would get much worse in the years to come. When we were next trying to survive Zimbabwe, in the crisis of 2018/19/20, everything was very different. On the streets brutality had gone from police with rubber truncheons to extended periods with armed soldiers  in towns and cities. Information technology and access to the internet had also changed when Zimbabwe went into its second collapse. By 2018 everyone had a cell phone with a camera and an audio recorder; WhatsApp allowed instant, affordable sending, forwarding and sharing of millions of images and messages; internet connections, Wi-Fi hotspots and Internet cafes were everywhere and so the State had to up its game, and so did we.

By 2018 the ability to send and receive information was country wide; booster towers enabled communication from most places and the only way the State had to stop the flow of information, in and out, was to switch off the internet to the whole country which they first did on the 15th January 2019. Luckily for Zimbabwe, after twenty years of experience

321

of the oppressive tactics of the government, the rumours had started hours before that the internet was going to be switched off. The first thought that came to mind was: "They wouldn't do that," but after twenty years of saying "shouldn't, wouldn't, couldn't," we knew that the government of Zimbabwe probably would do exactly that. The old saying 'ignorance is bliss' definitely wasn't true for Zimbabwe, ignorance was dangerous and messages started flooding our phones and WhatsApp connections telling people how to download VPN's.

It had been impossible to imagine that in 2019 we would be learning ways around complete internet shutdowns by the government but we were and we were quick learners. Suddenly everyone was talking about VPNs (Virtual Private Network) which enabled you to connect to an international server and send and receive data which was anonymous and secure online but more importantly couldn't be blocked by government. VPN's were of course dependent on you having lots of credit and mobile data on your phone because you were linked to an international connection and we soon learned to switch on and off the connection to the VPN for short periods of time only to send and receive messages. As the clamour to download VPN's onto phones spread, everyone was desperate for the settings; cellphones littered desks and tables, Bluetooth connections enabled, sending the settings to peoples phones so they could stay in touch.

South Africa's *Sunday Times* newspaper reported on how quickly Zimbabwe learned to get around the government's latest attempt to silence us: "On January 15 2019, Zimbabweans woke up to a total shutdown but those who had downloaded VPN settings stayed online until the internet was restored briefly around 4pm on Wednesday. About 30 minutes later the internet was blocked again but more people had downloaded VPN settings. "It's impossible to keep us out now. If they block a VPN server, there are many out there and most them are all over the world. The one I'm using is based in Japan" said a journalist. (Times Live, 2019)

## THE ASSAULT ON THE MEDIA IN ZIMBABWE: 2000-2009

Being a journalist was a dangerous occupation in Zimbabwe during the years of collapse and State oppression; the risks increasing with every election, every human rights abuse and every attempt to silence voices of discontent. This was particularly evident in the country's collapse between 2000 and 2009 when repressive legislation was introduced; regulations and restrictions on the media reached extreme levels. None were spared including film-makers, artists, playwrights, actors, authors, musicians, theatres and galleries. The chronological list below covering those years is not exhaustive but paints a graphic picture of just how desperate the government was to silence the press and the people working in it.

## 8 MARCH 2000

Parliament passes the Post and Telecommunications Bill which allows the government to monitor and intercept any communication in any medium, including the internet, if, "in the opinion of the President, it is necessary in the interests of national security or the maintenance of law and order."

## 22 APRIL 2000

A homemade bomb is thrown from a passing car at 9.00pm at Trustee House which houses *The Daily News.*

## 2 MAY 2000

Harare airport police arrest Associated Press photographer Obed Zilwa, who went to take pictures of the bombing of the *Daily News*. Zilwa spent 48 hours in custody.

## 23 MAY 2000

"The Supreme Court of Zimbabwe dismissed charges against reporters Mark Chavunduka and Ray Choto for publishing a report alleging a military coup plot against President Robert Mugabe. ... Chavunduka, editor of the *Standard* and chief reporter Choto were charged on January 21, 1999, with publishing false information "likely to cause fear and despondency." Military police arrested Chavunduka and Choto on the 12th and 14th of January. "The two journalists were detained at a secret location, where government agents allegedly beat them and applied electric shocks to their hands, feet, and genitals. The agents also submerged the journalists' heads in drums of water and demanded that they reveal their sources. When Chavunduka and Choto were brought to court on January 21, they both had cigarette burns on their bodies. Independent medical sources subsequently confirmed the allegations of torture." (CPJ, AP)

## 21 JUNE 2000

A mob of 20 people, one wearing a ZANU PF T shirt, attack a car carrying foreign journalists in full view of Commonwealth election observers. The journalists from AFP, *The Sowetan and ETV* are unharmed; car windows are smashed.

## 5 OCTOBER 2000

Police dismantle and seize *Capitol Radio*'s broadcasting equipment from its studio at the Monomotapa Hotel in Harare. The equipment included a CD player, console, mixer, microphone, amplifier, multiplex generator, modular, coaxial cables and an antenna.

## 6 OCTOBER 2000

The High Court of Zimbabwe orders the return of equipment confiscated from *Capitol Radio*.

## 18 OCTOBER 2000

Soldiers attack four international AP journalists in Dzivareskwa Harare. They were beaten when they left their vehicle to interview soldiers who had come to contain rioting crowds of citizens angered over recent increases in the price of bread, sugar and soft drinks.

### 9 JANUARY 2001

The printing presses of the *Daily News* are bombed.

### 16 FEBRUARY 2001

Mercedes Sayagues, Harare correspondent for the South African *Mail and Guardian* is ordered to leave Zimbabwe. Sayagues had been working in Zimbabwe since 1992.

### 15 AUGUST 2001

Police arrest *Daily News* editor Geoff Nyarota, reporter Sam Munyavi, editor John Gambanga and his assistant Bill Saidi. The four are charged with "publishing false information likely to cause alarm or despondency in the public." The arrests are a result of *Daily News* reports that police vehicles were used in the looting of white owned farms in Mhangura.

### 8 NOVEMEBER 2001

Geoff Nyarota, editor-in-chief of the *Daily News*, and Wilf Mbanga, the former CEO of the Associated Newspapers of Zimbabwe (ANZ) are arrested.

## 11 FEBRUARY 2002

The Access to Information and Protection of Privacy (AIPPA) Bill is signed into law. AIPPA requires all journalists in Zimbabwe to be licensed by a Media and Information Commission. Under the law, only citizens or permanent residents can be accredited as journalists, although foreigners can be accredited for an unspecified "limited" period.

## 28 MARCH 2002

Peta Thornycroft, Zimbabwe correspondent for the *Mail and Guardian* (South Africa) and the *Daily Telegraph* (UK) is arrested in Chimanimani where she was investigating reports that Zanu PF supporters were attacking members of the political opposition.

## 2 MAY 2002

Andrew Meldrum, Zimbabwe correspondent for the *Guardian* newspaper (UK) is arrested at his home and charged with "publishing false information" and "abusing journalistic privileges."

## 28 AUGUST 2002

Offices of *Voice of the People* (VOP) Communications Trust are bombed. Witnesses reported windows being smashed and explosives thrown into the building. The entire building was razed to the ground and all of the company's equipment destroyed.

## 11 NOVEMEBR 2002

Mark Chavunduka, 37, former editor of *The Standard* newspaper died in Harare. "After his release, [from detention in 1999] Chavunduka received treatment for post traumatic stress disorder in both Britain and the United States. According to the BBC, Chavunduka often complained of nightmares following the beatings and electric shocks he received during his detention." (CPJ, BBC)

## 28 FEBRUARY 2003

The following foreign media organizations and individuals are banned from covering the March 9-10 presidential election: The Associated Press; *Sunday Times; Mail & Guardian;* The Independent Newspapers Group; David Blair from *Daily Telegraph;* John Murphy from *The Baltimore Sun;* Sally Sara from Australian Broadcasting Service, and Gorrel Espelund from *Sydsvenska Dagbladet.*

## 6 MAY 2003

Police arrest Pius Wakatama, a *Daily News* reporter, and charge him with publishing false information and abusing journalistic privilege under AIPPA. Charges relate to an article he wrote about the eviction of a black farming family from their property.

## 12 SEPTEMBER 2003

Police officers order everyone out of the *Daily News* offices.

## 16 SEPTEMBER 2003

Detectives, security agents, armed paramilitary members, and riot police raid the offices of the *Daily News* and seize computers and other equipment belonging to the newspaper. (AP)

## 18 SEPTEMBER 2003

The High Court rules the *Daily News* can resume publishing and orders authorities to immediately return computers and other equipment that was confiscated.

## 18 SEPTEMBER 2003

Police occupy the offices of the *Daily News* in the evening and prevent journalists from putting out a Friday edition of the newspaper.

## 22 SEPTEMBER 2003

"Four directors of the Associated Newspapers of Zimbabwe (ANZ), the company that owns ...the *Daily News*, were arrested today and charged with violating AIPPA. Chief Executive Sam Sipepa Nkomo and three directors: Brian Mutsau, Rachel Kupara, and Stuart Mattinson were summoned to the Central Police Station in Harare and told that they were under arrest for publishing a newspaper without a license. According to journalists at the newspaper, police today re-confiscated more than 100 computers that had been returned to the newspaper on September 20. Police also asked Nkomo for a list of all ANZ employees ... He told CPJ that he plans to supply the list but fears that it will allow police to arrest and charge the newspaper's entire staff. "(CPJ)

## 14 JANUARY 2004

"Itai Dzamara, reporter with the *Zimbabwe Independent*, and the paper's general manager, Raphael Khumalo, are arrested after presenting themselves to police at Harare Central Police Station. The arrests followed the publication of a story in the January 9 edition of the *Zimbabwe Independent* co-authored by Dzamara alleging that Zimbabwean President Robert Mugabe had commandeered an Air Zimbabwe plane for his trip to East Asia, thereby stranding passengers who were slated to fly on the plane between Harare and London. The piece also quoted a source saying that the plane carried containers for storage of goods Mugabe might acquire on his trip." (CPJ)

[On the 9th March 2015 Itai Dzamara, journalist and pro democracy activist, was abducted from a barber shop in Harare by five armed men and has never been seen again.]

## 6 FEBRUARY 2004

The *Daily News* decides not to publish its Friday edition following a Supreme Court ruling upholding legislation that criminalizes the publication of unlicensed newspapers.

## 19 MAY 2004

Two journalists from *The Standard* are arrested. Editor Bornwell Chakaodza and reporter Valentine Maponga are charged with "publishing false statements prejudicial to the State."

## 10 JUNE 2004

The private weekly newspaper *The Tribune* is ordered closed by government's Media and Information Commission.

## 2004

The Committee to Protect Journalists puts Zimbabwe as third on the list of the worst places in the world to be a journalist. (Freedom House)

## 2005

Wilf Mbanga, exiled founder of the *Daily News*, begins publishing a weekly newspaper *The Zimbabwean* from the UK. The paper is circulated in UK, South Arica and Zimbabwe.

## 10 JANUARY 2005

President Mugabe signs into law the AIPPA Amendment Act which sets prison terms of up to two years for journalists found working without accreditation from the government's Media and Information Commission.

## 28 FEBRUARY 2005

The Media and Information Commission (MIC) closes the independent regional newspaper *Weekly Times* after just eight weeks of publication.

## 31 MARCH 2005

Toby Harnden, chief foreign correspondent for the *Sunday Telegraph (UK),* and photographer Julian Simmonds are arrested at a polling station in Norton, They are charged with violating AIPPA.

## 1 APRIL 2005

Fredrik Sperling a reporter for Swedish *Sveriges Television* (STV) is arrested in Harare and deported to South Africa despite having accreditation to work in Zimbabwe. Sperling was filming a large farm expropriated by the Zimbabwean government and now occupied by a relative of President Robert Mugabe.

## 15 APRIL 2005

Two British journalists, Toby Harnden and Julian Simmonds, detained in Zimbabwe during parliamentary elections, leave the country after being acquitted of the charge of reporting without accreditation. The journalists had spent two weeks in prison while standing trial.

## 20 APRIL 2005

Police bring criminal charges against *Standard* editor Davison Maruziva and reporter Savious Kwinika in connection with an April 10 story alleging election irregularities.

## 19 MAY 2005

Police detain freelance journalist Frank Chikowore who was filming police as they cleared Harare's central business district of street vendors.

## 18 JULY 2005

The Media and Information Commission again refuse to license the banned independent *Daily News* and its sister paper the *Daily News on Sunday*, both of which were shut down in September 2003.

## 31 AUGUST 2005

Kelvin Jakachira is acquitted of criminal charges of working without accreditation for the now banned *Daily News* between January and September 2003.

## 9 DECEMBER 2005

"Trevor Ncube, owner and director of Zimbabwe's two remaining independent newspapers and of South Africa's *Mail and Guardian, is* ordered to hand over his passport when he landed in Zimbabwe at Bulawayo airport from South Africa. Ncube told CPJ he was on a list of government critics whose passports the immigration authorities have been ordered to seize. The list includes journalists and media lawyer Beatrice Mtetwa, who won a CPJ International Press Freedom Award in 2005." (CPJ)

## 15 DECEMBER 2005

Three VOP staff members are detained by police who came to their offices looking for broadcasting and transmitting equipment. They were released three days later but VOP Director John Masuku was then detained.

## 27 JANUARY 2006

Sydney Saize, former journalist for the banned *Daily News*, is arrested and accused of working without accreditation and filing a "false" story for the *Voice of America*.

## 30 APRIL 2006

Two journalists from Botswana's state broadcaster are arrested by Zimbabwean police and held for two days, charged with violating AIPPA. Mokoba and Seofela were arrested near the Botswana-Zimbabwe border, where they had traveled to report on a recent outbreak of foot and mouth disease in local livestock.

## 13 SEPTEMBER 2006

Michael Saburi, freelance cameraman for *Reuters* TV, is assaulted by police and jailed for filming a banned trade union march in Harare.

## 31 JANUARY 2007

Bill Saidi, editor of *The Standard*, receives a hand delivered envelope containing a bullet and an unsigned hand-written note that read, "What is this? Watch your step."

## 11 MARCH 2007

Freelance photojournalist Tsvangirai Mukwazhi and freelance TV producer Tendai Musiyu are stopped by police while driving to cover an MDC gathering in Harare. The pair were ordered to lie face down on the ground before being beaten with wooden sticks and handcuffed. Police seized the car, cell phones, cameras and a laptop. "Mukwazhi and Musiyu were taken to separate police stations in Harare and repeatedly beaten, before being released without charge two days later. The car and equipment were not returned, Mukwazhi said." (CPJ)

## 27 MARCH 2007

Two ZBC journalists, Andrew Neshamba and William Gumbo are arrested and charged with "criminal abuse of duty as a public officer" in connection with film footage of diamond trafficking in Manicaland.

## 2 APRIL 2007

Gift Phiri of the *The Zimbabwean (UK) is* jailed, beaten, and charged by police in connection with coverage of the recent unrest in Zimbabwe.

## 31 MARCH 2007

Edward Chikomba, veteran ZBC cameraman is found dead in Darwendale. Chikomba had been abducted on March 29 by a group of armed men in a 4×4 vehicle near his home in Harare. "We are utterly dismayed by this murder, which comes at a critical time for independent journalists because, after years of harassment, they are now being subjected to extreme violence," Reporters Without Borders said. One of Chikomba's former colleagues said Chikomba was accused of providing the international media with video footage showing opposition leader Morgan Tsvangirai with his face badly swollen after being beaten while in custody. (Reporters Without Borders)

## 6 AUGUST 2007

The Interception of Communications Act is ratified; it "will target imperialist sponsored journalists with hidden agendas" the country's information minister Sikhanyiso Ndlovu said, describing the law as intending "to protect the president, a minister, or any citizen from harm." The Interception of Communications Act will allow authorities to intercept all phone, internet, and mail communications, and will establish a state monitoring center and require telecommunications providers to install systems "supporting lawful interceptions at all times," according to the Media Institute of Southern Africa. (CPJ)

## 28 SEPTEMBER 2007

Journalists express concerns about a purported government document that names 15 independent journalists to be "placed under strict surveillance and taken in."

## 16 APRIL 2008

"Award-winning *New York Times* journalist Barry Bearak and British freelance journalist Steve Bevan leave Zimbabwe after a Magistrate ruled that there were no legal grounds for their arrest. The two foreign journalists were arrested at the York

Lodge in Harare on April 3 and accused of practicing journalism without accreditation." (CPJ)

## 8 MAY 2008

Davison Maruziva, deputy editor of *The Standard* is picked up and accused of "publishing false statements prejudicial to the state and contempt of court" in connection with a column by Arthur Mutambara, leader of a breakaway faction of the MDC.

## 24 MAY 2008

A truck containing 60,000 copies of *The Zimbabwean* newspaper is hijacked and burnt to a shell. "On May 24, eight men armed with AK-47 rifles intercepted the truck's driver, Christmas Ramabulana, and distribution agent Tapfumaneyi Kancheta at Ngundu Halt …south of Masvingo. According to *The Zimbabwean on Sunday* Editor Wilf Mbanga, the armed group took over the 16-gear truck and drove the distributors in separate cars to a remote location in Madamabwe. The assailants beat Ramabulana and Kencheta with rifle butts and left them in the bushes." (The Zimbabwean/ CPJ)

## 17 DECEMBER 2008

Freelance photojournalist Shadreck Manyere disappeared after taking his car to a garage in Norton. Police raided Manyere's home the following day and confiscated equipment related to his work. (AP; BBC; CPJ; Freedom House; MISA; The Zimbabwean; Reporters Without Borders)

# CHAPTER 13

# CHRISTMAS

## THE VOICE OF HOPE: SW RADIO AFRICA, CHRISTMAS 2003

Three years after land invasions and political violence began to tear Zimbabwe apart, many people who had tried to stay but couldn't survive had left the country; trying to start new lives in new countries, get their children into school and find jobs. The days before Christmas 2003 in Zimbabwe were very emotional as the reality of friends and family who had left the country sank in. It was a time of sharing whatever we had: small gifts, money, food, toiletries. Never had I imagined a Christmas with 600% inflation; that a tube of toothpaste would give such joy to an unemployed man; that a single box of tampons would bring tears to the eyes of a desperate teenager; that a pencil and exercise book would be received with such gratitude from a budding writer.

The lifeline for so many of us was *SW Radio Africa*, the radio station broadcasting from London run by exiled Zimbabweans. The most powerful and compelling attraction of *SW Radio Africa* was that it was our voices, telling our story in recorded *telephone* interviews. The calls were often very emotional; eye witness accounts of horrific events that were happening in Zimbabwe, un-edited, raw and painful to listen to, providing a damning testimony of the abuses going on in the country.

For many of us whose families and friends had fled Zimbabwe, *SW Radio Africa* became our extended family, the voice of hope. Night after night, almost always by candlelight because of the power cuts, my wind up radio sat on the kitchen table tuned into *SW Radio Africa* for the two hours that they broadcast. More nights than I care to remember I sat and wept as I heard people telling their stories of un-imaginable terror, violence and brutality.

*SW Radio Africa's* Christmas broadcasts in 2003 included messages from hundreds of exiled Zimbabweans calling from countries all over the world. It was unbearably painful to listen to children and grandchildren in the Diaspora sending messages to their parents and grandparents in Zimbabwe. The pain of separation, voices filled with longing and loneliness, the anguish of being so far apart. The voices from Zimbabwe and to Zimbabwe told the story of the collapse of our country so graphically. Zimbabweans were scattered all over the world, but we were still one and that gave hope.

## MILLION DOLLAR PRESENTS, CHRISTMAS LUNCH AND CHRISTMAS CAKE MIX: 2005

In 2005 my hometown was a seething mass of people the week before Christmas. There were huge queues at all the banks, building societies and savings banks. In the supermarkets there was no sugar or milk and it was very hard to find eggs, flour, rice, maize meal and margarine. The prices of everything were monstrous and it was almost impossible to find anything priced at less than one hundred thousand dollars.

At home we had agreed that we weren't going to buy junky presents because everything was so expensive but of course as the days to Christmas got closer, I inevitably weakened. I spent two million dollars on little things for Richie: a small backpack for his schoolbooks, a shirt and a pair of swimming goggles. Another two million dollars bought a second hand exhaust pipe for a friend's car and two million dollars was spent on a box of groceries for a family in the village near our farm who had also lost everything during the farm invasions.

Christmas lunch was stir fry chicken, veggies from the garden and steam pudding and custard, all made with ingredients searched for far and wide and bought at outrageous prices from black market dealers for many weeks before Christmas. On Christmas afternoon we all had a slice of fruit cake thanks to Roger who had sent a Christmas cake-mix in a box by post. The instructions 'just add water and an egg' couldn't have been easier to achieve and the finished product of a rich, dark, moist cake were well worth getting up in the middle of the night to bake in the few hours when the electricity was on.

## HOME-MADE CHRISTMAS MINCE PIES: 2006
Determined to overcome despair and depression and to try and cheer up Christmas in 2006, I decided to make mince pies in an attempt to get into the festive spirit. Baking isn't my

thing and I'd never made mince pies before, even in the years when things were 'normal.' Family and friends always used to give them to me but as the exodus to the Diaspora has eradicated most of my friends and all of my family members, I decided to just roll up my sleeves and get on with it. How hard could it be, I thought, dragging out dust covered recipe books.

Looking at the recipe books I realised I didn't have half of the ingredients and most importantly I didn't have the fruit mincemeat. Determined not to be defeated I decided to carry on, improvise where I could and make things up as I went along. I chopped up a packet of dried fruit I had received in a parcel from Canada, snacking as I went, realising how much I missed the variety of such treats in my life. Next I added a packet of sultanas left over from my sister's visit from the Diaspora two years before and then, just as a bit of improvisation, I added some chopped up strips of dried guava and of tin of expired pears I found at the back of the pantry cupboard. The pears tasted fine, so I drank the juice and tipped the fruit into the bowl. Then came the alcohol and I sloshed in a generous amount of cheap, rot-gut brandy and gave everything a stir.

The mixture seemed too stiff, so I added more brandy bit by bit, having a healthy taste test of the mixture every time of course. Mixing and mushing everything together I added the only sugar I had, Old Fashioned Demerara Sugar, sticky and dark brown and something that had been a long time occupant of the back of the pantry cupboard, from when times were normal about five years ago. A few errant tears dripped into the mixture too as I thought about Christmases past but pulled myself together knowing that if I started crying, I wouldn't be able to stop; so much pain, so many losses incurred in surviving Zimbabwe. I added another glug of brandy and had another taste: Whew, it was getting very strong!

When I finally got the consistency of the mincemeat to what looked right, I realised that I'd used over half the bottle of rot-gut brandy and there was a pool of liquid sitting on top of the fruit. I decided I'd just go ahead and make the mince pies anyway and drink the pooled juice later. The mince pies, when they got made much, much later, did taste very weird, but nice!

## THE CHRISTMAS TREE: 2000 - 2006

In early September 2000 when men calling themselves war veterans and supporters of Zanu PF were squatting all over our Marondera farm, claiming fields, paddocks and dams, chopping down trees and erecting crude shacks everywhere, the writing was on the wall for me. It obviously wasn't going to be long before we had no option but to leave our farm and so one afternoon Richie and I went up into the plantation behind the farmhouse. Richie was eight years old at the time and 'the forest' as he called it, was a favourite place to play. Tall pine and gum trees, springy young branches to hang, bounce and swing on, soft ground underfoot, cool and quiet with a gentle, whispering wind. There were often guinea fowl, francolin and nightjars to see too, if you were lucky, and

Richie's forest was his favourite place to hide. The pain of leaving bit deep into my heart as we walked hand in hand into the forest.

Armed with a couple of little hand trowels and black plastic plant bags, we went in search of the perfect baby Christmas tree.

"We are going to take this to our new house," I told Richie.

"You mean we won't come to the forest and cut one down for Christmas like we always do?" he asked.

"No Rich, but that's why we're going to take one with us."

It didn't take long to find the perfect little Pine seedling. Richie helped to carefully dig the ground all-round the seedling, putting some of the soil into our black plastic bag, "so that it'll always have some of its very own farm soil," I told him, and then we carefully uprooted the little seedling, just five centimetres tall, and planted it in the bag. The Christmas tree of our future in a country starting to collapse was put carefully aside so that it could be packed and moved, along with our lives, hopes and dreams when we moved off the farm, knowing then for sure that we were soon to be evicted by the squatters.

In its new home off the farm the little seedling took hold and before long outgrew its black bag and was transplanted into a bigger container. In 2000 and 2001 our little farm Christmas tree came into the house for Christmas week, a link to our past, a reminder to me not to give up hope for the future. In December 2002 the Christmas tree lived up to its name when it was carried inside and it was strong enough to hold a few decorations ; we wound silver, green, red and blue tinsel between its thin young branches and put a silver star at its tip.

Every year as Zimbabwe's collapse continued and environmental devastation was so widespread, I determined to never again cut down a tree for Christmas and would use something else instead. I nurtured our farm Christmas tree, moving it into ever bigger pots, carrying it inside for Christmas week, decorating it and laying presents around it and then, after Christmas, back outside it went.

In December 2005 it was time to set the Christmas tree free. It had been raining almost incessantly for days and days. Before lunch on Christmas day, taking advantage of a break between downpours, Richie and I went out in the garden and we dug a big hole. It was an easy task, the ground was soft, saturated and easy to dig and we were finished in no time. A wheelbarrow load of compost was tipped into the hole and mixed with soil and then we were ready to plant. We dragged the Christmas tree in its pot to the edge of the hole and for a moment I was overcome with emotion and the significance of what we were about to do. Maybe it was symbolic, I thought, maybe planting it here meant that I'd accepted that we would never be going back now.

At first, after we planted the Christmas tree in the garden, it stood in shock for a long time; didn't lift its branches and didn't grow but then suddenly it took off. By December 2006 the Christmas tree was over two metres tall. That year I had made a skeletal Christmas tree from a dry palm tree flower head, bleached white from the sun, its flowers and berries long gone. Standing in a deep glass bowl held in place with river stones, my palm flower Christmas tree was minimally decorated with a few strands of fine silver tinsel and a few red and silver glass baubles. The tree stood about sixty centimetres high and its skeletal beauty was strangely significant for the state of our lives in Zimbabwe five years into the new millennium: skeletal and stoic while all around us everything was falling apart.

Outside in the garden was the 'real' Christmas tree which told its own poignant story of the first five years of our lives of surviving Zimbabwe's collapse. I took a ladder outside and climbed up onto the top step, stretched over and tied a silver star to the tip of the living, breathing pine tree where it stirred gently in the hot December breeze. There were many more Christmases to come from a country in continuing cycles of collapse but always I was hopeful that one day it wouldn't be like this anymore and that we would see the end of dictators and oppression, corruption and greed; that we would be able to thrive in Zimbabwe.

# SOURCES OF REFERENCE

AFDB (2011) Zimbabwe report 2011 (African Development Bank) www.afdb.org

Amnesty International (2019) "Zimbabwe: medical doctor found alive but tortured: Peter Magombeyi." www.amnesty.org

BBC News (2004) "Zimbabwe returning to stone age." www.bbc.com

Buckle, C (2019) "The winds of discontent" Letters From Zimbabwe www.cathybuckle.co.zw

Buckle, C (2002) "Little white stickers." Letters From Zimbabwe www.cathybuckle.co.zw

The Chronicle, Zimbabwe www.chronicle.co.zw

Chavisa, M (2007) "Zimbabwean's desperate quest for AIDS drugs." Institute for War and Peace reporting. www.iwpr.net

Cuneo,C, Sollom, R & Beyrer, C (2017) Health and Human Rights Journal The Cholera Epidemic in Zimbabwe, 2008–2009: A Review and Critique of the Evidence"

Deposit Protection Corporation, Harare (2003) www.dpcorp.co.zw

Freedom House (2006) "Countries at the Crossroads 2006- Zimbabwe" www.freedomhouse.org

Global health workforce alliance (2013) "National Health Strategy for Zimbabwe 2009-2013." www.who.int/workforcealliance

Hanke, S & Kwok, A (2009) "On the measurement of Zimbabwe's Hyper inflation." Cato Journal 29 (2).

The Herald, (2006, 2007) Zimbabwe www.herald.co.zw

Howden, D 2006 " Dead by 34. How AIDS and starvation condemn Zimbabwe's women to early grave." The Independent. www.independent.co.uk

IOL (2018) "Fired striking Zimbabwean nurses refuse dismissals." ANA (African News Agency) www.iol.co.za

IPI (2006) (International Press Institute)   www.ipi.media

IRIN (2013) "Is Zimbabwe's education sector on the road to recovery?" www.thenewhumanitarian.org

Khumalo, N (2007) Relief Web. OCHA (United Nations Office for the Coordination of Humanitarian Affairs) www.unocha.org

The Lancet (2004) "Health and Hunger in Zimbabwe." www.thelancet.com

Machipisa, L (1998) IPS, Rome. (International Press Service News) "Economy-Zimbabwe: Panic Grips the Banking Sector"  www.ipsnews.net

Matyszak, D (2017) Institute for Security Studies, reported in Daily News  www.dailynews.co.zw

Mawere,M & Marongwe, N (2018) "The End of an Era? Robert Mugabe and a Conflicting Legacy."

Ministry of Health and Child Welfare (Zimbabwe) (2010) Human Resources for Health information sheet. www.mohcc.gov.zw

MISA (2002; 2006;2014) (Media Institute of Southern Africa) www.zimbabwe.misa.org

Moore, D; Kriger, N; Raftopoulos, B (2013).'Progress' in Zimbabwe? The Past and Present of a Concept and a Country."

NUST (2007) (National University of Science and Technology, Bulawayo) (ICRC presentation) www.nust.ac.zw

Pambazuka News (2002) Voices for Freedom and Justice
www.pambazuka.org

Plus News (2005) "Zimbabwe: Price of ARV's rockets in declining
economy." www.news24.com

Reporters Without Borders (2005)  www.rsf.org

Samukange, T (2014) Newsday  www.newsday.co.zw

SIRDC (Scientific and Industrial Research and Development Centre)
2005  www.sirdc.ac.zw

The Standard, (2005) Zimbabwe  www.thestandard.co.zw

SW Radio Africa (2005) www.swrdarioafrica.com

Thompson, J (2019) "How Zimbabweans stayed online when
government shut down the internet."  Sunday Times, South Africa.
www.timeslive.co.za

Tren, R; Ncube, P (Archbishop); Urbach, J & Bate, R  (2007) "Tyranny
and Disease. The Destruction of Health Care in Zimbabwe"

UNICEF (2009) "Zimbabwe education crisis worsens"
www.unicef.org

United Nations - World Population Prospects  www.un.org

UNDP (2004) Human Development Report

USDA (2008) (United States Department of Agriculture)
www.undp.org

WHO (2005; 2006; 2007) www.who.int

World Bank  www.worldbank.org

The Zimbabwe Independent (2008; 2014)
www.theindependent.co.zw

The Zimbabwean (2008) www.thezimbabwean.co

The Zimbabwe Situation   www.zimbabwesituation.com

Zim Online (2005) zimonlinenews.com

ZIMSTAT Business Tendency Survey, 2006-2009 www.zimstat.co.zw

ZTA  (2009; 2017) (Zimbabwe Tourism Authority)

www.zimbabwetourism.net

*D I D 2 9 4 6 0 1 8 *

L - #0287 - 091120 - C0 - 210/148/19 - PB - DID2946018